Time Within Time
THE DIARIES
1970–1986

ANDREY TARKOVSKY

Time Within Time

THE DIARIES

1970–1986

ANDREY TARKOVSKY

Translated from the Russian by
KITTY HUNTER-BLAIR

faber and faber
LONDON · BOSTON

First published in Great Britain in 1994
by Faber and Faber Limited
3 Queen Square London WC1N 3AU

Original © Verlag Ullstein GmbH Frankfurt a. Main/Berlin, 1989
English version © Seagull Books Private Limited, Calcutta, 1991

Kitty Hunter-Blair is hereby identified as translator of this
work in accordance with Section 77 of the Copyright Designs
and Patents Act 1988.

A CIP record for this book is
available from the British Library

ISBN 0-571-16717-9

2 4 6 8 10 9 7 5 3 1

Contents

A Note from the Translator

In 1985–6, I had the privilege of translating Andrey Tarkovsky's book on cinema, *Sculpting in Time*. The work was a constant source of exhilaration, despite the difficulties. I had long admired Tarkovsky as one of the key figures of late twentieth century culture, whose films, unmistakably part of the aesthetic and spiritual tradition of Russia and Europe, have about them something timeless and universal. At the same time they are always overwhelmingly personal. What was remarkable about the book was that it too, while treating of supremely important things, spoke intimately with the reader. In the few years that have passed since its publication, *Sculpting in Time* seems to have become an important part of the lives of an extraordinarily wide range of people.

Translating *Time Within Time* has been a different kind of experience. The notes and diaries do not address the reader; Tarkovsky wrote them, often on the spur of the moment, for himself, and they are disjointed. This volume represents only a portion of all that the director wrote down in the course of his working life. And yet throughout these pages I have been held by the same magnetic, personal spell that makes all Tarkovsky's work so compelling to his admirers.

Hermann Hesse, whom Tarkovsky so often quotes, wrote that 'every man is not only himself; he is also the unique, particular, always significant and remarkable point where the phenomena of the world intersect once and for all and never again.' Working on this book I have repeatedly felt how perfectly those words apply to Andrey Tarkovsky.

A Biographical Note

Andrey Tarkovsky was born on 4 April 1932. His mother, Maria Ivanovna, was a talented actress, and his father, Arseniy Tarkovsky, a respected poet and translator. Both his parents have featured in his work—his mother as an actress; and his father through the haunting poems which Andrey has used in several of his films.

When his parents separated, Andrey and his younger sister Marina continued to live with their mother. In 1939 his schooling in Moscow was interrupted; but he returned to the city in 1943. In addition to regular classes at school he began to study music and drawing. In 1951 he joined the Moscow Institute for Oriental Languages, but he couldn't complete the course due to illness. In 1954 he successfully applied for admission to the prestigious All-Union State Institute of Cinematography (VGIK) in Moscow. Here Mikhail Ilych Romm became his most influential teacher. His friendship with Andrey Mikhalkov-Konchalovsky led to the joint script for *The Steamroller and the Violin,* Tarkovsky's debut film which earned him the degree at VGIK, and which already reveals significant elements typical of his later work.

Tarkovsky's first major feature film was shown in Moscow in April 1962. *Ivan's Childhood,* based on a story by Vladimir Bogomolov (who was also involved in the filming), won the Golden Lion in the very same year at the film festival in Venice. The international recognition following this success triggered off considerable ideological concern in his own country, which subsequently—around the end of 1966, after the première of *Andrey Rublyov*—mounted to intensive criticism and led to immense working difficulties for Tarkovsky. This political-ideological position inevitably had an effect on the distribution policy. For example, *Andrey Rublyov,* which was shown out of competition at the Cannes Festival in 1969 and won an award there, was cleared for export by the Soviet Film Department only in 1973. Similarly *Mirror,* an autobiographical film, which was completed in 1974 against strong bureaucratic resistance, reached west European cinema halls only years later.

With *Solaris* (1971/1972), based on a science fiction novel by Stanislas Lem, Tarkovsky touched upon a subject that was still relatively innocuous in the Soviet Union at the time—man forging ahead into space—but even here his approach generated a long list of criticisms and objections. *Stalker*, Tarkovsky's last film made in the Soviet Union, is based on *Roadside Picnic*, a story by the Strugatsky brothers. It deals with themes underpinning the world view of the director: the rift between natural science and belief, the future of mankind in view of current atomic threats; and, ultimately, the dim glimmer of hope still left to man.

After a stage production of *Hamlet* in Moscow, Tarkovsky travelled to Italy in 1982 to shoot *Nostalgia*. A Soviet–Italian co-production, it is based on a script written jointly with the poet Tonino Guerra. The theme is, however, typical of the Russian dilemma: that of the artist abroad, smitten by homesickness, unable to live in his country or away from it—a fate that befell Tarkovsky himself in the last years of his life.

In the autumn of 1983 he staged *Boris Godunov* with great success at the Covent Garden Opera in London. A year and a half later, in 1986, his widely acclaimed book *Sculpting in Time* got published. Around the same time he was carrying on preparations for his last film from Berlin, where he was staying in 1985 on a fellowship from the German Academic Exchange Service: *Sacrifice*, often referred to as Tarkovsky's legacy.

At the end of 1985, after completing the shooting of *Sacrifice* in Sweden, Andrey Tarkovsky returned to Rome, already afflicted by the disease to which he succumbed a year later, on 29 December 1986, at a Parisian cancer clinic. He is buried in a graveyard for Russian *émigrés* in the town of Saint-Geneviève-du-Bois, France.

ANDREY TARKOVSKY

MARTYROLOGY

30 April 1970

When you are bored, sitting all day long in front of your ink-bottle, aimlessly jotting down the odds and ends that come into your head—you can find that what you have written is enough to drive you mad.

Kenko-Khosi, *Notes to Relieve Tedium*, 1; 14th c.

[Translation of title page of 1970 MS]

1970

30 April, Moscow

Sasha Mishurin and I again talked about Dostoievsky. First, of course, it has to be written: it's too early to start thinking about how to direct it.

There's almost certainly no point in screening the novels. We must make a film about the man himself. About his personality, his God, his devil, his work.

Tolya Solonitsyn could make a wonderful Dostoievsky. For the moment I must read. Everything Dostoievsky wrote. Everything that's been written about him; and Russian philosophy—Solovyov, Leontiev, Berdyaev, etc.

'Dostoievsky' could become the whole point of what I want to do in cinema.

Now *Solaris*. For the moment progress is agonizingly slow, because things at Mosfilm have reached crisis point.

Then—*The Bright Day*.

10 May, Moscow

On 24 April 1970 we bought a house in Myasnoye. The one we wanted. Now I don't care what happens. If they don't give me any work I'll sit in the country and breed piglets and geese, and tend my vegetable patch, and to hell with the lot of them!

We shall gradually put the house and garden in order, and it will be a wonderful country house; stone.

The people here seem nice. I've installed a beehive. We'll have honey. If only we could get hold of a pick-up we'd be all set. Now I must earn as much as possible so that we can finish the house by the autumn. It has to be habitable in winter as well. Three hundred kilometres from Moscow—people won't come dragging out here for nothing.

The two important things now are:
1. *Solaris* has to be in two parts.
2. Maximum distribution for *Rublyov*.
Then I'd be free of debt.
And—the agreement in Dushanbe.

To be done in the house:
1. Reroofing.
2. Re-lay all floors.
3. Make second frame for one window.
4. Use tiles from house to roof shed.
5. Make stove for steam heating.
6. Repair cracks in gallery.
7. Put up fence all round house.
8. Cellar.
9. Remove plywood from ceilings.
10. Open up door between rooms.
11. Put stove in gallery.
12. Build bath-house in kitchen garden.
13. Make lavatory.
14. Install pump (electric) from the river to the house (if it's not going to freeze up in winter).
15. Shower (by bath-house).
16. Plant garden.
17. Paint floors and walls of gallery, and beams.

25 May

Went to see Bazhanov. He promised to ring Surin about its being in two parts. It has to be quickly! Work is at a standstill.

We ought to do some trial takes as soon as possible. The actors are all there, apart from Khari.
Actors:
Chris—Banionis
His father—Grinko
Berton—Massiulis
Snaut—Yarvet
Sartorius—Solonitsyn
The Mother—Tarkovskaya (?—if she agrees)
Messenger—Stevens
Larissa's not well. She'll be having the baby very soon now. Oh, Lord!

4 June

Things are gradually coming together. The Committee is apparently allowing *Solaris* to be 4000 metres = 14 parts = 2 hours 20 minutes. And apparently the Central Party Committee is going into the question of filming in Japan.

Larissa went to the doctor and was told it might be twins.

13 June

Yesterday Bibi Anderson was introduced to me. I spent the entire evening wondering if she would make a Khari. Of course she's a marvellous actress. But she's not that young, although she looks very well. I don't know, I haven't yet decided what to do about her. She's willing to work for our currency. She's going to be filming for Bergman through the summer and she'll be free in the autumn. We'll see. For the moment I haven't made any decision. I must talk to Ira.

On the 12th I took Senka to school. My impression was that he had failed, but the headmaster is liberal-minded and didn't say anything, so for the moment everything is all right as far as school is concerned.

15 June

Went to see Ira yesterday. She was surprised by my suggestion about Khari, but she didn't refuse. She is thinner, and there is something acute about her, a lightness, exactly what is needed for Khari. It will be tremendous if she plays that part. Only we still have to find the Mother. Perhaps Demidova?

Kolya Shishlin is coming today. (He's an extraordinarily nice, decent man.) I want to read him *The Bright Day*.

The only way is to approach the thing 'from the top'. Maybe he'll have some good advice.

11 July

I haven't written anything for ages. Bibi Anderson and her husband were here. She is very keen to be in *Solaris*. Of course she's a brilliant actress. I'll do one more test with Ira, using the new make-up, and if I'm still in any doubt about her I'll start 'testing' Bibi. Incidentally, she's willing to work for Soviet currency, in other words, for all practical purposes—unpaid.

Larissa is going into hospital the day after tomorrow.

We've found the location for Kelvin's house. I think it's very good. White willows and a pond. And in another place a river, again with white willows. We must start building the decor. I don't have to worry about the actors; Yarvet and Banionis are wonderful. Solonitsyn and Grinko are going to need a bit of work—Russian school—quasi-dilettante.

(Woman—from the country—to a man who complains about his age: 'You still have everything in front of you!')

Bibi could be tremendous as the Mother in *The Bright Day*.

Yesterday I saw an unbelievable cutting copy by Karasik for Chekhov's *Seagull*. This time I think he is going to blow it.

12 July

Yesterday I got drunk. And shaved off my moustache. I only realized this morning. And on all my document photographs I've got a moustache. I'll have to grow it again.

I do love my Larochka, she is wonderful. Why, when I love her, do I go on the booze . . . presumably because what is missing is that notorious thing, freedom.

If only Larissa would have the baby soon. What frightens me most is taking her to hospital myself. It's a terrifying thought.

15 August

On 7 August at 6.25 in the evening Larissa gave birth to a son, Andriushka. She was a month overdue. But it was a quick birth. They were brought home today; or rather, not today, yesterday. The only people in the team who congratulated us were Rubina and Tamara Georgevna. Blow them all. They want to club together to buy a pram. Bother them. For some reason Yussov wanted to know—'Why such an expensive present?' People are crazy, they've lost their human image.

Andriushka is seven days old. He looks like a one-month-old baby. He's peaceful. Doesn't cry. He sometimes breathes noisily, through his nose, or chirps, or squeaks.

Things aren't going well for the team. Dvorzhetsky still hasn't been sent his reference from the Omsk Regional Committee. It's touch and go with Japan. They're not giving out enough film. The set for Kelvin's house is not going to be done in time. So there'll be no winter filming on location this year.

Did another test with Ira. She's good. But as for 'things in general—' I don't know.

Work on the script—both Lenya Kozlov's and mine—has stopped.

There's no time. Friedrich has arrived from the south. He's going to start making a few changes in the screenplay.

Not a word from Dushanbe about the treatment we sent on Belyaev's instructions. We're depending on it for cash. Penniless. And appalling debts. What's going to happen? I just can't imagine.

Andriushka has gorged himself and is fast asleep. He's a clever boy, doesn't cry, and so peaceful.

The house in the country must be reroofed; and repaired generally.

Rereading Thomas Mann. He's a genius! *Death in Venice* is astounding! Despite the ridiculous plot.

Teynishvili of Soyuzinfilm has suggested making a film for the foreign market. We'll see. Perhaps about Dostoievsky? But not until after *The Bright Day*.

26 August

Andriushka is so funny. When he's had his feed he smiles. Full of attention when you call him by name. Altogether—he's delightful. Actually he's got a bit scabby. The doctor told us to use ointment.

Japan seems to be gelling. They're going to give us 2000 dollars to take, for the five of us. It's a joke! The Zvenigorod set is going to be left standing till the end of May 1971.

Larissa is not well. Heart and chest. Thank God the mastitis went down quickly. But she had a very high temperature for two days.

Things at the studio are awful. It's a reflection of the general situation. Where is it all heading? God alone knows. There are idiots in charge.

27 August

Reading Ovchinnikov's brilliant vignettes of Japan in *Novy Mir*. Wonderful! Subtle and intelligent. How lucky I managed to read them before going to Osaka.

1 September

Yesterday I took Senka and Mama to Kursky Station. Senka has grown up. His sadness seems somehow to have broken away from his cheerfulness. In some ways that's good and in some ways—bad.

He's dreadfully scatter-brained, doesn't concentrate, doesn't pay attention. I spent a whole hour explaining to him how to tell the time. He seemed to have understood; then I asked him an hour later—and he had forgotten it all!

Though perhaps it is natural that he should be so lacking in concentration.

Actually it may be that he is in fact concentrating very hard on something.

A child doesn't have to be a prodigy. He has to be a child. The only thing that matters is that he shouldn't become 'stuck' in childishness.

Read Vonnegut's *Children's Crusade*. Yes, he's a pacifist, and a good man. Writes with verve.

But where are our senseless, useless, great, Russian depths?! How sad.

'I don't want to have a new daddy. Why can't I have the same one!'

'What's all that? What new daddy?'

'Mummy said I would have to have a new daddy.'

'We'll see, we'll talk about it another time.'

(Conversation with Senka).

Why did Ira put it like that? Why a new *daddy*? I'll have to talk to her about it.

It would be good to illustrate the cinema book (*Juxtapositions*) with some of Uncle Lyova's photographs.

Going through old papers I came across the transcript of a university debate on *Rublyov*. God, what a level. Abysmal, pathetic. But there is one remarkable contribution by a maths professor called Manin, Lenin Prize winner, who can hardly be more than thirty. I share his views. Not that one should say that about oneself. But it's exactly what I felt when I was making *Andrey*. And I'm grateful to Manin for that.

'Almost every speaker has asked why they have to be made to suffer all through the three hours of the film. I'll try to reply to that question.

'It is because the twentieth century has seen the rise of a kind of emotional inflation. When we read in a newspaper that two million people have been butchered in Indonesia, it makes as much impression on us as an account of our hockey team winning a match. The same degree of impression! We fail to notice the monstrous discrepancy between these two events. The channels of our perception have been smoothed out to the point where we are no longer aware. However, I don't want to preach about this. It may be that without it life would be impossible. Only the point is that there are some artists who do make us feel the true measure of things. It is a burden which they carry throughout their lives, and we must be thankful to them.'

It was worth sitting through two hours of rubbish for the sake of that last sentence.

This isn't the moment for complaints and indignation in the corridors. It's too late for that—complaints seem pointless and undignified. We have to think very seriously about how we can carry on living: any rash move could have disastrous consequences.

It is not a question of safeguarding particular advantages, what is at stake is the very life of our intelligentsia, our nation, our art. If the decline of art is obvious—which it is—and if art is the soul of the nation, then our nation, our country, is suffering from a grave psychic disease.

(I'm inclining more towards Bibi.)

I'd love to show *Rublyov* to Solzhenitsyn. Mention it to Shostakovich.

3 September

'They say that the true carver works with a slightly blunt chisel.' —Kenko-Khosi, *Notes to Relieve Tedium*, 14th century.

'The autumn moon is unutterably beautiful. Anyone who thinks the moon is always like that has no concept of difference, and is to be pitied.'—ibid.

'. . . And when all sorts of different ideas come crowding unbidden into our souls, it may be because there is no soul in us. If our soul had its own master, then surely our breasts would not be bursting with such a multitude of cares.'—ibid.

Yesterday I went to see N. P. Abramov about an interview for the Polish periodical *Cinema*. He's a nice, inoffensive man, but terribly limited. He was thrilled by what I said about the nature of cinema and about science fiction. Had he really never thought of it himself? He gave me his clumsily-written and unspeakably empty books. What a bore.

How vain those old men are—those Gerasimovs! How desperate they are for fame, acclaim, awards, prizes! They apparently think it's going to make them better filmmakers. They're pretty pathetic.

Poor little dilettantes earning money with this and that. And highly professional with it, I may add.

Heyse said something apt about that, incidentally: 'A dilettante is a curious person who derives pleasure from doing things he is not capable of doing.'

I also feel sorry for those so-called artists, poets and writers who feel that they are in no fit state to work; what they are really talking about is not working but earning.

One doesn't need a lot to be able to live. The great thing is to be free in your work. Of course it's important to print or exhibit, but if that's not possible you still are left with the most important thing of all—being able to work without asking anybody's permission.

However, in cinema that is not possible. You can't take a single shot unless the State graciously allows you to. Still less could you use your own money. That would be viewed as robbery, ideological aggression, subversion.

If a writer, despite his natural gifts, gives up writing because no one will publish him, then he is no writer. The artist is distinguished by his urge to create, which by very definition is a concomitant of talent.

5 September

Today I have to answer Abramov's idiotic questions.

Andriushka has an inflammation of the mammary gland. The hospital gave him an ichthyol bandage; poor little boy. He's been smiling all morning.

I'm worried about the Japanese visa. Of course we don't know when it'll come. The set-up is enough to drive you mad. If we don't arrive until the end of the exhibition we shan't have time to film anything. We'll have to film in the town. What idiots, God forgive me!

You'd think I was a private individual making films for my own pleasure and reward and coming up against protests and resistance.

What are we going to do now about a production manager and a costume designer?

O. Teynishvili told my assistant that it's not worth 'pushing' Bibi— too difficult, not a good idea, and so on. That's it. I'll come down on him on Tuesday. We'll see. Officials have invented a new approach —criticizing everything and everyone and making out that they themselves are the only decent people in the entire system; and explaining their own indolence by the fact that it's 'impossible to work'. But G. I. Kunitsyn is quite different. That's why he was given a bad time—he tried to take his own decisions.

What is truth? The concept of truth? It must be something so human as to have no equivalent in objective, supra-human, absolute terms.

And since it is human, it is limited, rigidly confined, in human terms, within the framework of the human milieu. There is no conceivable link between what is human and the cosmos. And the same applies to truth. To attain greatness within our own limits—which are Euclidean and insignificant in juxtaposition with infinity—is to illustrate that we are merely human. Anyone who does not aspire to greatness of soul is worthless; as insignificant as a field-mouse or a fox. Religion is the one area set aside by man to define what is powerful. But 'the most powerful thing in the world', said Lao-Tzu, 'cannot be seen or heard or touched.'

By virtue of the infinite laws, or the laws of infinity that lie beyond what we can reach, God cannot but exist. For man, who is unable to grasp the essence of what lies beyond, the unknown—the unknowable—is GOD. And in a moral sense, God is love.

Man has to have an ideal in order to be able to live without tormenting other people. An ideal as a spiritual, ethical concept of law.

Morality is within a person. Ethical precepts are something external that have been thought up in place of morality. Where there is no morality, ethical precepts hold sway—bankrupt and worthless. Where morality exists there is no call for precepts.

The ideal is unattainable, and in its understanding of this phenomenon lies the greatness of human reason.

The attempt to present something attainable and specific in the guise of the ideal subverts common sense, it is a way to madness.

Man is estranged. It might seem that a common cause could become the basis of a new community; but that is a fallacy. People have been stealing and playing the hypocrite for the last fifty years, united in their sense of purpose, but with no community. People can only be united in a common cause if that cause is based on morality and is within the realm of the ideal, of the absolute.

That is why labour can never in itself be elevating. That is why there is such a thing as technical progress. If labour were a moral category, a valour, then progress would be reactionary, which would be absurd.

'To claim that labour is virtue is as great a distortion as it would be to equate a man's nourishment with virtue and morality', said Lev Tolstoy.

He needed to stitch boots and to plough for quite another reason: in order to experience, with special intensity, his own flesh—that flesh of which he was the singer.

If it's not possible to 'grasp what cannot be grasped' then, apart from God, man has not justified his existence in any way.

Religion, philosophy, art—those three pillars on which the world has rested—were invented by man in order symbolically to encapsulate the idea of infinity, setting against it a symbol of its possible attainment (which in real terms is of course impossible). Humanity has found nothing else on such an enormous scale. Admittedly man found it by instinct, without understanding why he needed God (easier that way!) or philosophy (explains everything, even the meaning of life!) or art (immortality).

What an inspired idea is the notion of infinity in juxtaposition with the brief span of human life. The very concept is infinite. Not that I am convinced so far that man is the yardstick of this whole construction. What about plants? There is no yardstick. Or maybe it is everywhere—in each tiny particle of the universe. That would not be too good for man; there's a lot he would have to give up; nature would not need him. At least on Earth, man has realized that he is standing face to face with infinity.

Or perhaps it's just a muddle? After all, nobody can prove that there is a meaning. On the other hand, of course, if someone were to prove it (to himself, naturally) he would go off his head. His life would become meaningless.

H. G. Wells has a story called *The Apple*, about how people were frightened to eat the apple from the tree of knowledge. It's a brilliant idea.

I am by no means certain that after death there'll be nothing, a void, as clever people assure us, a dreamless sleep. Nobody has dreamless sleeps like that: as if a person could fall asleep (which he remembers) and then wake up again (he remembers that too) and remember nothing of what went on in between—something happened, only he cannot remember what . . .

Of course life has no point. If it had, man would not be free, he'd become a slave to that point and his life would be governed by completely new criteria: the criteria of slavery. Like an animal, the point of whose life is that life itself, the continuation of the species.

An animal carries out its slavish activities because it can feel the point of its life instinctively. Therefore its sphere is restricted. Man, on the other hand, claims to aspire to the absolute.

7 September

What will our children be like? A lot depends on us. But it's up to them as well. What must be alive in them is a striving for freedom. That depends on us. People who have been born into slavery find it hard to lose the habit.

On the one hand it would be good if the next generation could enjoy some measure of peace; on the other hand peace can be a dangerous thing. Philistinism and all that is petty bourgeois in us inclines heavily towards peace. Whatever happens, they mustn't slide into spiritual lethargy.

The most important things to instil in children are virtue and a sense of honour.

Whatever happens I must make *The Bright Day*. That is part of the same work. A duty.

How terrible and ignoble to feel that you do not owe anything to anybody. Because that can never be the case. It's an attitude that can only be adopted with great effort; by shutting your eyes.

There are a lot of people like that nowadays. I think I've seen through Arturo M.; a very weak man. To the point where he actually betrays himself; the ultimate abasement.

Lenya Kozlov and I are working on *Juxtapositions*. It's tough going. We want to talk about everything, and talk truthfully. But some questions are taboo, and one way or another they'll be edited out. We'll just have to go for the theory.

I think constantly about *The Bright Day*. It could make a beautiful picture. It will actually be an instance of a film built in its entirety on personal experience. And for that reason, I'm convinced, it will be important to those who see it.

If only I had finished *Solaris*, and it isn't even started. A whole year to go; and what a miserable year . . . there's no one to work with.

I've sacked the production manager. And the wardrobe mistress as well. And who is going to take their place? There's no one at all in the studio.

A telegram has just arrived from Banionis: 'American trip postponed to spring.' Just when we're going to need him. Each day is more alarming than the one before. If there's no Banionis, then who is there? Maybe Kesha Smotkunovsky?

I must do something about Bibi straightaway.

But from what angle? How should I start? Teynishvili just mutters and is not convinced.

Quite by accident I came across Evtushenko's *Kazan Universities* in *Novy Mir*. What awful stuff. Staggeringly bad. Low-brow avant-garde. The Siberian was infinitely more talented than that before. And what's left of him now? 'Pineapples in champagne' and contemptuous smiles.

It's pathetic the way Zhenya flirts to win admiration.

He once came up to me in the VTO,* drunk, and said, 'Why are you so cruel, Andrey?' I didn't answer.

'You know, you remind me of a blue-blooded White who took part in Kolchak's retreat over the ice. Only my grandfather or father were probably lying in the snow at that point, as partisans, settled in with their old guns. All those officers were frozen into the ice, you know, they couldn't budge.'

A true humanitarian, that Zhenya.

Possible films:
  I. *Kagol* (Borman's trial)
  II. *Physicist-Dictator* (various versions)
  III. *The House with a Tower*
  IV. *Echo Calls*
  V. *Deserters*
  VI. *Joseph and His Brothers*
  VII. Solzhenitsyn's *Matryona's House*
  VIII. *Dostoievsky*
  IX. *The Bright Day*—as soon as possible!
  X. Dostoievsky's *A Raw Youth*
  XI. *Joan of Arc, 1970*
  XII. Camus' *The Plague*
  XIII. *Two Saw the Fox*

Screenplays:
  I. *The Last Hunting Trip* or *The Clash*
  II. *Catastrophe*
  III. *The Flying Man* (based on Belyaev)

In a good period I could have been a millionaire. Making two films a year from 1960 on I could have made twenty films . . . Fat chance with our idiots.

*All-Union Theatre Society.

'There are some fools in the world, but this lot's solid fool.'
'Stupid. Aksyon's stupid, moving his hut three times. Looking for something better.'—Country conversations.

Playwrights often overdo the clever line or turn as the curtain's about to fall. It shows lack of taste. You don't find it in good plays.

The strange thing is that when people come together in a community for the purpose, simply, of production, or for reasons of geography, they start to hate each other and do one another down. Because each one only loves himself. Community is an illusion, as a result of which sooner or later there will rise over the continents evil, deadly, mushroom clouds.

An agglomeration of people aiming at one thing—filling their stomachs—is doomed to destruction, decay, hostility.

'Not by bread alone.'

Man is made up of opposing characteristics. History demonstrates vividly the fact that it always moves in the worst possible direction. Either man is not capable of directing history, or else he does direct it, but only by pushing it down the most terrible, wrong path there is.

There is not a single example to prove the opposite. People are not capable of governing others. They are only capable of destroying. And materialism—naked and cynical—is going to complete the destruction.

Despite the fact that God lives in every soul, that every soul has the capacity to accumulate what is eternal and good, as a mass people can do nothing but destroy. For they have come together not in the name of an ideal, but simply for the sake of a material notion.

Mankind has hurried to protect the body (perhaps on the strength of that natural and unconscious gesture which served as the beginning of what is called progress) and has given no thought to protecting the soul.

The church (as opposed to religion) has not been able to do so. In the course of the history of civilization the spiritual half of man has been separated further and further from the animal, the material, and now in an infinite expanse of darkness we can just make out, like the lights of a departing train, the other half of our being as it rushes away, irrevocably and for ever.

Spirit and flesh, feeling and reason can never again be made one. It's too late. For the moment we are crippled by the appalling disease of spiritual deficiency; and the disease is fatal. Mankind has done everything possible to annihilate itself, starting with its own moral annihilation—physical death is merely the result.

How insignificant, pitiful and vulnerable people are when they think about 'bread' and only about 'bread', and don't realize that thinking like that can only lead to death. The one achievement of human reason is its recognition of the dialectical principle. And if only man were consistent, and not suicidal, he would understand so much by being guided by that principle.

Everyone can be saved only if each saves himself.

The time has come for individual prowess. The banquet during the plague. You can only save everyone else by saving yourself: in a spiritual sense, of course. Concerted efforts are useless. As people we lack the instinct for the preservation of the species that ants and bees possess. On the other hand, we have immortal souls, which humanity has spat on with vicious delight. Instinct cannot save us; the lack of it will be our downfall. And we don't give a rap for our spiritual, moral foundations. So where does salvation lie? No good turning to our leaders, that's for sure.

Now only a genius can save humanity—not a prophet, no!—a genius who will formulate a new moral ideal. But where is he, this Messiah? There is nothing left for us but to learn to die with dignity. Cynicism has never saved anyone yet; it's the lot of the faint-hearted.

Human history looks all too like some monstrous experiment with people, set up by a cruel being incapable of pity. A kind of vivisection. And will it ever be explained? Surely human fate cannot just be the cycle of an endless process, the point of which people are not able to understand? The thought is terrifying. After all, despite everything, despite the cynicism and the materialism, man does believe in the Infinite, in Immortality. If you were to tell him that not one more person was to be born into the world, he'd put a bullet through his brain.

It has been drummed into man that he's mortal, but faced with something that really threatens to take away his right to Immortality he will resist as if he were about to be killed.

Man has simply been corrupted. Or rather, little by little people have corrupted each other. And all through the centuries, right up to the present day, those who thought about the soul have been— and still are being—physically eliminated.

The one thing that might save us is a new heresy that could topple all the ideological institutions of our wretched, barbaric world.

The greatness of modern man lies in protest.

Thank God for people who burn themselves alive in front of an impassive, wordless crowd, or who walk out into squares with placards and slogans condemning themselves to reprisals, and all those who say 'No' to the go-getters and the godless.

To rise above the opportunity of living, to acknowledge practically the mortality of our flesh in the name of the future, in the name of Immortality . . .

If humanity is still capable of that, then all is not lost. There is still a chance.

Humanity has suffered too much, and man's sense of suffering has atrophied. That is dangerous; because it means that it is no longer possible now to save humanity by means of blood and suffering. God, what a time to be alive!

10 September

Andriushka is already smiling and laughing and saying 'goo', and follows things with his eyes, even turns his head, and he recognizes me. Tries to roll over onto his tummy. Nobody believes us when we tell them. And it is hard to believe, after all he was only a month old on the 7th. When he makes faces he looks like Dopey in Disney's *Snow White*.

11 September

Yesterday Zavattini sent Larissa some roses and a note saying, 'Long live the new Tarkovksy, Zavattini.' (Valery Sirovsky translated it and congratulated us warmly.) We must write and thank him.

Sasha Mishurin seems to have vanished off the face of the earth. I'll have to get hold of him.

Yesterday there was a party to celebrate Lenya Kozlov's doctorate, in the House of Architects. I came back from there with Frehlich. I think he's a nice man, but he surprised me by making the rather unexpected suggestion that I might make a film from his screenplay. Just what I need! Oh, dear. The moment anyone offers me their screenplay I make a run for it. And for some reason the person always falls in my estimation, even though really he has done nothing dishonourable. But surely Frehlich, who I thought knew something about me, must know that I shall only ever make films from my own screenplays? In any case, I am not sure that he's capable of writing a screenplay. Then he told me that Otar Teynishvili had said that *Rublyov* was going to released soon. So why hasn't Otar said anything to me about it? Something odd is going on . . .

Андрюшка уже улыбается, слегка угукает, следит глазами, даже поворачивая голову, узнает меня. Пытается поворачиваться на пузо. Никто не верит, что мы не распеленываем.

Да и трудно поверить, ведь ему исполнилось только месяц.

Своими угуканьями он поет на "прогулка" из Диснеевского фильма о белоснежке.

Вчера Дзаваттини прислал Ларисе розы и запи...:

un evviva al
nuovo Tarkovsky
Zavattini
Roma 31. 8. 70

Да здравствует Новый Тарковский!
Дзаваттини
(Перевел и об ней души по-
здравил Валерий Боровский)

Надо послать ему письмо и поблагодарить.

Саша Мишарин словно сквозь землю провалился.

Надо его разыскать.

Вчера в Доме Архитектуры праздновалась защита лепет Козловым кандидатской диссертации.

Возвращались оттуда вдвоем с Фрейдлихом. Он хороший по-моему человек, но удивил меня нес-

Andriushka can follow a rattle with his eyes, and turns his head to see it. It's really very early.

12 September

The other day I talked to our sound editor, Yuri Mikhailov. He really is excellent. According to him we shouldn't use Bach in the film, it's in fashion. Lots of people are using Bach.

Teynishvili said today that after *Solaris* he'd like to offer me some sort of work abroad. I wonder what he has in mind. And whom? Gambarov?

In any case it would be worth explaining to him that I'm not going to make anything just for money.

I think that after *Solaris* I must make *The Bright Day*.

I wonder if I shall ever earn enough to pay off all my debts and buy the most basic essentials—a sofa, the odd bit of furniture, a typewriter, the books that I'd like to have of my own? Then there are repairs to be done in the country—that means more money.

I haven't seen my father for ages. The longer I don't see him the more depressing and alarming it becomes to go to him. It's patently clear that I have a complex about my parents. I don't feel adult when I'm with them. And I don't think they consider me adult either. Our relations are somehow tortured, complicated, unspoken. It's not straightforward, any of it. I love them dearly, but I've never felt at ease with them, or their equal. I think they're shy of me too, even though they love me.

It's extraordinary—Ira and I have separated, I have a new life, a different life, and they go on as if they hadn't noticed. Even now, when *Andriushka* has been born (NB: tomorrow or the day after—go to Registry Office and register him). They are too inhibited to talk to me about any of it. And so am I. It could go on like that for ever.

It's very difficult to talk if you're playing at 'you can't say yes or no or black or white'. Whose fault is it? Theirs, or perhaps mine. Everybody's, up to a point.

All the same, I must go and see my father before I leave for Japan. It's a torment for him too, our relationship being as it is. I know that for certain. I just can't imagine how things would develop if I were the one to break the ice. And it's so difficult. Perhaps I should write a letter? But a letter won't decide anything. Afterwards we would meet and both pretend the letter had never happened. It's a kind of Dostoievskyism, or Dolgorukyism.* We all love each other and are

*A reference to Dostoievsky's *A Raw Youth*.

shy, afraid of one another. For some reason it's far easier for me to relate to total strangers . . .

Now I shall go to bed and read Hesse's *The Glass Bead Game*. I've been tracking it down for ages, and today, at last, it has actually reached me. How scared I am of funerals. Even when my grandmother was being buried it was frightening. Not because she had died, but because I was surrounded by people who were expressing their feelings. I can't bear seeing people express their feelings, even sincere ones. I find it intolerable when my nearest and dearest give expression to their feelings.

I remember my father and I were standing by the church, waiting for the moment when we could take grandmother's coffin away (the service and burial were in different places) and my father said (it doesn't matter what it was about), 'Good is passive. And evil is active.'

During the burial service for my grandmother and the others (I think there were seven or eight of them) in the church in the Danilov cemetery, I was standing at the head of her coffin, not far from Marina and Mother. Marina kept starting to cry. The priest wrote down the names of the departed and the service began. When the priest, in the course of the service, read out the names of all the departed, I thought he had forgotten to mention Vera, that he'd left out my grandmother's name by mistake. I was so horrified that I started pushing my way through to the priest in order to remind him of my grandmother's name. I felt that if I didn't do that something terrible would happen to my grandmother. She knew before she died that she would be given a funeral service. And now there she was, lying there, believing that the burial prayers were being said for her, and the priest had absent-mindedly left out her name. She was lying there dead, but I knew that she too would have been horrified if she had been able to feel and realize that her name had been forgotten during the service. I was right beside the priest who was just starting to list the names for the second time when I heard— Vera . . . So I must have just imagined it. But how it scared me!

That was the only burial I had been to. No—the first time I was at a cemetery was when Antonina Aleksandrovna, my father's second wife, was being buried. But at that time I was really only a child. All I remember is the dead woman's fine, sharp profile and heavily powdered face. She had died of a brain tumour. Cancer. It was winter and my head was freezing. Then, too, my father was beside me.

I remember when I was still quite small and was visiting my father in Party (!) Street, Uncle Leva (I think it was) appeared.

My father was sitting on the sofa wrapped in a blanket, I suppose he was unwell. Uncle Leva stopped in the doorway and said, 'You know, Arseniy, Maria Danilovna has died.'

My father sat there for a moment, not taking it in, then he half turned away and started to cry. He looked terribly unhappy and alone, sitting on the sofa in a blanket. Maria Danilovna was my paternal grandmother. My father hardly ever saw her. He seemed somehow ill at ease as well. Perhaps it runs in the family, anyhow on my father's side? Or maybe I'm mistaken about my father and grandmother Maria Danilovna. They may have had a quite different sort of relationship from my mother and me. My mother has sometimes said that Arseniy only ever thought about himself, that he was an egoist. I don't know whether she's right or not. She'd have every right to say that I'm an egoist, too. I must be. But I do love my mother, and my father, and Marina, and Senka. Only a stupor comes over me and I can't utter my feelings. My love is not active, somehow. Probably all I want is to be left in peace, even forgotten. I don't want to count on their love, nor do I demand anything from them, apart from freedom. But there is no freedom, nor will there be. Then they blame me for Ira, I can feel that. They love her, normally and simply. I'm not jealous, only I don't want them to torment me and think I'm a saint. I'm not a saint and I'm not an angel.

What I am is an egoist, who is afraid more than anything else in the world of pain suffered by those he loves.

I'm going to go and read Hesse.

18 September

Just read Zamyatin's *Us*. Feeble and pretentious. All that would-be racy, 'dynamic' prose. It's somehow a nasty little book.

Today I saw Bondarchuk's *Waterloo*. Poor old Seryozha! It's embarrassing.

An Italian came up to me today, I think he's called Roberto Coma. He's in charge of *Waterloo* on the Laurentiis side. He wanted to know what possibility there might be of inviting me to make a film. I advised him to read Mann's *Joseph*; you never know. If that comes off, it would be good to film Camus' *The Plague*.

Sasha Mishurin and I could certainly write the screenplay.

Incidentally, I met Alla G. It turns out that Sasha had gone on a tremendous binge. And now for the next two months he's going to be doing army training. Poor fellow.

Sasha! At least he's apparently managed to get himself onto the newspaper. The army and Sasha—two mutually exclusive concepts.

> Through roadway dust, through mists on furrowed fields,
> Escape the prison grip of fall aslant,
> All-piercing incandescent whispering
> Expanse of childhood! Sharp as a dry awn
> Will stab you, while white towers are tilting,
> Transpierce with whitewashed wall and heady barm,
> The town's collapse, the burst of childish fear,
> A quivering of lace along the paths.
> Like glowing tan concealing a disease
> Decay in woody fibres. Painted
> With deathly paleness of remembrance.
> How fearful suddenly the fearless jump
> From off the rotting roof . . .

Vladimir 1964—
Moscow 1970

I saw a very bad film by Bunuel—I forget the name—oh, yes, *Tristana*, about a woman who has her leg amputated and who sometimes dreams of a bell with her husband/stepfather's head in it instead of a clapper. It's unbelievably vulgar. Just occasionally Bunuel allows himself lapses like that.

Read Akutagawa's story about water-sprites—'kappas'. Rather mediocre and limp.

Chukhrai asked me to bring them the screenplay of *The Bright Day*. He wants me to make it with their team. They're allegedly thinking of buying *Ariel* as well. We'll see. I don't trust Chukhrai. He's often let people down. Betrayed them.

20 September

Several people have complained about it.

Since the war culture has somehow collapsed, fallen apart. All over the world. Along with spiritual criteria. Here, quite obviously, apart from anything else it's the result of the consistent, barbaric, annihilation of culture. And without culture society naturally runs wild. God knows where it's all going to end. Never before has ignorance reached such monstrous proportions. This repudiation of the spiritual can only engender monsters. Now, as never before, we have to make a stand for everything that has the slightest relevance to the spiritual.

How readily man turns away from immortality; surely he is not quintessentially brutish?

It's far harder to maintain a high moral state than to vegetate in insignificance.

In *The Glass Bead Game* Hesse has some wonderful things to say about Chinese music. He refers to it a lot and ends with these words: 'Truth has to be lived, not taught. Prepare for battle!'

Reading *The Glass Bead Game*—what a brilliant book. Again: 'Our entire life, both physical and spiritual, is a dynamic phenomenon, from the fullness of which the Game catches only the aesthetic side, and indeed for the most part it does so only in the form of rhythmic processes.'

This is the height of art, based on the universal, on the experience of all knowledge and all discoveries. A spiritual symbol of life. A novel of genius. It's a long time since I read anything like it. An even, benevolent attitude is a sign of good upbringing.

21 September

Late yesterday evening E. D. rang and said that Chernoutsan had just telephoned him: Suslov signed the document for the release of *Rublyov* immediately after the Congress. I must find out from Kolya straightaway which cinemas and how many copies. Of course if the Committee insists on cuts I'll tell them to go to hell. So I must see A. N. Kosygin as soon as possible. He apparently wanted to meet me and spoke highly of the film.

Tomorrow Vadim and I are going to Yalta—flying—to choose locations.

He's just rung to say that there doesn't seem to be any point in going until we know definitely about Japan. That's what I always said. What are they all fussing about?

'. . . The music of a well-ordered age is calm and joyful, its guiding principle is balance. The music of a troubled age is restless, sullen, its guiding principle is against nature. The music of a decadent state is sentimental and cheerless, its guiding principle is under threat.'—Li Bu-vey, *Spring and Autumn*.

I've just spoken to Andron on the telephone. He had a conversation with Seryozha Bondarchuk, who is organizing his own team at Mosfilm. He's inviting Andron, Saltykov, S. Surin, Panfilov from Leningrad, and me. In charge will be young Dostal, chief editor

V. Solovyov, and Bondarchuk will be artistic director.

He's been talking about it for some time. He wants the people making films to make two a year.

If only . . .! Somehow I can't believe it. How many wonderful films one could make. But I don't think that even Sergey—even supposing he wanted to—could actually manage to create a state within a state.

The Bright Day would have to be made there, in that case. I'd better wait a bit with Chukhrai.

'But what I would really like is that when the time comes to break away and jump, I shall jump not backwards, not down, but forward to something higher.'—Joseph Knecht in Hesse's *Glass Bead Game*.

'What you call passion is not moral energy but friction between the soul and the external world.'—Hesse.

Today, before it's too late, I must find out where Surin stands on the question of our trip, and put him in touch with the Committee, otherwise he'll fly to Yugoslavia and then it really will be too late.

They've found a wardrobe mistress to replace I. Belyakova who was sacked (utterly useless)—N. Fomina. If she has Misha's drawings I think she'll cope.

When I telephoned Surkov he told me that there's a connection between the release of *Rublyov* and a memo about the film that was presented at the Congress. Now they're all going to make out that they were responsible. Anyhow the main reason was the fact that Kosygin talked to Kozintsev and Shostakovich. And none of the bureaucrats had anything to do with it.

Today some official, a journalist, said to Kozlov, 'Apparently Tarkovksy has been given permission to take a condemned prisoner into *Solaris* so that he'll die on screen' . . . ! ! ! ?

2 *October*

The studio has refused to make preparations for the transport of the sets in Yalta. They can't afford it. Now they're going to apply to the Committee for a limit of 1,800,000 on our estimate, plus six months' preparation period.

Those are quite substantial demands. I only hope they're not made an excuse for cancelling the film. We urgently need a production manager. Who? Where is this production manager?

Sasha Gordon showed the material for *Theft* today. We watched it together. A dreadful spectacle. Really bad. Such a pity.

Tomorrow is Marina's birthday. I must go whatever happens.

3 October

I went to see Marina on her birthday. My father and I travelled home together. He reminded me of the day when Uncle Leva Gornung told my father that Maria Danilovna had died. It was in March 1943. But my father already knew about it. He had heard earlier, in the hospital.

8 October

I had a letter from Georgiy Malarchuk, from Kishinyov. And a periodical with his American travel journal. The journal is bad—tendentious and full of loyal clichés. Depressing.

Georgiy writes that his fellow villagers in his native district want him to be president of the collective farm.

An extraordinary concatenation of circumstances. There's something behind it. But things are not likely to be any easier for him as president; not under our system, which makes even the running of a collective farm dependent on central administrators, who apply endless pressure entirely in their own interests.

Roberto Coma telephoned again about my invitation to Italy to make *Joseph and His Brothers*, based on Thomas Mann. They've agreed in principle. Their Communist Party helps with the production and hiring of films.

Roberto said that Visconti wanted to make a Mann film, but for some reason it fell through.

It would be wonderful to make *Joseph*. Only how will the Committee react? It's hardly likely to get through. They're like a brick wall. Bondarchuk is the only one to break through it. If it were to come off, it would be important to have conditions written into the contract, guaranteeing me a free hand: actors, cameraman, designer, etc.

Yussov and Abdusalimov are supposed to be coming. Shavkat is sensitive to the torrid, biblical feel of the thing.

What we must do—first and foremost—is write the screenplay. I think Sasha and I can do that together. I'll ring him now (he's just back from his army training). He's thrilled at the prospect of *Joseph*. It'll be hard work. In fact, hellishly difficult.

17 October

A lot has happened in the last few days. Saw Alov and Naumov's film, *The Flight*. It's terrible! It makes a mockery of everything Russian—temperament, individual character, officer. Bloody hell!

There was a row over the 1,850,000 that we (i.e. the studio) requested from the Committee. And over the extension of the preparation time. We're going to ask for 1,250,000. If they let us have 1,000,000—that'll do (or will it?).

We want to cut 'Prometheus'. And go straight from 'The House' to landing at Solaris station. I've written a letter to the Committee—to Chernoutsan. We must have a trip abroad in order to film a 'town of the future'. Japan fell through for a whole series of reasons. But basically it was Chutkin being silly.

Yesterday we were given the choice of two production managers—Gostinsky or Polyak (sacked from the committee apparatus for stealing or something of the sort). I'm for Polyak.

Went to see Malarchuk in Moscow. His talk of wanting to be president of the collective farm is serious. Well, good luck to him!

'What would a person gain from the liberation of the whole world if his soul were not free?'—George Santayana (1863–1952).

'If on the last day the entire created world is singing alleluia while there remains a single cockroach whose love is unrequited, it will disturb the peace of the *boddhisattva* (enlightened one, almost Buddha) but will not affect the self-absorption of the *arahaut* (or hermit, totally detached from the world).'—William James (1842–1910).

It is meaningless, and therefore absurd, to make a distinction between idealistic and materialistic philosophy on the basis of a spurious watershed arbitrarily introduced into the question of whether primacy lies with matter or with consciousness. You might as well argue about which came first—the chicken or the egg. Put like that, the question can't lead anywhere—except to war between the 'big-enders' and the 'little-enders'.

20 October

On the 18th we had a telegram from Scherbakov: there's been a fire in our house in Myasnoye. The whole middle section has been destroyed. All the wood. Tosia was there the day before, and lit the stove—maybe that was how it happened. Anyhow, the house has been burnt down. The roof must have collapsed, and the tiles fallen in. We must find out about the tiles. One way or another it's not too good.

In the spring we must do all the rebuilding we wanted to do earlier. It'll take about three thousand. We'll see. Whatever happens it must all be done by the summer. We must find out about a garage in our yard.

We shall almost certainly not be given more than 1,000,000 for the picture. And because of the dates Bibi won't be able to be in it. We have to look for an actress.

24 October

Seryozha must really draw a plan for the building work at Myasnoye; then it can be sent to Shilovo for them to give us a price for materials and labour. As far as I can gather it's going to cost 4000. I'll get 1000 for *Ariel*, which I'll have to spend on a sofa and the bedroom. And what'll be left? What about my debts? In February (roughly) I'll get another 2600 or so. That's the only money I can count on as far as the house is concerned. Maybe the family will chip in. If it doesn't get built in the spring the whole project will collapse. Perhaps I shall start getting royalties for *Rublyov* in the spring. If work is being done on the house then someone has to be living there all the time. Otherwise there's no point in embarking on it at all. It all has to be thought out.

The studio's in a mess. They're not willing to ask the Committee for more than 900,000. That is useless. Polyak refused to be our production manager. What's going to happen? Yesterday I wrote a desperate letter to Chernoutsan. Larissa promised to get it to him through some friends. Will it help?

The Japanese trip has fallen through. We're 350,000 short for the film. There are no rolls of film. We're short of an actress. There are no costumes. The team can't work without an estimate confirmed by the Committee.

It's a crazy situation. And of course no one does anything to help. At best all they do is chat.

With all that's going on there's not a hope of getting down to my book. It's hanging over me like the sword of Damocles.

Kolya S. suggested we meet at his place in a week's time and read *The Bright Day*; and in a gentle sort of way start getting ready to make the film. He wanted to invite one or two people, including Chernoutsan. I'd like Sasha Mishurin and Felix Kuznetsov to be there.

Andriushka is growing. He's a delightful little boy. Funny and cheerful. Only he never seems to be able to get enough for his size—

he's large. From tomorrow Larissa wants to supplement with porridge and juices.

In a word, this is a madhouse, apart from Andriushka and everything connected with him. I must write to Ira. Senka and I must have some sort of more regular arrangement. Ira thinks it doesn't matter that much that we don't have a straightforward relationship. How stupid! I know all too well what it means not to see one's father. Children understand everything, after all.

7 November

Andriushka is three months old today. Good, sweet little boy. Actually he's terribly dribbly and has started to play up. As for work, it's all bad. No money, no production manager, no actress. All bad.

Went to see Grisha Poshenyan yesterday. Altogether feeling thoroughly low. To hell with them all.

14 November

Things are gradually falling into place. A. E. Yablochkin has agreed to take on our picture. Admittedly I am going to have to let him have 500 roubles out of the production money.

We must have the house done up in the spring. Our money in the country: 50 roubles with Grigory Al., 110 in the form of roofing paper, fencing, etc., was burnt in the house.

I'm a bit below par. Heart spasms: my aorta wasn't functioning properly. The doctor (Sasha) has forbidden me either to smoke or to drink. Absolutely strictly. Not a single cigarette. I gave up smoking that same day (12 November '70). Andriushka is delightful. More like an angel than a baby.

15 November

I really have to make a note of the fact that on 12 November 1970 I gave up smoking. Frankly, it was high time. The last few weeks I've been feeling somehow empty and dull-witted. Either because I've been ill, or because I feel frustrated. You could very easily expire without ever having done anything. And there's so much I want to do . . .

Reading Thomas Mann's stupendous *Joseph and His Brothers*. The whole approach is as it were from the far side. Kitchen gossip from the far side. I can see why the typist, as she finished typing out *Joseph*, said, 'Now at least I know how it really happened.' Yes, . . .

but as for screening it, I really don't know what to say. For the moment, I don't see how it would come across.

I want to restore the house in the country—then there'd be some point. Build a bath-house, cultivate the garden. The children could graze. I must ask Fedya about the GAZ-69. It looks as if it's all talk (on his part). My father came to see us yesterday. He was introduced to his grandson who wore his smart blue suit for the occasion. Please God.

17 November

There's a great furore over Solzhenitsyn. The awarding of the Nobel Prize took everyone by surprise. He's a good writer; and above all—citizen. Rather embittered, which is entirely understandable humanly speaking but harder to understand if one thinks of him primarily as a writer. His best thing is *Matryona's House*. But as a personality he's heroic. Noble and stoical. His existence lends a point to my life too.

My father has had a heart attack. He categorically refuses to go into hospital—he's got a thing about hospitals altogether. He doesn't want to see the doctor. And there he is with his aneurysm!

I think he has a contract—or if he hasn't got it yet he will any minute now—for another book. Marvellous. I so want him to write more poetry now. Only—God grant him health.

There's a new production manager in the studio, someone called Sizov; from Mossoviet. He's also deputy chairman of the Cinema Committee. In the right hands that's an asset, in the wrong ones— a disaster. Is there ever going to be order in Russia, or will there never be anything until the whole thing disintegrates?

There has never before been such universal, total repudiation of order. They've all become inveterate liars, time-servers, crooks. Life is impossible.

Oh, it's so vital to organize the house in Myasnoye. And a car. Garden, vegetable patch, household, sauna, house, car—all that together would solve most of the problems arising from the physical lack of work.

22 December, Rovno

Here I am in Rovno. A good, easy journey in a separate compartment. Fedya came to meet me.

I must telephone home tomorrow. I'm already missing Andriushka and Lara.

I must buy either a candlestick for New Year or some glasses—nice ones, I saw them in a shop. I'll have to rest a bit, do nothing, and then think about how to make *The Waiting Room*.

24 December

Not feeling too good; throat, head—a cold. I hope it's not 'flu. Boris and I talked together. Really homesick, missing Lara and Andriushka.

If she rings—ask about the Hungarian money. It would come in very useful at this moment.

Khari worries me terribly. We'll have to do a lot more tests. We must try out Terekhova, Terentieva, Orlova. Must tell Larissa to organize some trial takes with Vera Fyodorovna.

Have been reading about the Kennedy assassination. Of course they were pretty slack over Oswald, but all the same the way the whole thing was handled is very impressive. Compared with the American leaders, our lot are cretins.

1971

I'm very strongly affected by diaries and archives and 'laboratories' of every kind. They're a wonderful catalyst.

1971

1 January

No entries for some time. My mood has somehow not been right for cerebral exercises.

I went over to Fedya Rykalov at Rovno. Stayed a week there. Spent it pretty pointlessly. We probably shan't start filming before the middle of February and from now till then I'm going to have to spend quite a lot of time doing nothing.

Yussov and I must discuss making *The Waiting Room* sometime in the future. Naumov assured me he had spoken to Demichov about *Rublyov* and its release, and that he had been encouraging. It will apparently come out after the Congress. If there really is any question of doing *Joseph* with the Italians, I'm going to feel rather unsure.

How can Mann be filmed? It's obviously not possible.

2 January

If only we could start filming.

6 January

Reading the report of the discussion about *Rublyov* and its being passed for general release. There's a lot of interesting stuff.

This is the first file, dated 19 January 1966. There are things that are worth copying out.

V. M. Kreiss: '. . . Among the new material being proposed is a series of new scenes which I like very much; I think they improve the film, and that it would be worth cutting somewhere else in order to include the scene where the cat is killed.' (?!)

8 January

Romanov telephoned me today, very embarrassed. The Ambassador in Paris wired Romanov telling him to talk to me, and that as a result of that talk I was to refuse (officially) the prize (only just) awarded me by the French critics.

The point being that the president of that organization, Madame Voulmann, according to the Ambassador and Romanov, is a Zionist engaged in anti-Soviet propaganda. (?!)

I suggested dissociating ourselves by saying nothing. Not react to the prize at all. Kozyryov (the deputy foreign minister) thinks the same.

The trouble is that Romanov wants to talk to Demichov about it.

If need be I shall have to make the point that the prize is being awarded not by Voulmann but by the French critics.

31 January

On Friday I went to see the new production manager for the first time—someone called Nikolay Trofimovich Sizov. For the moment nothing is clear. He wants to have a talk with me this week about *Solaris*. What could that be about?

Read Clarke's *Odyssey 2001*. It breaks off before the end. There's a postword by I. Yefremov *explaining* why the end has been 'cut off' —as he puts it. I was so indignant I wrote a letter to the editor. Not that it will lead to anything, of course. Or only to something unpleasant.

11 February

Yesterday I returned from Yalta, which is snow-bound. Terrible wind, very cold. Very hard to travel around looking for locations in weather like that; particularly on the Crimean roads. We didn't find anything suitable. And because of today's art committee meeting about the first version of *Ariel*, I had to leave Yussov and Gavrilov in Yalta and come back to Moscow.

17 February

Missing Larochka terribly—she's gone to the country to organize the materials for doing up the house.

She's stuck there now, thanks to our hopeless, slovenly Russian ways. They all promise to help but they are terrible windbags. Time just doesn't matter to them. Bletherers. When Larochka's not there something always goes wrong. I went to House of Cinema and had a fight with Vassya Livanov. He was drinking, I was drinking, and we bashed each other up to such an extent that now neither he nor I can go out of the house. The next day he rang to apologize. He

Вчера вернулся из Ялты, которую всю
занесю снегом. Везер страшный
Очень холодно. Трудно ездить
на выбор натуры в такую погоду
особенно по крымским дорогам.
Ничего подходящего не нашли.
А из-за сегодняшнего худсовета по
II варианту "Аэлита", я вынужден
был оставить в Ялте Юсова и
Гаврилова и вернулся в Москву.

Есть идея пригласить
на роль Кэри одну финскую
актрису

Очень соскучился без
Ларочки — поехала в
деревню хлопотать насчет
материала для восстановле-
ния дома.
Застряла она там из-за
нашей российской безалабер-
ности. Все ей обещают помочь,
но болтуны страшные
Время — гром и, трепачи
А когда Ларочки нет
меня всегда неприятно. По-
шел в Дом кино —
напился и подрался
с В.Ливановым. ни он
ни я не мошел выйти из
дома — друг друга поласкали

must have started it. I don't remember a thing.

That's what happens when Larochka's away for a long time.

Andriushka's an angel.

The screenplay for the Experimental Association is finished. It turns out to be useful only for me. An excellent script. No question of a pot-boiler. Friedrich and I started to write for money, but finished up on a grand scale. Not much to be earned that way.

How we worked:

1. We made a strict plan (with myself in the foreground).

2. Friedrich did the writing, straightaway (not brilliant—dialogue and other small points).

3. Before the shooting version I'll revise the dialogues and everything (without letting Friedrich have it).

What has Belyaev got to do with it?

If only Larochka would come back.

18 February

'Fear of the aesthetic is a first symptom of weakness.'—Dostoievsky's notebooks, about *Crime and Punishment*, p. 560.

'The supreme idea of socialism is machinery. It turns a person into a mechanical person. There are rules for everything. And so man is taken from himself. His living soul is removed. It is understandable that one may be calm in such Eastern quietism, and these gentlemen say they are progressives! My God! If that is progress, then what is Eastern quietism!'

'Socialism is despair at the impossibility of ever being able to organize man. It organizes tyranny for him and says that is freedom itself!'—ibid., about Svidrigailov, p. 556.

I'm very strongly affected by diaries and archives and 'laboratories' of every kind. They're a wonderful catalyst.

So—*Ariel* has turned out really well. Only no one must be told what the script is about.

It's about—

1. The creative pretensions of the mediocre.

2. The greatness of simple things (in a moral sense).

3. The conflict within religion. (The ideal has collapsed. It's not possible to live without an ideal, no one is able to invent a new one, and the old one has collapsed: the church.)

4. The emergence of pragmatism. Pragmatism cannot be condemned because it is a stage and a condition of society: indeed an inevitable stage. It started at the turn of the century. Life can't

be condemned. It has to be accepted. It is not a question of cynicism. The war of 1914 was the last war to have a romantic aura.

5. Man is a plaything of history. The 'madness of the individual' and the calm of the socialist order.

Parallel between *Ariel* and the turn of the next century. Super-pragmatism on a state scale, as viewed by the man in the street. Consumerism.

I showed *Ariel* to Klimov, he said he liked it. Whatever happens I must let Yussov have it, so that he can be ready.

12 March

It occurred to me that the film made by Kelvin the elder, which Chris takes with him, should be made like a poem. (Base it on one of father's poems.)

Yussov has read *Ariel* but still hasn't said anything about it. We'll see.

Andriushka has an upset tummy. Either teeth, or by itself. He's even lost weight, poor little mite.

I telephoned Kulidzhanov yesterday about a flat. He said the Union of Cinematographers should be having two flats by the beginning of the Congress, and that the first would go to me. That would be good.

Yablochkin asked to work on *Solaris*. Although Nagornaya is a very bad production manager, it's too late now. There'd be a row at Party level in the studio; and Nagornaya is a member of the Party Office.

17 March

Winter filming today at Zvenigorod. We decided that the film Chris takes with him must have Khari in it. Chris shows her the film deliberately, in order to see how she reacts. He's checking her out, and at the same time Snaut's words about the guests.

I think our Mother (O. Barnet) is good. Ira hasn't replied either to the note which Kushnerev left her, nor to my letter about Senka. (I dreamed about her again last night—my heart was really painful again.)

Andriushka has been poorly—teeth and tum. He's getting better. He's so heavenly one can go on watching him forever.

I've decided on Natasha Bondarchuk as Khari. At the last costume test she was superb.

I must now start collecting *everything* I possibly can about Dostoievsky.

Golgotha would be a good title. I'll almost certainly have to write it myself.

24 April

At last I've managed to get rid of Nagornaya. Now the production manager is V. I. Tarassov. He used to be head of the personnel department of the Committee and was dismissed as a result of some row. He has no experience of working on a team or in production; on the other hand he has fantastic connections. With two or three good deputies everything will be fine. In any case he's an obliging and pleasant man.

We're waiting for an opportunity to go to Yalta.

Repairs on Myasnoye have begun. Larissa has gone off there and for several days there hasn't been a word from her. Terribly inconsiderate of her. Doesn't she realize that the most solidly built relationship can be shaken by those things that 'don't matter'?

Read Valenkin's *Modigliani*. Weak, illiterate and dull. Oh, how I long to be filming! What sort of a country is this that doesn't even want to earn money on me?!

Went to see Romanov. Sitting there were Gerasimov, Bondarchuk, Kulidzhanov, Pogozheva, someone from the Central Committee (Yermash's spy) and Baskakov. And Sizov. More corrections to *Rublyov*. It's more than I can bear. I lost control rather, and blew my top at them. The worst of it is that Sizov is categorically for the changes, even if Demichov agrees to let the picture go without them. I'll have to go and see Demichov, apply to the source of all this misery. We'll see.

12 July

My God, what a long time since I touched this notebook. When you're working you become stupefied, you don't have any ideas, and in any case there's no time. But now there's a break. A lot has happened in the meantime:

We started filming and—

1. Yussov and I disagreed over the graphic realization. I am against having a milieu equivalent to an actor. I am for a 50.75 lens, Yussov is for a 35. Our basic disagreement was over that.

2. We came to the conclusion we had been right to choose Natasha Bondarchuk as Khari.

3. We're going to shoot three scenes all over again. All that work is being thrown away.

(*a*) first meeting between Chris and Snaut

(*b*) second . . .

(*c*) and half the library.

4. The Kodak film is finished, and we haven't finished filming. Will they let us have more? What can we do?

I so want to make *The Bright Day*. Probably it should be mixed, black-and-white and colour depending on memory. It's important to start at least collecting the material for Dostoievsky.

There's apparently a character known as Hippopotamus who deals in books. The complete works of Dostoievsky including the diaries costs 250 roubles. I must buy it.

10 August

No time at all for writing. Work on *Solaris* has been hell. We're behind schedule. But we've got to get it finished by New Year. During the time that we're filming I want to finish the sound and the editing. God, how hard it is these days to work at Mosfilm. It's beyond all description.

Beata Tickiewicz was here at the Festival. She advised me to go and make a film in Poland. (Would they let me go?)

I've sent their deputy minister for cinematography—Vishnevsky —the script of *Ariel*. I'm asking for permission to use three Russian actors, and to invite Shavkat as designer.

Yussov and I are constantly arguing. It's very hard to work with him now. In a week's time we go to Zvenigorod, and at the end of September to Japan.

11 August

I'm very much afraid that there's going to be a restlessness about *Solaris*. Those blasted corridors, laboratories, instrument rooms. Perhaps it's impossible. God knows.

I felt the whole thing should be filmed with a 50.80 lens. But for a lot of it we've used a 35. What the result will be I don't know. I'm very worried.

Filming is very difficult. Very, very difficult. Making *Rublyov* was a holiday picnic compared with this business. What we're doing now is completely stupefying.

Rublyov was not shown at the Festival. Will they release it at all? Again I'm beginning to wonder.

I really want to start work on a new picture. I'm fed up with *Solaris*, just as I was at a certain point with *Rublyov*; Soviet directors are doomed to spend too long on each film.

14 August

Culture is man's greatest achievement. But is it more important, say, than personal worth? (If one doesn't take culture and personal worth as being one and the same thing.) The person who takes part in the building of culture, if he is an artist, has no reason to be proud. His talent has been given him by God, whom he obviously has to thank.

There can be no merit in talent, since it is only yours fortuitously. The mere fact of being born into a wealthy family does not give a person a sense of his own worth and thus the respect of others. Spiritual, moral culture is created not by the individual—whose talent is accidental—but by the nation, as it spontaneously throws out that individual endowed with the potential for artistic creation and the life of the spirit. Talent is common property. The bearer of it is as insignificant as a slave on a plantation, or a drug addict, or a member of the lumpen proletariat.

Talent is a misfortune, for on the one hand it entitles a person to neither merit nor respect, and on the other it lays on him tremendous responsibilities; he is like the honest steward who has to protect the treasure entrusted to his keeping without ever making use of it.

A sense of self-respect is available to anyone who feels the need for it. I don't understand why fame is the highest aspiration of the artistic confraternity. Vainglory is above all a sign of mediocrity.

Reading extracts in *Novy Mir* of S. Birman's memoirs, with the pretentious, tasteless title, 'Meetings Granted Me by Fate'. God help us! It's about Gordon Craig and Stanislavsky. She quotes from a conversation between them about *Hamlet*, in particular where they are talking about Ophelia.

What rubbish it all is!

Craig's interpretation of *Hamlet* is metaphysical and pretentious and stupid. *Hamlet* as construed by the idiot, megalomaniac Stanislavsky is equally absurd.

At the same time Craig is right when he says that Ophelia falls out of the tragedy, that she is insignificant, whereas Stanislavsky, with one eye forever on the audience because he was scared to death of their verdict, maintains she was a pure, beautiful girl. I'm irritated by this silly claptrap from a silly old woman who wants to attract attention.

15 August

Stanislavsky did great harm to future generations of the theatre; roughly the same as Stassov did for painting. All those lofty ideals— that so-called 'sense of direction' as Dostoievsky put it—falsified the functions and the meaning of art.

20 August

Tomorrow we're moving to Zvenigorod. We must shoot the scenes on location as quickly as possible, to be ready to go to Japan.

No assistant director. We're going to use Soviet film for shooting on location.

Discussing *The Bright Day* with Chukhrai. They seem to want it to be a one-part film. That is not likely to be possible. For it to be a one-part film, 2700 metres, I would need a script of 45–50 pages. In other words a printed page is equivalent on average to 60 metres.

But *The Bright Day* is 72 pages, of which 18 consist entirely of the answers to the questionnaire. It's going to be difficult to get the two parts.

Maybe we could take them by surprise?

If we make one part—53 pages × 60 metres = 3200 metres, and we film the questionnaire in parallel. The result will be 4000 metres. Will they then need a second part?

Who is going to play the Mother? Demidova? She does everything too hard, and she's an awful person to work with. Bibi Anderson? They won't allow it.

I must collect L. V. Gornung's photographs. I'll ring my sister as soon as things are clear with the production.

Beata took *Ariel* with her to Poland. Will anything come of it?

Andriushka has started walking—he can take a few steps. Lara and I miss him terribly. Tonya says he is becoming unbelievably funny.

What's going on with Senka? In fact Ira has done everything she can to stop us seeing each other. She's turned out a real Kalashnikov. Will things ever be all right between Senka and me? I hope to God they will.

6 September

The Bright Day really does have to be in one part—3100. The shooting-script should be written roughly around August.

We've been in Zvenigorod for a week. The weather is frightful, rain all the time, it makes things really hard.

Organization here is nil. By the 15th we must have done the whole of Banionis—the morning scenes, Berton's arrival, one scene with the Father, the Return. Everything else must be filmed in the course of three or four days after the 15th.

We've decided to film 'The Fire' in black and white; and Chris in the twilight. In other words, dusk and a brief stretch of daily routine, just before nightfall. And the Return. I think the scene with the 'blue' sun on Solaris could also be in black and white. That could be good.

We must finish off in Zvenigorod as soon as possible and fly to Japan.

13 September, Zvenigorod

Liuka Fayt brought the first Dostoievsky books to me on the set:
1. Articles on Dostoievsky by Cornfeld and Remizov, 1921.
2. D. by his daughter, L. Dostoievsky, 1922.
3. One volume of the complete—souvenir—edition of 1883.
4. I have his letters to his wife (A. G. Snitkina) at home.

On 24 September we're flying to Japan. Before the 24th we have to finish filming everything out of doors, apart from the Return, which we are going to do after we go back to Moscow.

So:

before the 14th—Banionis
14th to 22nd incl. all the summer scenes
22nd – 8th Oct.—Japan
8th – 15th Oct.—'Return'
15th – 25th Oct.—Chris's room in the space station
25th – 30th—Chris's room in the house
1st Dec.—everything else
1st – 7th Dec.—corridor and labyrinth
7th – 10th Dec.—refrigerator

14 September, Zvenigorod

Dostoievsky read by the light of two candles. He didn't like lamps. He smoked a lot while he worked and occasionally drank strong tea. He led a monotonous life, starting off in Staraya Russya (the prototype of the town where Karamazov lived). His favourite colour—the waves of the sea. He often dresses his heroines in that colour.

19 September, Zvenigorod

We're flying to Japan on the 24th and we still haven't filmed the sun. The weather is awful. The sun scenes are going to have to be handed over, to be filmed while we're away.

We have to decide what we're going to film in Japan, and how. The question is—exactly what?

I am beginning to have the impression that Dostoievsky had an extraordinarily reserved and pedantic temperament. In fact, looked at from the outside, perhaps actually dull. It's going to be hard to write a screenplay.

For the screenplay:

The fit on the landing. Reality, intermingled with a scene from *The Idiot*—Rogozhin and Prince Myshkin, also . . .

Irritation at Turgenev's Europeanization. *The story of an enmity.* Letters. Academia. Karmazinov in *The Possessed. Merci.*

14 October, Moscow

We came back from Japan on the 10th. Utterly exhausted. And with my nerves shattered. Masses of impressions. But it's better not to write them down straightaway; let them settle a bit. We filmed a certain amount for Berton's drives through the 'town'. At the moment I seem to have neuralgia—chest pains and really high blood pressure. Muzzy head and aching behind the ears. We filmed the scene with Gabarian (back in the studio—Sos Sarkisian). I've seen the Zvenigorod material. At present I can't make head or tail of it.

23 October

Yesterday the art committee had a meeting about our material. They liked it. For some reason one or two people don't appreciate the way Grinko talks. Generally speaking there's no problem. They approved of Yussov and of the costumes. Volodya Naumov said, 'Superb quality. World class.' What he doesn't realize is that the film is altogether outside world classification.

Today Lara is bringing Andriushka and his granny back from the country. My God, how I've been missing him.

Yesterday I saw V. A. Pozner, who has been in Paris and promised to let me know about the possibility of *Solaris* going to the Cannes Festival if in the end it's good enough. We'll see. As usual the Committee could ruin everything.

Japan is a wonderful country, of course. Nothing in common

with Europe or with America. A great country—nobody accepts tips. There's no unemployment.

Tokyo is an amazing city. There's not a single factory chimney, not a single house that looks like any other. Architecturally, of course, it is very advanced.

Polite, well brought up people. In Tokyo and Yokohama together there are 22 million inhabitants. But you don't find the kind of senseless crowd there that you have in Moscow.

The Japanese promised to invite me over for the première of *Andrey Rublyov*. I think the invitation has already arrived. I wonder what the Committee will say?

I'd like to finish *Solaris* as quickly as possible. Even though I still have 1500 metres to go I feel as if the picture is already finished. I'd like to start on *The Bright Day* as soon as I can. It occurred to me that parallel with the 'destruction of the church' we could film 'morning on the field of Kulikovo'* which we weren't able to do in *Rublyov*.

It could be interesting.

And father's poem 'As a Child I Once Fell Ill . . .', finishing with an angel standing at the edge of the wood.

Not a word from Beata Tickiewicz. Has she shown *Ariel* to Vishnevsky or not? It would be good to make a film in Poland. I shan't be allowed to make *Ariel* here.

3 November

Mikhail Ilych Romm died on 1 November. A week ago we met in a corridor of the editing studio. He looked worn out, dejected, unable to concentrate.

A. M. Room came past. Mikhail Ilych and I talked about how full of life he was. Mikhail Ilych said, 'I shan't last as long as him.'

It's tragic.

I can't imagine that Elena Aleksandrovna will survive M. I. for long. Why is it always the best people who die? Society must go downhill because of that as well. As a result of moral entropy.

4 December

I haven't opened this notebook for a month. The picture has got to be finished before the end of the year. I'm working from 7.30

---

*The battle of Kulikovo, 1380, was a decisive victory for Grand Duke Dmitri Donskoy over the Tartars. For financial reasons, A.T. was not able to include the battle scenes in *Andrey Rublyov*.

till midnight every day, and have been for the last month. I'm utterly exhausted.

Natasha B. has outshone everybody. I'm glad of it, because it keeps the balance right.

I think the actors could be graded as follows:
1. Natasha Bondarchuk
2. Yarvet
3. Solonitsyn
4. Banionis
5. Dvorzhetsky
6. Grinko

I am very much afraid that I shall have to go through the same sort of hell over *Solaris* as I did over *Rublyov*. I'm afraid that's how it will be.

Still not a word from Beata Tickiewicz.

Friedrich and I have finished the second version. Chukhrai's group like *The Bright Day*.

Solaris is almost finished. After handing it over it will still need one or two small touches, and then have to be copied.

Why did Sizov have to go and surround himself with scum like Ivanov, Agafonova and Sviridova?

There are rumours that Romanov is soon going to be retired.

29 December

Tomorrow (or the day after if the copy is not ready by tomorrow) I shall give *Solaris* in to Sizov. Then of course they're all going to come running, from the Committee, from the board, probably from the Central Committee.

I'm sure there'll be a row.

I haven't seen the whole film myself yet, I only know the parts, which for me do not add up to any unified impression.

30 December

Mosfilm are taking the picture at 6.0 this evening.

I still do not have an impression of the film. It'll happen after the showing. Some bits have turned out not at all bad: the scenes with the mother, the suicide, the city, the return to the pond, the night conversation, Chris's delirium. But will the picture be a whole? Will there be an impact? Will the idea be alive within the filmed material?

Natasha of course is the best of the lot. She is one with her role. That is the optimum in cinema.

It's a pity we didn't do the filming with Chukhrai; of course the audience will come to the film.

In the lab, when Yussov was watching the duplicated film as it came out of the printer, he was confronted with this picture: in order not to get in the way, people were kneeling all the time the work was going on just so that they could see another bit of *Solaris*.

Larissa went to see Sizov, who told her that he likes *The Bright Day*, likes it 'very much'.

The first article (since *Andrey* was released) has appeared in *Komsomolskaya Pravda*. By someone called Gr. Ognev. A nasty little piece, which will have the effect of bringing the public to see the film.

There is no announcement in any paper about *Rublyov* being on. Not a single poster in the city. Yet it's impossible to get tickets. All sorts of people keep telephoning, stunned by it, to say thank you.

1972

For many years I have been tormented by the certainty that the most extraordinary discoveries await us in the sphere of Time.

1972

12 January

Yesterday Sizov dictated comments and criticisms of *Solaris* collected from various bodies—the cultural department of the Central Committee, Demichov's office, the Committee and the governing board.

I have made a note of some thirty-three of these observations. Here they are. There are a great many of them, and if I were to comply with them (which is not actually possible) the whole basis of the film would be destroyed. In other words, it's even more absurd than it was with *Rublyov*.

The comments go like this:

1. There ought to be a clearer image of the earth of the future. The film doesn't make it clear what it's going to be like (the future, that is).

2. There ought to be some landscapes of the planet of the future.

3. What form of society was the starting-point for Kelvin's flight— Socialism, Communism or Capitalism?

4. Snaut ought not to speak of the inexpediency (?!) of studying space. It leads to a dead-end situation.

5. Cut out the concept of God. (?!)

6. The encephalograph ought to be run to the end.

7. Cut out the concept of Christianity. (!?)

8. The conference. Cut out the foreign executives.

9. The Finale:

(*13 January*)

(*a*) Can Chris's return to his father's house not be made more realistic.

(*b*) Can it not be made clear that he has completed his mission.

10. The suggestion that Chris is an idler should be unfounded.

11. The motive for Gabarian's suicide (not in Lem) ought to be

that he is sacrificing himself for his friends and colleagues. (!?)

12. As a scientist Sartorius lacks humanity.

13. Khari ought not to become a person. (!?)

14. Shorten Khari's suicide.

15. Cut out the scene with the Mother.

16. Shorten the bed scene.

17. Cut the scene where Chris is walking around with no trousers on.

18. ?! How long did it take for the hero to complete his flight out, the return flight, and his work.

19. There should be a written introduction to the film (from Lem) explaining it all. (?!)

20. Restore the conversation in the shooting-script between Berton and his father about their youth.

21. Put in some quotations from Kolmogorov (about the finite nature of man).

22. 'The Earth' is too long.

23. The scientific conference looks like a trial.

24. Clarify the situation at the conference in terms of the plot.

25. Have the flight to *Solaris*.

26. Why are they (Snaut and Sart.) afraid of Chris?

27. It is not made clear that the Ocean is responsible for the situation. (?)

28. Is science humane or not?

29. 'The world cannot be known. Space cannot be understood. Man has to perish.'

30. 'The audience are going to be completely baffled . . .'

31. What is Solaris? And the visitors?

32. The necessity for contact must be made more explicit.

33. They have to come through the crisis.

34. Why does Khari vanish? (The Ocean has understood.)

35. Take-home message: 'There's no point in humanity dragging its shit from one end of the galaxy to the other.'

This crazy list finishes with the words: No further comment.

I might as well give up.

It's some kind of provocation . . . Only what is it that they want? Do they want me to refuse to make the changes? What for? Or to agree to them all? But they know that I won't.

It makes no sense.

21 January

I simply cannot work out what they meant, or rather, what was in their minds, when they gave me those corrections.

The corrections can't possibly be made, they would ruin the whole film. And if I don't make them? The whole thing is like a provocation, but I don't see the point of it.

I've decided to make just those alterations that are consistent with my own plans and will not destroy the fabric of the film.

If that doesn't satisfy them, then there's nothing I can do about it.

I went to see Yermash. Didn't say a word about *Solaris* and the alterations. I asked him if I was an underground director and how long this persecution was going to go on, and would I be able to go on making two films a year (ugh!—I couldn't even bring myself to write the truth: two films in ten years). Yermash replied that I was entirely Soviet and that it's a disgrace that I do so little work. I said in that case, please support me and guarantee me work. Otherwise I shall have to start taking defensive action myself.

In fact they are going to have to allow *Solaris* if they don't want a serious row. Because I'm not prepared to sit there quietly without work, not saying a word, looking on while they violate the constitution.

23 January

The Association—with myself taking part—has drawn up a list of the changes that we accept. These we shall carry out, particularly as they are almost as full of demagoguery as the comments I was given.

There are rumours that our Association is going to be reorganized according to guidelines laid down by Chukhrai. If that is the case, we shall have to make *The Bright Day* in our own studios. Chukhrai is untrustworthy and suspect.

Rublyov is on at the moment in Vladimir, with tremendous success. There are crowds outside the cinema and it's impossible to buy tickets.

Larissa has been to Rovno and has managed to arrange for a pick-up.

9 February

Today is the last day for editing the soundtrack to synchronize the alterations. We have realigned the sound in six places, but my impression is that something still remains to be 'clarified' (in the terminology of our committee colleagues). In other words, formally speaking the alterations have been made, only the film has not become any less sophisticated as a result. That may worry Sizov. I don't know! Anyhow I shall try not to touch the picture any more.

It looks as if I shall be making *The Bright Day* in our own Association —they want to change to self-financing methods as well. We'll see. Vadim and I will start shooting in August or September. It won't be easy. I am going to have to 'strip naked', and Vadim is not close enough to me, not enough of a kindred soul (I'm not even convinced that he has a soul) for me to want to confide in him. At one level he is a pleb.

Should I invite Rerberg to work on the film?

14 February

Apparently Ivanov (!?) said in Sizov's hearing that *Solaris* ought to be sent to the Cannes Festival. What has it got to do with Ivanov?

'The Field of Kulikovo' and 'As a Child I Once Fell Ill' must go into *The Bright Day.*

15 February

The film was sent to the Committee without any discussion. Sizov telephoned today and said that the film is now much better and more harmonious. But he hinted that there would have to be more cuts. I shall resist them. The length is actually an aesthetic consideration.

I'm going to see Sizov on the 17th; he asked me to; he has to talk to me about something. I can't bear surprises, they're always unpleasant.

I am tired. In April I shall be forty. But I'm never left in peace, and there is never any silence. Instead of freedom Pushkin had 'peace' and 'will', but I don't even have those.

People are sending me letters after seeing *Rublyov*. Some are very interesting. Of course audiences understand the film perfectly well, as I knew they would.

A STORY

Someone is given the opportunity to become happy. He is afraid to use it, because he thinks happiness is impossible, and that only a madman can be happy. Circumstances somehow convince our hero to use the opportunity and—by some sort of miraculous means—to become happy.

And he goes mad. He is drawn into the world of the insane, who may not merely be mad; they are also able to link up with the world by means of threads which are inaccessible to normal people.

For many years I have been tormented by the certainty that the most extraordinary discoveries await us in the sphere of Time. We know less about time than about anything else.

16 February

Our film industry, of course, is in the most abysmal state at the moment. Just because it provides the money, the State is able to ride roughshod over new ideas and wallow in a slough of vapid, boot-licking muck.

Dignitaries bedecked with honours and incapable of stringing two words together have demolished our cinema; here and there among the ruins there still smoulders the shell of some sort of construction. I recently read through a history of the pre-war Italian cinema. My God, how it reminds me of the story of Soviet cinema. We've never been as low as this before.

I have finished my *Solaris*. It's more harmonious than *Rublyov*, more purposeful, less cryptic. More graceful, more harmonious than *Rublyov*. Not that there's any comparison. It's finished and done with and that's that. Now it's time to start thinking about *The Bright Day* and to find some way of pushing through *High Wind*. (New title for *Ariel*.)

Incidentally the names of those three characters have to be invented or changed. Let's have:

Ariel—Phillip
Hide—Lecker
Fox—Claff, Brook, Royce, Fields, Crookes
Must not forget—the short story
memory—reality
      —dream, fantasy

21 February

Romanov hasn't accepted the film, won't sign the paper. He doesn't consider that I've made any alterations. Sizov is expecting to see me on Thursday. He obviously intends to bully me into making corrections. What corrections? It's going to be the *Rublyov* saga all over again.

Evening.
Bagrat telephoned from Yerevan to say that in *L'Humanité* there

was an account of the celebrations in honour of Louis Aragon, and that he had said that he has two favourite films (that he'd like to see). One is by Godard (*Pierrot le Fou*) and the other is *Rublyov*. I must get hold of the paper.

I want to find out about Savonarola. About his relationship with Botticelli.

22 February

I've written to Beata about *Ariel*. Andriushka is ill. 'Flu, he must have caught it from me. I'm terribly worried . . . He didn't sleep all night, he was crying. He must have had a temperature. He started muttering and murmuring—he sounded so funny. His teeth are still coming on with gusto.

If only he were better.

Now what can I hope for? As likely as not I'm going to spend the next few years unemployed.

It's urgent that we rebuild the house, change flats in Moscow, get hold of the pick-up, and dig down in the country.

Do they really want a row like they had over *Rublyov*? It's hard to believe. Anyhow that's what Romanov is going to get. I wonder how they're going to react to the foreign press coverage of the *Solaris* furore. And what about the Poles?

How can they be so stupid?

I shall wait a little while, then I'm going to tell one or two people what it's all about.

I've just heard that Naumov is trying to have the film accepted. Even if he succeeds because Romanov happens to be away at present—Romanov will eventually be back.

23 February

Am I really going to be sitting around again for years on end, waiting for somebody graciously to let my film through?

What an extraordinary country this is—don't they want an international artistic triumph, don't they want us to have good new films and books? They are frightened by real art. Quite understandably. Art can only be bad for them because it is humane, whereas their purpose is to crush everything that is alive, every shoot of humanity, any aspiration to freedom, any manifestation of art on our dreary horizon.

They won't be content until they have eliminated every symptom of independence and reduced people to the level of cattle.

In the process they'll destroy everything: themselves and Russia.

Tomorrow I'm going to Sizov and he'll explain what is happening about *Solaris*. No doubt he'll try to persuade me and win me over and convince me. The usual story.

I must read the Korolenko story Friedrich was talking about; it's all about peasant life miles from anywhere in Siberia, and their prejudices and so on . . . It may be a bit like *Echo Calls*? Screening an existing book is an easier way of doing things.

I somehow think that it's better to screen inferior literature, which nonetheless contains the seed of something real—which can be developed in the film and grow into something wonderful as a result of going through your hands.

25 February

Romanov has not accepted the film. I have been sent a list of alterations which I cannot make.

1. Shorten the film (by not less than 300 metres)?!
2. Cut out the scene of Khari's suicide.
3. Cut out the city.
4. Cut out the scene with the mother.
5. The dress that Chris cuts must also go.
6. Cut out the scene at the end with the flowing water. Obviously I am not going to do any of it.

28 February

Late this evening I looked at the sky and saw the stars. I felt as if it was the first time I had ever looked at them.

I was stunned.

The stars made an extraordinary impression on me.

31 March

Romanov came to the studio on the 29th and *Solaris* was accepted without a single alteration. Nobody can believe it. They say that the agreement accepting the film is the only one to be signed personally by Romanov. Someone must have put the fear of God into him.

I heard that Sizov showed the film to three officials whose names we don't know and who are in charge of the academic and technological side of things; and their authority is too great for their opinion to be ignored. It's nothing short of miraculous, one can even begin to believe that all will be well.

2 April

Today (or rather, yesterday) T. G. rang and assured me that Sizov is sending *Solaris* to Cannes. It's perfectly possible.

One of the organizers of the Cannes Festival is coming today. (Pozner telephoned to tell me.)

I must move on to the next film as soon as possible. Either *The Bright Day* or *The Renunciation* (new title for *Ariel*).

There must be a reading of *Ariel* as soon as possible at K. Shishlin's (as I thought). Then we must go to Yerevan. In any case I must start on a new film as quickly as possible so that I'm not left without any income.

Evening.

I'm very excited by Zen. At present I'm reading somebody's dissertation (or simply research notes) about Koan. Very interesting.

'. . . In order to write well you have to forget the rules of grammar.' (Goethe)

'Dostoievsky gives me more than any thinker, more than Gauss.' (Einstein)

'We are being sentimental when we attribute more tenderness to a person than the Lord God has endowed him with.' (R. T. Blice)

6 April

Here I am forty. And what have I done in all this time? Three pathetic pictures. So little! So ridiculously little and insignificant.

I had a strange dream last night: I was looking up at the sky, and it was very, very light, and soft; and high, high above me it seemed to be slowly boiling, like light that had materialized, like the fibres of a sunlit fabric, like silken, living stitches in a piece of Japanese embroidery. And those tiny fibres, light-bearing, living threads, seemed to be moving and floating and becoming like birds, hovering, so high up that they could never be reached. So high that if the birds were to lose feathers the feathers wouldn't fall, they wouldn't come down to the earth, they would fly upwards, be carried off and vanish from our world forever. And soft, enchanted music was flowing down from that great height. The music seemed to sound like the chiming of little bells; or else the birds' chirping was like music.

'They're storks', I suddenly heard someone say, and I woke up.

A strange and beautiful dream. I do sometimes have wonderful dreams.

Sizov is going to America and taking *Solaris* with him.

24 April

Sizov hasn't taken *Solaris* to America, in order not to spoil the chances for Cannes. It is going to Cannes.

The Festival is from 4 to 19 May. Baskakov is going, Banionis and myself, and Natasha B.

7 May

Larissa and I have been to Yerevan. Bagrat seems to be in a bit of a mess, he can't get down to shooting.

I think I've had enough of working with Armenians. They're a pretty useless lot.

Sos is really nice.

Flying to Paris on the 10th.

The première of *Solaris* is in Cannes on the 13th. I can't really believe there's going to be any sort of prize. There are some very good films in the programme, by Petri, Pollack, Jancsó. Anyhow, we shall see.

I went to see Sizov. He's going to draw up the documents we need in order to be paid for *Rublyov*.

Volodya Vissotsky has suggested we go to France in September at Marina's invitation. Perhaps that is a possibility.

8 May

I've sent *The Bright Day* and *The Renunciation* to be retyped. I shall go ahead with whichever goes through. *The Bright Day* could be a great picture, but it's going to be very hard to make. *The Renunciation* could be a major, traditional film with an anti-intellectual bias and a grandiose finale.

What am I to do about Yussov? He's really touchy, neurotically so, and conservative. It's becoming very hard to work with him.

9 June

It's a feature of any kind of acclaim that it eventually leads to depression, disappointment, even to something rather like a hangover, a feeling of guilt.

Lots of people accepted *Rublyov* because it had been kept on ice for so long. *Solaris* hasn't been kept on ice, which is why so many of my good friends and comrades are furious.

I've given Sizov and Yermash both scripts—*The Bright Day* and

The Renunciation—and on Monday I'll give them to Baskakov.

Actually if *The Renunciation* comes off I probably shan't go back to *The Bright Day*.

I must start work. As soon as possible. Though Sizov said that what is 'expected' of me is a *topical, relevant* picture, and so neither of my scripts is any good.

I said that my work had to do with maintaining the standard of Soviet cinema and not with what is 'relevant' and 'topical'.

All I can think of is paying off my debts, changing flats and doing the rebuilding. Otherwise we shall be in a mess.

14 June

Opposition (relationship) between—on the one hand—the spiritual; the traditional; continuity; and—on the other—a tendency towards something tortured, constricted, emasculated, cold, its metaphysical details separated and isolated. Thomas Mann's *Faustus*.

There is always the same relationship between the myriad links connecting a creative individual with reality (of which the history of culture has accumulated a vast number).

A desire to start reading afresh the links between the individual and reality, excising the traditional ones (which is impossible).

A model of the old conflict between spirit and the senses, idea and flesh, God and the devil, good and evil . . .

The rhythm of editing, the length of a frame—these are not merely dictated by the professional need to establish a link with the audience (as they are thought to be). They express the character and originality of the author of the film. At the present time cineastes use editing rhythm to gild the pill that has to be swallowed by the unfortunate audience. According to me, entirely in order to make money.

My father categorizes *Solaris* not as a film but as something akin to literature. Because of the internal, authorial rhythm, the absence of banal devices and the enormous number of details each with a specific function in the narrative.

22 July

It's a long time since I opened this notebook. I've been in Armenia with Larissa, in connection with the business with Bagrat and the Propaganda Bureau. Things are not going too well for Bagrat. I have the impression that he doesn't know himself what to do with his *The Wine Press*. The boy is not up to much. The screenplay and dialogue are positively bad. I don't know. I can't stay with them for ever. Nothing came of the payment from the Propaganda Bureau: despite the fact that Gukasyan spent several months persuading us to come we didn't earn anything. Either we were swindled or else they don't know how to work.

We went to Zangezur with Arayk and M. Razmik. Stunning.

Before Sizov went off to Karlovy Vary I went to see him about the screenplay. He said, 'Neither of those scenarios has any support.' Surely not another spell of nothing being done!

On the 1st of August Larissa and I are going to Locarno (Switzerland) for the Festival. I've been asked to be on the jury. Then I think there'll be some more travelling.

Things are still not right in the country. The walls have to be rebuilt completely. The money that came in from *Solaris* was not even enough to pay off my debts.

Oh, if only I could start on *The Bright Day*!

Tyapa is in the country and I miss him terribly.

Volodya Vissotsky has promised to put me in touch with Pushkaryov, who is in charge of exchanges. We must change flats as soon as we can, it's impossible to live here now. Leva Kulidzhanov promised to help as well.

19 August

Larissa and I are back from Switzerland. I was president of the jury in Locarno.

It was all fine. The committee was pleased with the results. *Rublyov* was much praised.

According to Kamshalov *The Bright Day* will be allowed through provided they are given a clear and detailed explanation of the idea of the film (which they misunderstood).

The Committee is being reorganized. Everyone is panicking: they don't know who is going to be president. Sizov has promised to help over the exchange. There's an awful lot happening, and several trips abroad coming up. But the one thing that matters is starting work. There are fires all around Moscow—peat and forests burning. More than 500 hectares. Terrible. There's smoke actually in Moscow. I'm very worried about Tyapa. Maybe in September we'll be able to rebuild the house properly.

23 August

Switzerland is an incredibly clean, well-maintained country, very good for people who are tired of hustle and bustle. It's very like a lunatic asylum—quiet, polite nurses, smiles . . .

It looks as if *The Bright Day* may be happening. I have to convince Baskakov, Sizov and Kamshalov, who have only met over it once. Work must start soon.

Romanov has been removed. F. T. Yermash has been appointed in his place.

Up till now he has been well-disposed towards me.

Larissa is going to the country today. Apparently someone has been found who will be able to rebuild the house quickly.

17 September, Moscow

There was a meeting about *The Bright Day* in Yermash's new office. Apart from him and myself Sizov was there, and Kamshalov, Baskakov and Naumov.

Sadly enough, the one who behaved the worst was Baskakov. (I went to see him the day before to ask permission to go to Paris, with Larissa, in connection with *Solaris*. He refused on the grounds that he didn't want to set a precedent from the point of view of my colleagues. It was a bad, careless argument, because there have already been precedents—Ozerov and Bondarchuk have been to Paris for the same sort of business trips.) He even blurted out something about Communism, glancing nervously around as he said it. So much for Baskakov.

I explained to them how I see the film. I had to talk about the 'connection between the characters and the country', or rather, the 'life of the country' and all that. They all wanted me to make something new and important for the country, involving scientific, technological progress. I told them that was not my line at all, and that I am more at home dealing with humanitarian questions.

Anyhow the conclusion of all our talk was that I must write a paper (which I've already done) setting out in detail my plan of the film, which of course they hadn't understood. They are not capable of reading anything beyond the salary bulletin twice a month. I must also indicate what changes there will be in the shooting-script, as opposed to the literary scenario with which they are already familiar. Very reluctantly they agreed that once they had read my bit of paper (which they've already been sent), provided they found it satisfactory, I could embark on the shooting-script.

At the beginning of next week—i.e. tomorrow—I should ring either the studio or Naumov to find out what is going to happen.

Oh, yes, they are also insisting that the shooting-script should be shortened to 3200 metres—1 hour 50 minutes.

If I go about it in a constructive way, I think all may be well. Only, of course, I shall be paid less if it's just one part.

I'm principally worried about my mother and the hidden camera. In fact, what I mean is—I'm afraid of how she may react to material being filmed without permission—without her permission.

Larissa and Tyapa and Anna Semyonovna are in the country. Lara hasn't written. I'm worried: I don't know anything—how they are, whether the work is being done on the house, whether I ought to be sending money.

I am to go to Italy on the 20th. A wonderful country but ghastly company—Gerasimov, Ozerov, Khrabrovitsky . . . The only way is to go having decided not to talk to them about anything. Just smile and talk about things that don't matter. We'll see.

18 September

Razmik of Armenfilm telephoned this morning. He asked me to go to Bagrat after Italy. He's having a difficult time there for some reason. But he's not all that competent. No imagination.

I must send him the final monologue for Varya, urgently, otherwise he'll give up altogether.

23 December, Moscow

Three months since I touched this notebook, and so much has happened. I have been in Italy and Brussels and Luxemburg and Bruges. And then in Paris where I cut *Solaris* by 12 minutes for the French version. In Belgium I saw Erasmus's house, and the paintings of Memling, Van Eyck and Brueghel.

Paris is beautiful. You feel free there: nobody needs you, and you don't need anybody.

I didn't like Italy this time. Maybe it was because of the company, maybe because this time it struck me as twee, picture postcardish. (We went to Sorrento and Naples.) Rome was overwhelming. It's an amazing city. If in other cities you can see year rings like on a tree, in Rome what you see are the rings of decades, or even perhaps of epochs.

They seem to be letting me start on *The Bright Day*, which I've renamed *The Raging Stream*. It probably won't get through, which is a pity.

Yussov let me down at the last minute by refusing to work on the film. Mercifully Gosha Rerberg is free (for the moment). As for Yussov, I'm sure he deliberately chose a moment when his refusal to work with me would cause me the greatest possible distress. He always disliked me, without saying anything. He's spiteful. He is filled with class hatred for the intelligentsia.

Misha R., and Larissa for that matter, say he often used to insult me. I must say I don't remember.

I'm glad it's happened the way it has. It was time we parted company. Even in *Solaris* there was a lack of direction about the images. Yussov was trying to hang on to what had already been achieved; and there's no future in that. And he couldn't bear the concept of *The Bright Day*. In his lower-middle-class way he was infuriated by the fact that I was making a film about myself.

Larissa has brought Tyapa and Anna Semyonovna back from the country. Tyapa has grown, and chatters away nonstop. A bit less at the moment, because he's under the weather. He's adorable, and incredibly funny.

1973

The artist is a being who strives (but not in secret or in hiding, nor moving in circles, nor in the spaciousness of some kind of ecological niche) to master ultimate truth.

The artist masters that truth every time he creates something perfect, something whole.

Ведь посредственность ненавидит художников. А наша власть сплошь состоит из посредственностей.

Если удастся сделать "Белый день", надо будет подать заявку на фильм, т.е. пока на сценарий о Достоевском.

Пора уже....

А может быть ликвидировать не всё?

Какое самое красивое дерево? Вяз, наверное. Но оно слишком для резьбы.

А что про резьбу говорить? Ветла или серебристый тополь?

Серебристый тополь — красивое дерево

Перерыв, удастся мне через Федю получить автомобиль? Это единственный путь. Сам я, конечно, машину никогда не куплю. А как хочется пожить внизу в деревне!

камень у крыльца

окно со ставнями

дверь

ставни с вырезанными ...

1973

9 January

The revised script was sent to the Committee the day before yesterday. Sizov has promised that over the next three weeks the whole question of whether it can be produced will become clear. Help me, O Lord!

24 January

There was a time when I thought that film, unlike other art forms, (being the most democratic of them all) had a total effect, identical for every audience. That it was first and foremost a series of recorded images; that the images are photographic and unequivocal. That being so, because it appears unambiguous, it is going to be perceived in one and the same way by everyone who sees it. (Up to a certain point, obviously.)

But I was wrong. One has to work out a principle which allows for film to affect people individually. The 'total' image must become something private. (Comparable with the images of literature, painting, poetry, music.)

The basic principle—as it were, the mainspring—is, I think, that as little as possible has actually to be shown, and from that little the audience has to build up an idea of the rest, of the whole. In my view that has to be the basis for constructing the cinematographic image. And if one looks at it from the point of view of symbols, then the symbol in cinema is a symbol of nature, of reality. Of course it isn't a question of details, but of what is hidden.

26 January

For the last few days we have all been ill. And I've been lying here for the last three weeks. And yet again I find myself in the ghastly state of expectation and uncertainty. I mean about whether *The Bright Day* will be permitted. It's misery not being allowed to work.

Sasha Mishurin made rather a good suggestion: a screenplay based on Auesov's *Abalo* for the Kazakh studio.

Only I'll have to tread carefully, and not let the pay packet be grabbed out of my hands.

I've just read the Strugatsky brothers' science fiction story, *Roadside Picnic*; that could make a tremendous screenplay for somebody as well.

It's well worth considering earning some money from Central Asian studios now if I'm to pay off my debts—and they come to 8000 roubles. Now I even regret refusing to take on the artistic directorship of the short film based on Aitmatov's story. It would have meant a regular monthly salary after all. I shan't be so stupid next time.

There are two kinds of dreams. In the first, the dreamer can direct the events of the dream as if by magic. He is master of everything that happens or is going to happen. He is a demiurge. In the second, the dreamer has no say, he is passive, he suffers from the violence done him and from his inability to protect himself. What happens to him is exactly what he doesn't want, all that is most horrible and painful. (As in Kafka's prose.)

'A painter's moments of illumination must not come to him through his consciousness (any more than do those of any other artist). His discoveries, mysterious even to him, must bypass the long road of deliberation and go so fast into his work that he has no time to notice the transition. If he lies in wait for them, observes them, holds them back, they will turn to dust like the gold in the fairy-tale.' Rilke, *Letters to His Wife* (*about Cézanne*), *21 October 1901*.

27 January

How sad life is! I envy anyone who can carry on with his own work without reference to the State. In fact, practically everybody, apart from people in theatre and cinema, is free (I don't include television because it isn't art). They are free of salary as well, of course, but at least they can work.

How crass the authorities are! Do they actually need literature, poetry, music, painting, cinema? Of course not. On the contrary, how much simpler life would be without them!

Boris Leonidovich [Pasternak] was obviously right when he said that I would make another four pictures. I've made the first—*Solaris*. That leaves another three. And that's all!

I want to work, nothing more than that. Work! It's surely crazy, criminal, that a director whom the Italian press called a genius should be unemployed.

Frankly, I think the mediocrities who have hacked their way up to positions of power simply have it in for me. After all, mediocre people can't bear artists. And our bosses are mediocrities to a man.

If I succeed in making *The Bright Day* then I must do a treatment for the film, or at least the screenplay, about Dostoievsky. It's high time . . .

Or should I just say to hell with it all?

What is the most beautiful tree? It must be the elm. Only it takes so long to grow. Which grows faster? A white willow or a silver poplar? Silver poplars are beautiful trees.

I wonder whether I'll be able to get hold of a car through Fedya. That's the only possibility. I could never buy one myself, obviously. And I so want to make life in the country tenable!

29 January

On 5 February *Solaris* is going to be on release in Moscow. The première will be at the Peace, not at the October or the Russia, but at the Peace. The bosses don't consider my film good enough for the best screens. So much the worse for them. Let them watch bloody Gerasimov at the Russia.

I shan't ask them for any favours, obviously, but neither shall I go to the première.

It's time to realize that nobody needs you. And to start behaving accordingly. You have to be above it. I am Tarkovsky, after all. And there is only one Tarkovsky, unlike the Gerasimovs of this world, whose name is legion . . . My business is to make films, and not to have any part in the general mêlée and fuss that goes on around so-called artists.

Tarassov telephoned. The organizers of the Peace première had contacted him. Larissa explained the situation, and said I really was ill and couldn't go to the première. In order to know how it's going to work out for me in the future I must make *The Bright Day*. (I still cannot decide what to call that film.)

Little plots and stories, acted out and screened, can't possibly be called cinema. They have nothing whatever to do with cinema. A cinematographic work is above all a work which would not be possible in any other art form. In other words, it can be created by means of cinema, and cinema alone.

Oh, if only there were someone who would sign a contract with me for five years, obliging me to make as many films as I could in that time. Films that I want to make.

I shouldn't waste my time. I think I would make seven films in the course of those five years.

31 January

Our fraught way of life gives each of us a narrowly defined role, creating conditions conducive to developing only those elements in our psyche which allow us to grow within the confines of that role. The other areas of our psyche waste away. Hence lack of contact. Here psychological and social factors combine, and produce fear, distrust, moral baseness and the death of hope.

1 February

Today is Larochka's birthday, and I am ill. And we are penniless. Poor Larochka! Never mind, we'll have to celebrate her birthday a bit later, when we've recovered.

An idea: *The Idiot* for television. In seven parts; in colour. I'll have to discuss it with Lapin. With no middlemen and with no unnecessary officials. It's not a bad idea!

2 February

The Idiot would be several instalments. The film about Dostoievsky —*Father Sergey* also for television. It would be good to do *The Idiot*; in seven parts.

For the moment I must think of ways of earning money. Sasha Mishurin and I could write screenplays quickly, to order. If only we could fix two or three contracts for three-hour screenplays. Valery K. is helping. He has already spoken to someone from Moldavia.

I think Ageyev is in Kazakhstan. One could write a screenplay for him with no risk at all.

Kirillin rang today, he's in charge of distribution within Moscow. He seems to be very worried about my illness because of the première. I gathered from our conversation that he had been talking to Rokachov. Tarassov evidently didn't make any bones about my views on the *Solaris* première. So much the better. Send the lot to hell, it's what they deserve.

4 February

There's a rumour that Baskakov has given the go-ahead. In that case we must start work as soon as we possibly can.

If only I could get better. This 'flu is terribly persistent.

Rereading *The Idiot* yet again. I can't say it will be easy to film. The script will be very hard to write. The novel divides roughly into 'scenes' and 'descriptions of scenes'; in other words accounts of anything important that has happened, in terms of the development of the plot. Those 'descriptions' cannot of course be entirely left out. Some of them will have to be made into scenes.

But that will be for later. For the moment the most important thing is *The Bright Day*. Of course the most closely structured of Dostoievsky's works, the most harmonious, the one that lends itself most readily to adaptation is *Crime and Punishment*, but Lyova Kulidzhanov has already done that.

I don't like *The Bright Day* as a title. It's limp. *Martyrology* is better, only nobody knows what it means; and when they find out they won't allow it. *Redemption* is a bit flat, it smacks of Vera Panova. *Confession* is pretentious. *Why Are You Standing So Far Away?* is better, but obscure.

'. . . Almost any reality, even though it has its own immutable laws, is almost always unlikely and improbable. And in fact the more real it is the more improbable it is.' (Lebedev in *The Idiot*)

5 February

Rublyov has been awarded the Grand Prize at the International Festival in Yugoslavia.

It is the festival of festivals, and in the course of '71 and '72 I think all the prize winning films of every country have been shown there. Apart from *Rublyov* we put in *Tamed Fire* and *Dawns Are Quiet Here*. Of course those didn't win anything. They are only awarded prizes in this country because the authorities arrange it. I wonder which foreign films were shown at the festival. Naturally I heard about this independently of both the Union and the Committee.

Yesterday Urusevsky telephoned to congratulate me. He had heard the announcement on the radio. My bosses are still behaving abominably.

This is the fourth international prize to be awarded to the 'illegitimate' *Rublyov*.

6 February

They say *Solaris* was well received. There were no empty seats and no one walked out. In fact at the end somebody even shouted, 'Long live Tarkovsky!' We'll have to see what's going to happen.

THE BRIGHT, BRIGHT DAY.

7 February

'. . . Never have a second arrow. If you rely on a second arrow you will be careless with the first. Every time you must be convinced that you have only one chance, and that you must hit your target with your one and only arrow!' XCII. *Notes to Relieve Tedium*, Kenko-Khosi.

'If you deliberate about whether or not to do something, then as a rule it is better not to do it . . .' From the collected sayings of the leaders of the Buddhist Jodo sect, 1287.

17 February

Rostotsky has just telephoned. He recently returned from Yugoslavia. He says he didn't know that he was the only one going to the festival. I don't believe a word.

It was *the* festival for all the award winning films of the last two years. *The Godfather* was shown, they say it's being promoted by the Mafia. That could be true.

The festival opened with *Rublyov*. It was given fourth place in the audience rating. *The Godfather* and two others had higher marks.

Rublyov was given the first place overall by the international critics. Every single one of the 160 (I think) critics voted for *Rublyov* in first place.

Rostotsky also said that the festival was pro-American. Who knows? Poor old Rostotsky.

18 February

I have never once seen a performance that did not suffer from the same, invariable flaw: they start by 'assessing', then they go on to think; and only then do they utter.

That terrible, unnatural sitting around, that absence of thought or inner state, the incapacity for unbroken thought, the inability to utter words for the sake of a thought and not merely for the sake of the word itself. All that sequentiality where there should be synchronism of word, deed and inner state. All those things taken together amount to what is known, apparently, as the Russian school of acting.

And they contain a fundamental error, lie, untruth.

N. Pokrovsky told me he handed over his late father's manuscript to Gamzatov at the latter's request, and that Gamzatov has now had it for the better part of two years. He won't give it back and in the mean time two doctoral theses have been written on the strength of the book in Daghestan. Its title is *The Struggle for Independence of the Mountain People of the North-eastern Caucasus in the First Half of the Nineteenth Century*. So much for an Avar!

Lots of historians (only historians) are critical of the balloon in the prologue to *Rublyov*. Interestingly, it was the late Svechev who encouraged me to use it. (I met him through Yamschikov.)

I feel more and more that the principles of unity (in the name of wholeness) are of supreme importance in cinema; more so, perhaps, than in any other art form. What I mean is, so to speak, hitting the same spot. An example, to make myself clear: if *Crime and Punishment* comes close to that structural ideal, then *The Idiot*, for instance, is considerably further from it. It is more 'dislocated'.

'. . . We have enjoyed those advantages which society is so ready to give to writers and to which writers themelves are so strongly attached. As we know, they are subject to nothing and obliged to no one, apart from the dictates of their mind and conscience.' (1862—Strakhov on the years between 1861 and 1882).

'. . . At that time his [Dostoievsky's] attitude to Herzen was very friendly, and in his *Winter Notes on Summer Impressions* can be felt something of that writer's influence; later, however, towards the end of his life, he often used to express his indignation at Herzen's inability to understand the Russian people, or to appreciate certain elements of their way of life. The pride he took in education, his fastidious contempt for simple, naive ways—these characteristics of Herzen exasperated Fyodor Mikhailovich, who condemned them even in Griboyedov, not just in our revolutionaries, and scribblers of diatribes.'

'. . . Frenchmen are quiet, *honest*, polite, but *false*, and money is everything to them.' (From a letter to Strakhov, Paris, 26 June 1862).

'. . . Fyodor Mikhailovich was not a great traveller; he was not particularly interested in nature, or historic monuments, or works of art, except perhaps the most outstanding. All his attention was directed towards people, all he would take in was their nature and character, and possibly a general impression of life in the streets. He once explained to me with some feeling that he despised the ordinary, accepted way of sightseeing famous places with the aid of a guide book.' (Strakhov, *Memoirs*).

'. . . Altogether I would say that Fyodor Mikhailovich was extraordinarily moderate in that respect. (As regards wine—A. T.) I do not remember a single occasion in the course of those twenty years when he betrayed the slightest sign of any effect from the wine he had drunk. He may perhaps have had a slight weakness for sweet things; but in general he ate very moderately.' (ibid.)

Maria Dimitrievna died of consumption on 16 April 1864.

I don't know why, but I find myself extraordinarily irritated of late by Khutsiev. He has changed as a result of his cosy place on television. He has become more careful. Age hasn't made him any less childish. And as a director, of course, he is completely unprofessional. All his ideas are small-scale, like a young Pioneer.

I find all his pictures thoroughly irritating, apart perhaps from the last one, about the end of the War. Although even that is pretty contrived, and the hero is appalling. You feel the Pole from the concentration camp might have been hired from some pool. And the little vignettes of tourists and ruins just don't work. The odd thing is that he's a bit pathetic.

After my unsuccessful perusal of *The Idiot* I have decided to reread *A Raw Youth*. The discussion of *The Idiot* with Lapin has been postponed. At the end of this month I'm supposed to be going to East Germany. Perhaps I should use that as an opportunity for a possible joint production, or even simply a German production?

Is it worth thinking about Thomas Mann? I must reread one or two things, starting with a novella. What about *The Magic Mountain*? No, maybe it's not the right moment.

In that case *Doctor Faustus*.

19 February

There's something odd happening to Yussov. He was already terribly hard to work with on *Solaris*. He was fed up with everything, and spiteful, kept offending everybody in a sly, vicious way. He drove everyone mad. And he let us all down—Misha Romadin and V. Fyodorovna and myself. Several people told me afterwards that they were surprised by the way I reacted, they thought I didn't notice. In fact I was just trying to look as if I didn't notice, because otherwise we should have had nothing but rows and shouldn't have been able to work. That's exactly what happened with Danelia's last film, *Huckleberry Finn*.

Vadim always had a need for success and professional acclaim. He is a pleb and hates anything original or independent. Or rather, he envies it. The funny thing is that his views epitomize the attitude of the masses towards the intelligentsia. He has a class hatred of able, creative people with a persona of their own. He is in love with himself. And when it became clear that he was not kingpin he was furious.

When we were working on *Solaris* it was obvious that he had already become a 'master', that he worked only with certainties, using what he had achieved on earlier occasions; that he wanted at all costs to perpetuate those achievements and not look any further.

That's bad. Now he either has to resign himself to the fact that he is not a genius, work on films that are doomed to State and Lenin prizes, and thereby win laurels in return for losing his self-respect and sense of individuality; or else become a director himself (he'd love to do that, but he's inhibited about saying so—he's a frightful humbug on top of everything else) and make pulp films. There are plenty who do that: Bondarchuk, Volchek, Shatrov, Gubenko, Khrabrovitsky, Monakhov—a multitude that cannot be counted.

Murashko (the photographer) says that when Vadim was working on the film with Danelia they had a really bad time. Vadim could well destroy himself as an artist. The rot is to a great extent due to his Innochka; she wants her husband to have honours and money and easy fame for a day.

As for the breakup between him and me, I'm glad it's happened. The loss is Vadim's: he was hoping that he would walk out, breaking his promises, at a moment that would be fatal from my point of view because there would be no one for me to work with; and that would be the end of me. He really hoped that would happen.

In fact Gosha Rerberg and I are preparing to shoot, and I have never worked so easily, agreeably and interestingly with any other cameraman. We respect each other in our search for new methods. It's giving me a taste for real work.

And Vadim has lost out as a result.

18 March

We still haven't been able to start. There are difficulties with

Dvigubsky. At the London Festival, *Solaris* was awarded the prize for the best film of 1972. *Rublyov* has had six prizes already, and *Solaris* three. I must get down to work as soon as I can. The time is dragging on again . . .

23 March

Something has been happening to me recently. Today *that* feeling is particularly strong and significant, I'm preoccupied by it. I have started to feel that the time has come when I am ready to make the most important work of my life.

The guarantee that this is so is, first, my own certainty (which of course can be deceptive and turn out—dialectically—to be a run-of-the-mill disaster); and, second, the material which I am going to use—which is simple, but at the same time extraordinarily profound; familiar and banal—to the point where one will not be distracted, not drawn away from what matters.

I would even call it ideal material, because I feel and know it so well, I'm so aware of it. The only question is—shall I be able to do it? Shall I be able to imbue the perfectly constructed body with a soul?

Yesterday I went to see Mama. Marina has gone off to the coast at Riga. She and I have quarrelled over Larissa, seriously and with good grounds.

6 April

The Hungarians have brought *Rublyov* out as a separate volume.

Columbia (USA) have bought *Rublyov*. They have asked me to shorten it by fifteen or twenty minutes. I can certainly do so, starting with the balloon flight.

For some reason I've just remembered how I lost the script of *Rublyov* (when I had no rough draft). I left it in a taxi at the corner of Gorky Street (opposite the National). The taxi drove off. I was so miserable I went and got drunk. An hour later I came out of the National and went towards the All-Union Theatre Society. Two hours after that, as I came down again to the corner where I had lost the manuscript, a taxi stopped (breaking the law) and the driver handed me my manuscript through the window. It was miraculous.

14 April

Cinema has degenerated into something insignificant. Basically this is because so-called cinematographers have cut it off from their own inner world. In their view cinema is a pleasant way of earning money and a way of achieving acclaim.

I want my picture to be so real that it is tantamount to an action. *Of course they will all be offended and do their best to crucify me.*

Lara, Masha C. and Murashko have gone to Leningrad to look for actors. Then they'll go to Pskov, Novgorod and Petrozavodsk. I don't know . . .

I'm reading Bernard Shaw.

'It is not surprising that the most unforgivable sin for an actor is to *be* the person he is portraying instead of portraying him.'

15 April

Rublyov is showing all over Hungary.

2 June

> No sound of movement, no knocking
> No floor boards sing in the hall,
> The dull desperation of parting
> Looked us in the eyes.
>
> Nobody now believes
> My worthless prophecies
> Just now in the empty house
> The doors were gently closed.
>
> They've taken the lace from the window,
> And boarded up the frames.
> The low sun has slipped across
> The light mist on the road,
> Lighter than roadway dust.

———

3 June

> And now goodbye my dearest,
> My dearest birthplace.
> Fleeing, I can't remember
> The window of our home.
>
> I run beyond the spinney
> The distant blue horizon

To unhappiness—[a makeweight]*
From unhappiness—[a screen.]

I run on, not thinking
Some things to the end,
From someone else's yoke
From an enchanted crown.

How should I live, how think
About the joyous earth
How am I to conceive
What it is you want?

———————

I thought you were my girlfriend,
You are not even that.
In the mist—my horse is tired,
The saddle-girth has snapped.

Joy has come upon me.
I no longer feel fear.
Whatever I think of now
I shall be able to realize.

———————

My friend, my true friend,
The heart asks to be forgiven
And there is no hope for my joy.

More and more often my friend brings me
A cheerless rebuke—more painful every time.

———————

What cannot be said in a word
Will not be explained by pretence
Nor describe the way I'm in love.
I'll help with a wonder-working saint
On the well-trodden path through the ploughed fields.

*The words in brackets were apparently written in by way of stopgap rhymes
and the poems were not subsequently revised or finished.

Rain has fallen onto the earth
Making earth mingle with sky,
Taking account
Of your anonymous beauty
Like the celebration *today*
Of a rite for friends long lost
Live through a bad stage by the end of this month.*

---

17 June

Rublyov is being shown in Sweden. According to Bibi Anderson, Bergman called *Rublyov* the best film he has ever seen.

22 June, Moscow

Solaris is a great success in London.

Because of the shoot-out at the aerodrome in Buenos Aires, the the Argentina trip is being postponed for a week. That means that I personally shan't be going at all.

I want to make a film called *Thomas Mann*. I could offer it to the West Germans for their festival. A joint venture would not be a good thing. Yet again the money won't be available.

Must reread *The Magic Mountain*. Khamreyev telephoned from Tashkent. Sasha and I are to write a screenplay for him—a three hour film: a T[adzhik] Western.†

11 July, Moscow

On Monday 9th I went to see Pavlyonok. He's an unpleasant, coarse, *louche* character. He was bawling at Erica M. and Karayev and trying to drive a wedge between them. He and Yermash (or rather, Yermash) had been given a directive.

The result, we heard yesterday, is that we are being given both money—622,000 roubles—and 7500 metres of Kodak film.

That means up to three takes. We shall have to get the other 3000 metres × 4 from Konoplyov.

There is talk of making *Doctor Faustus* in Federal Germany. 6 June '75 is the hundredth anniversary of Mann's birth. I shall be

---

*Despite the unpolished state of these verse fragments, an attempt has been made at an English version.

†Similar to 'Spaghetti Western'.

meeting the Germans in a day or two. It all has to be done quickly, because it is less than two years to the anniversary.

30 September, Moscow

After a long interval: We came back from Tuchkovo a week ago. We filmed the summer outdoor scenes. It's not at all easy working with Gosha, he's rude to people. Shwedov, his assistant, walked out.

For the moment the material is good.

There will have to be a lot of changes in the script; it will be much better.

On the West German front everything went quiet to start with. Now I'm pursuing things through other channels, they say with some success. We'll see.

Sasha Mishurin and I have decided to write a screenplay for Khamreyev.

5 October, Moscow

NB: I've let Alyosha Artemiev have half the house—for 1500 roubles.

14 October, Moscow

In the mean time—between getting back from Tuchkovo and starting filming—I met M. Zakharov, artistic director of the theatre on Chekhov Street. He wants me to direct something for him. I don't like his approach. He has no programme, no idea of theatre, no prospects. He's a petty ideologue with a cushy job who never dares to make any criticism openly. To hell with him. Little squit.

Larissa is in Myasnoye, getting on with the rebuilding. This should see it through. Next year we shall only have to do the water supply, shower, outside toilet with a shed (and garage?).

20 October, Moscow

A bad thought: nobody needs you, you are utterly alien to your own culture, you have done nothing for it, you are a nonentity.

But if anyone in Europe, or indeed anywhere, asks who is the best director in the USSR, the answer is—TARKOVSKY.

But here—not a word, I don't exist, I'm an empty space. What is known as a moment of weakness. It is very hard not to be needed by anyone. And I should so hate to have standing on the strength of something inferior. What I want is totally to fill someone's life, or several lives.

I feel restricted, my soul is restricted inside me, I need another living space.

7 November, Moscow

I was hurrying because I wanted to write down something very important, but I was too late. I've forgotten it . . .
Why are they all trying to make me into a saint?
Oh God! Oh God!
I want to do things. Stop turning me into a saint.

17 November, Moscow

Reading memoirs about Bunin. What a sad, utterly Russian story. What childishly ungratified ambition. An unhappy, deeply unhappy man!

26 November, Moscow

I'm again starting to reread *Doctor Faustus*. I think the Germans are coming soon to discuss the production.

29 November, Moscow

A telephone call today from Sovexportfilm. *Solaris* has been bought by some big firm and I am being invited to the première in Rome in January '74.
I don't think our studio will be ready yet in January; maybe I shall be able to go to Italy.
Yes, I was right! Gerasimov seems to have been put forward for the Lenin prize. (Or rather, he has put himself forward.) I must check.

2 December, Moscow

Not a word about *Doctor Faustus*—their producer still hasn't appeared.
Rereading the novel. Incidentally, Thomas Mann was very fond of Hesse's *Glass Bead Game*. He found the book romantic, vague, nervous; but significantly he saw in it the same essence as in his own *Doctor Faustus*.
You have to take off all the covers, approach it directly, not come towards it from a distance. You have to peel off the husk; read it in your own way. Most important of all is the tragedy of the artist's loneliness, and the price he pays for understanding the truth.

As for Mark Zakharov and his theatre, I am inclining towards Shakespeare's *Julius Caesar*.

We just have to decide how to treat the crowd scenes—Anthony's speech to the people and the battle of Philippi. The sound will be very important. Artemiev must be brought in.

5 December, Moscow

Constitution Day. Non-stop rejoicing on the television about our achievements in industry, agriculture and international politics. Yet food prices for some reason are going up—roe, fish, shoes. Apparently the greater our achievements the worse we have to live.

Blow the lot of them.

I am taking on an immense burden.

Mann's *Doctor Faustus* is an elaborate amalgam of the author's past life, his shattered hopes, longing for his lost homeland, thoughts about suffering, about the torments of the artist, about his *sinfulness*. On the one hand he (the artist) is an ordinary person. On the other he cannot be ordinary, and consequently he pays for his talent with his soul. Talent is not given to man by God; rather man is doomed to carry the cross of talent. For the artist is a being who strives (but not in secret or in hiding, nor moving in circles, nor in the spaciousness of some kind of ecological niche) to master ultimate truth.

The artist masters that truth every time he creates something perfect, something whole.

But here one is assailed by a thousand other sounds, a thousand other questions. It is important to compare the man who is looking for the truth with the man who ignores it, or is simply not interested.

Probably our Committee will simply not give me this work; so I shall have to fight for it.

I must also do something about more work in case *Doctor Faustus* is delayed.

I must start working on *Renunciation*.

6 December, Moscow

Going to Yurevetz this evening for a day or two.

It's quite disturbing. I haven't been there for thirty years, after all. What will it be like? My feeling is that it will be quite different from all those years ago, when I was twelve. Perhaps I ought not to go at all, so that I don't lose yet another illusion?

Too late now. I have to go.

8 December, Moscow

Returned from Yurevetz this morning. We went as far as Kineshma by train, and after that by taxi.

It was cold, everything was covered in snow. Yurevetz made no impression on me. It was as if I was seeing it for the first time. I recognized the school I used to go to, and the house where we lived during the War. The sandy hill behind the school has been levelled and there's a skating pond where it used to be. St. Simon's Church has a hedge all around it, and in the main square they've built two hideous buildings—the consumer services centre and the town hall, 'next to the school'. Part of the boulevard beside the river has been demolished, in fact all of it has, and where the street used to be they have built a dam, to protect the town from the spreading waters of the Volga. If you ever go there . . .

12 December, Moscow

Today I saw the list of members of the cinema section responsible for awarding state prizes.

S. Bondarchuk, Gerasimov, Kulidzhanov, *Solntseva, Rostotsky*. Envious and unaccomplished, no further comment required. I shall never receive any prize of any kind while those people are around. They dislike me intensely. Only Kulidzhanov may not be my enemy. I now have two places for wonderful nature scenes: Vladimir and Yurevetz.

Marina is pregnant, in her fifth month already. Sasha is working as an assistant director. Do they really not see that it's impossible for them to have another child at the present time? Mama is ill, they have no money—it is ridiculous. Well, yes, of course Gordon is not very clever, not very clever at all.

For today the title for the film— *Why Do You Stand So Far Off?*— is the best.

16 December, Moscow

All three rooms have leaking ceilings. I wrote to Sizov. Our only hope is for him to help us get a flat in a new block near the studio. We are having no luck with the exchange.

A title for the film! I cannot think of anything good, precise.

I feel very unwell. Aching all over and my nerves are shattered. I shall go to the doctor tomorrow.

And I am penniless. And there's the problem of the flat. And the film. What is going to happen?

17 December, Moscow

Larissa went to see Sizov. It doesn't look hopeful as far as a flat in the Mosfilm block is concerned. Even though Sizov was the one who suggested it in the first place, now he says that if I am given a flat 'there will be a revolution' in the studio. What's he doing, going back on his word? Altogether our living conditions are awful. There's water pouring into all three rooms.

I should so like to move, and live on Sretensky Boulevard. How is this whole business going to be solved? I am tired. I shall soon be forty-two, and I have never had my own place.

18 December

The Myasnoye house is nearly finished. All that has to be done now is glaze the veranda, and make the summer room out of it. Lay on the water. Tiles on one kitchen wall. Gas. Outside lavatory. Bath-house.

The stove and fireplace have turned out superbly. They draw really well. The fire heats up the house, which retains the heat.

When shall I be able to stop worrying about house, mod. cons., and my chances of working!

25 December, Moscow

This is what is left from the trip to Yurevetz: a beer label.

29 December

Feeling very unwell. Could be because of the treatment, could be for lack of it. Aching all over, stiff, very low.

As for the film—it's all incomprehensible. Everyone is enthusiastic about the workprint. Olga Surkova was staggered, she says I have excelled myself. Sasha Gordon saw a few sequences and was also muttering something (I met him in the corridor of Mosfilm). I could see from his face that he really was rather stunned.

Even Alov and Naumov were weeping during the screening, let alone our lady editors.

Kremnev is thrilled. I really don't understand any of it. I don't see what they think is so special about it. I must press for Dostoievsky's *Idiot*. Terekhova could be a brilliant Nastasia Fillipovna. If the Committee cannot take the decision, I shall go and see Demichov.

A great deal of work is planned for the spring and summer: (1) write a screenplay for Khamreyev; (2) write a screenplay of

Дом в мягком приближается к завершению. Остались застеклить террасу, отделить маленькую комнату от общей, провести вод. капель на одну стену в кухне. Газ. Баня.

Улицу убрать. Баня.

Печи и камин вышли замечательно.

печь

камин голландка

Печь хорошая мягкая. А камин весь прогревал дом и держит тепло.

Когда, наконец, кончается хлопоты о жилье, удобствах, о возможности работать?

Вот что осталось от поездки в Юрьевец:

Жигулёвское пиво

29.XII.73 Очень плохо себя чувствую. То ли это результат лечения, то ли наоборот от его нехватки. Всё болит, ломит, нехорошо.

С картиной как будто всё хорошо. Все хвалят материал. Ольга Суркова призналась и говорит, что я превзошёл сам себя.
Саша Гордон видел кусочки и

The Idiot so that we can start work on the film in the autumn. That being so, I don't think there is any point in doing *Julius Caesar* for Zakharov, and in any case there isn't time. And this blasted illness on top of it all.

Not a word out of the Germans about *Doctor Faustus*.

It's looking more hopeful about the flat. We are going to be able to exchange for something on Sretensky Boulevard; or else have two flats from Mosfilm. I don't know which is better. It will all become clear when we know for certain, there'll be definite arguments for and against the two possibilities and the thing will decide itself.

The only arguments in favour of Sretensky are the architecture, and the fireplace in the study. And it's central. In favour of the Mosfilm flat are the two bathrooms, two lavatories, two kitchens, in other words six rooms. A loggia and good air.

We don't yet know what we are being offered at Mosfilm. Sretensky needs about five thousand roubles' worth of repairs.

The screenplay for *The Idiot* could start with a flashback: Nastasia Fillipovna's childhood and her first meeting with Totsky.

Myshkin's meeting with Rogozhin can be left out, it doesn't matter how they became acquainted. (The novel does not leave an impression of space, or crowd scenes, so they should be avoided.)

The row at the station with the whip must be omitted—too much fuss and movement in one spot.

It is interesting what one remembers most clearly from the novel—and obviously not just by chance.

On a small, intimate scale.

I have acted *The Idiot* more than once.
1. Myshkin meets the Yepanchins. The execution.
2. Ganya's slap.
3. Nastasia Fillipovna at the Ivolgins'.
4. Nastasia Fillipovna's biography.
5. The 100,000 roubles.
6. Ippolit's dream.
7. The Chinese vase.
8. At Rogozhin's (the mother) and Totsky.
9. Aglaya and Nastasia Fillipovna.
10. Nastasia Fillipovna's death. The Prince at Rogozhin's.
11. And of course the fit in the Scales Hotel, and Rogozhin's murder attempt.
12. The Prince with the children.

30 December, Moscow

I saw Kurosawa at the studio, we had dinner together. He is in an appalling position: they won't give him any Kodak film, and keep assuring him that Soviet film is wonderful. They have wished Tolya Kuznetsov onto him. His team is frightful, informers and cretins. He must somehow be warned that everybody is lying to him.

31 December, Moscow

My aim is to place cinema among the other art forms. To put it on a par with music, poetry, prose, etc.

There must be nothing slavish in our treatment of *The Idiot*. It must not be a literal reproduction of the details of the plot. We must body forth in the real world the ideas, stage directions, author's (director's) thoughts.

Андрей Тарковский

Андрей Тарковский

(Заголовок претенциозный и лживый, но пусть останется, как память о моём ничтожестве — неистребимом и суетном)

начата 74

Andrey Tarkovsky

MARTYROLOGY

(Pretentious and false as a title, but let it stay there as a reminder of my ineradicable, futile worthlessness.)

Begun '74

[Translation of title page of 1974 MS]

1974

3 January, Moscow

I saw a play called *Tourcentre* in the Mossovet theatre (inferior, pretentious title); the play is by Radzinsky, directed by Efros.

Not only is the play bad (very) but so is the production (very).

Neylova is a very good actress—first class. Only there is nothing for her to act.

QUESTIONNAIRE

1.	Your favourite landscape?	dawn, summer, mist
2.	Season?	autumn, dry, sunny
3.	Musical work?	Bach, *St. John's Passion*
4.	Russian prose work (novel, novella)	*Crime and Punishment*, *Death of Ivan Ilych*
5.	Foreign prose work (novel)	*Doctor Faustus*
6.	Novella (Russian)	Bunin—*Sunstroke*
7.	Novella (foreign)	Maupassant
		Tonio Kruger—Thomas Mann
8.	Favourite colour	green
9.	Poet	Pushkin
10.	Film director (Russian)	none
11.	Foreign	Bresson
12.	Do you like children?	very much
13.	What is a woman's driving-force?	submission, humiliation in the name of love
14.	And a man's?	creation
15.	The colour of a woman's hair?	red
16.	Favourite clothes	
17.	Favourite period	

7 January, Moscow

Someone says there is an interview somewhere with Bergman, who considers me the best contemporary director, even better than Fellini(?!) which is what he says in that interview. I must find where it is, what paper and when. I wonder if it can be true. It doesn't sound right.

My name is mentioned in one of Svetlana Alliluyeva's books, but I don't know in what connection.

25 January, Moscow

I went to Zakharov's première at the Lenin Komsomol Theatre. Altogether quite spirited and fun, but of course not on a par with European theatre. All rather noisy and provincial. Like a puppet show. Mark's actors are a disaster. Particularly the ladies.

I must turn down *Julius Caesar* and write two screenplays by the end of the summer, one for myself and one for Khamreyev; and I must go to Truskovetz.

27 January, Moscow

The Idiot. Smotkunovsky is trying to 'push it through'. He has gone to Leningrad for that purpose. Why Leningrad? Evidently no decision has been taken yet, certainly not by the Moscow board.

Must start pressing for *The Idiot* immediately.

On Monday I must go to Yermash. According to Kushnerev the Germans have something to tell me about *Doctor Faustus*.

Surely Smotkunovsky is not going to go and ruin Dostoievsky? I must see that he doesn't; go and see Shauro straightaway.

Yesterday there was a telephone call from the editorial office of Soviet Culture, asking me to do a piece on Solzhenitsyn. Larissa (thank God it was she who answered) said I was away, filming. They need the copy by Monday. Bastards! They've come to the wrong place.

3 February, Moscow

The latest news on *Faustus*: the delay was allegedly because of the nomination of the producer. He, or rather she, had government approval, and is apparently some highly influential, wealthy film-producer. She is supposed to be coming here in three weeks' time at the latest.

This week I shall submit my application for *The Idiot* to Sizov. If I have time, I'll let Shauro have a copy.

Attributed to Pushkin—'. . . contemporary society is as despicable as it is stupid; what is this lack of public opinion, this indifference to every kind of duty, justice, right, truth, to everything that does not constitute *necessity*. This cynical contempt for a man's thought and dignity.

'One should add (not as a concession but as the truth) that the government is still the only European in Russia. And however uncouth and cynical it may be, it could, if it wanted, be a hundred times worse. Nobody would pay the slightest attention . . .' (French).

It is very significant that Pushkin should have written both *The History of Pugachov's Rebellion* and *The Captain's Daughter*.

As a historian, an objective observer (and the greater the personality of the historian the cooler, the more untroubled is his gaze) he saw Pugachov as a bloodthirsty rebel, a fiend out of hell, a fiery sword, a scourge of God. And yet the writer's view of Pugachov as a national figure, as the quintessence of the people, led to his being idealized.

Pushkin could not envisage a national figure remarkable only for violence and bloodshed. It would not be historically justifiable, and, more important, it would not be viable. Historic truth could become an artistic lie, an artistic image with a minus sign.

An artistic image is one that ensures its own development, its historical viability. An image is a grain, a self-evolving retroactive organism. It is a symbol of actual life, as opposed to life itself. Life contains death. An image of life, by contrast, excludes it, or else sees in it a unique potential for the affirmation of life.

Whatever it expresses—even destruction and ruin—the artistic image is by definition an embodiment of hope, it is inspired by faith.

Artistic creation is by definition a denial of death. Therefore it is optimistic, even if in an ultimate sense the artist is tragic.

And so there can never be optimistic artists and pessimistic artists. There can only be talent and mediocrity.

4 February, Moscow

It is curious that performances of what is known as the 'Theatre of the Absurd'—Beckett, Ionesco—should as a rule produce an impression almost of naturalism; or at any rate of total truth.

That is how the problem of truth in art resolves itself; for such truth is intimately connected with the specifics of a given genre.

A film in cinema is what in theatre would be realism—and vice versa.

In cinema—as in life—the text, the words, are refracted in everything apart from the words themselves. The words mean nothing—words are water.

I don't believe that cinema is many-layered. In cinema polyphony comes not from a multiplicity of levels but from succession and accumulation—Take 1, Take 2, Take 3—constantly building up.

Not only that. The multiple meanings of an image are inherent in the quality of that image.

23 February, Moscow

Faustus—some new developments. I've been asked if I could make a picture in collaboration with East German television. I told them that in principle I could, that it would simply be a question of agreeing over the details. The producer will be coming at the beginning of March.

As for *The Idiot*—

1. I have handed Sizov an application for a two-part film.

2. Lollobrigida has been in Moscow and suggested to Sizov a joint production of *The Idiot* (with herself as Nastasia Fillipovna). She had Konchalovsky in mind as director. Sizov told her that there was also Tarkovsky, at which Lollobrigida was apparently delighted, but promptly went back to the idea of Konchalovsky.

That has to be stopped, and *The Idiot* must be made with Mosfilm.

8 March, Moscow

We have nearly finished shooting. It seems to be working. We shall see. Artemiev has refused to write the music for *Mirror*. He says he is overworked and exhausted. Oh, well, to hell with them.

It can be a compilation.

Bessy (from the Cannes Festival) wants me to go to the festival. He said he would take my film with his eyes shut. I must try and have it finished in time. We still don't know about the two parts. The Germans are supposed to be coming to Moscow soon. Chukhrai is said to be interested in *The Idiot* and wants me to make it for him. We shall see.

17 March, Moscow

Mirror is going really badly. Nobody has any idea of what it's about. All hopeless. Sizov saw it in order to decide the question of the two parts, and he had no idea what it was about either. The material keeps falling apart, it doesn't make a whole. Altogether it is all hopeless.

I must say something to Sizov on Monday about what length I can count on. I think the East German producer is coming today. I feel terribly low.

22 April, Monday

R. Baloyan (a friend of Seryozha Paradzhanov) came here. Shklovsky and I sent a letter to V. V. Scherbitsky:

To
The First Secretary of the Central Committee of the Ukraine
Comrade V. V. Scherbitsky.

In an article in *Evening Kiev* signed by the deputy procurator of Kiev we have been given the sensational news of the crimes of Sergey Paradzhanov, Soviet director, who 'works at the Dovzhenko studios'.

As we understand it, inherent in the Soviet legal tradition is the notion that the accused cannot be called a criminal before sentence has been passed. Yet this article puts Paradzhanov on a par with drunks and hooligans, and totally fails to convey what sort of a man he is.

The article is signed by a lawyer who must be aware of legal procedures. Despite that, the article accuses a man before he has been tried, which could have an effect both on his trial and on public opinion. Such an article is alien to Soviet practice and prejudicial to the processes of law.

We, the undersigned, are professional filmmakers whose lives as artists have not been easy.

In our opinion Sergey Paradzhanov is at the height of his powers, but too little used.

It is unfortunately the case that most Soviet directors have only a few films to their credit.

In the last ten years Sergey Paradzhanov has made only two films: *Shadows of Our Forgotten Ancestors* and *The Colour of Pomegranates*. They have influenced cinema first in the Ukraine, second in this country as a whole, and third—in the world at large.

Shadows of Our Forgotten Ancestors proved not only to the Ukraine, but to all Ukrainians scattered about the world by centuries of turmoil, that only in the Soviet Union has the voice of Ukrainian art spoken fully and clearly.

We are not familiar with the case against Paradzhanov, but feel ourselves to be responsible for his fate, responsible for him, both as an individual and as an outstanding artist.

We saw Dziga Vertov being ignored for decades; we saw the Party painfully rehabilitating the work of Sergey Eisenstein by making changes in the leadership of the arts.

A great number of films exist, but very few that will stand the test of time. We carry a responsibility for world cinema.

We are confident that the Soviet court will protect this most distinguished director.

If the man has become involved in something reprehensible, he needs help. We need him. We need his potential.

We are not asking for mercy; we would point out that artistic reserves have to be used sparingly.

Artistically, there are few people in the entire world who could replace Paradzhanov.

He is guilty—guilty in his solitude.

We are guilty of not thinking of him daily and of failing to discover the significance of a master.

21 April 1974　　　　　　　　　　　　　　V. B. Shklovsky
　　　　　　　　　　　　　　　　　　　　　A. A. Tarkovsky

12 June, Moscow

An answer addressed to Shklovsky and myself from the office of the Procurator of the Ukrainian SSR arrived a few days ago. Here it is—

Office of the Procurator of the Union of
Soviet Socialist Republics
Deputy Procurator
Ukrainian Soviet Socialist Republic
No. 04-458–74
24 May 1974
Kiev

Comrades Tarkovsky, A. A.
Shklovsky, V. B.
Moscow, Mosfilm Studios.

Your letter referring to the case of Paradzhanov, S. I., addressed to the Central Committee of the Communist Party of the Ukraine, has been noted by the Procurator's Office of the USSR.

For crimes stipulated in articles 122, parts I and II, and 211 of the Criminal Code of the Ukrainian SSR, Paradzhanov has been sentenced by Kiev Regional Court to five years' loss of freedom.

Paradzhanov was sentenced for a similar crime on a previous occasion. He partly admitted his guilt in the present case. Furthermore his guilt was confirmed by the evidence of numerous witnesses.

There are no grounds for appeal.

State Councillor of Justice III Class
M. Samayev

27 June, Moscow

Last night I dreamt that I had died. But I could see, or rather feel, what was going on around me. I could feel that Lara was beside me, and one of my friends.

I felt I had no strength or will, I was only capable of witnessing my own death, my own corpse.

Above all, I could feel in my dream something long forgotten, something that had not happened to me for a long time—the feeling that it was not a dream but real.

It is such a powerful sensation that a wave of sadness fills your soul, of pity for yourself, and a strange, as it were aesthetic way of seeing your own life. When you feel compassion for yourself in that way, it is as if your pain were someone else's, and you are looking at it from outside, weighing it up, and you are beyond the bounds of what used to be your life. It was as if my past life was a child's life, without experience, unprotected. Time ceases to exist, and fear. An awareness of immortality.

I could see (from above, from somewhere on the ceiling) the spot where they were setting up supports for the coffin, and everyone was very busy because I had died.

And then I came back to life, and no one was surprised.

They all went off to the public baths, and I wasn't allowed in because I didn't have a ticket. I pretended I was the bath attendant, but I couldn't produce any proof of identity.

But all that was just a dream, and I knew it was a dream.

It's the second time I have had a dream about death. And each time I have felt an extraordinary sense of freedom, of not needing any kind of protection. What can it mean?

The interview with Bergman where he says I am the best contemporary director is in *Playboy*.

17 July

Apparently Tito Kalatozov is ill. Lord, let this cup pass by. I cannot even utter the name of the illness.

27 July

Yesterday Yermash rejected *Mirror*; and while it was being discussed he talked such rubbish, it was obvious that he had not the slightest understanding of the film, nor of why he was rejecting it.

What else could one expect of them?

I am tired. I must find some way of earning money, and then go off into the country and live there.

29 July

Again all hell has been let loose—over the film. On Thursday Yermash rejected it: he found it all incomprehensible ('Make it comprehensible!'), some bits he didn't like ('Cut them out! What's the point of them?') and so on.

It was a ridiculous row, and very odd. As if Yermash were playing a badly rehearsed role, or trying to demonstrate how 'principled' and 'strict' he was being. Whatever the explanation, he made an appalling impression—overbearing and utterly lacking in imagination. He's hardly of the stature to preside over Goskino.

T. G. Ogorodnikova suggested I might write two or three adaptations for television. I want to offer her *Oblomov*, *The Life of Klim*

Samgin, and Pomyalovsky's *Seminary Sketches*. I must talk it over with her and if it works out—sign a contract and go and live in the country.

But then—what will happen to *Mirror*?

1 August

I have worked out a plan of campaign.

1. Write to Yermash, refusing to make the corrections and asking him to clarify his attitude towards my future work prospects (by August 6th or 7th).

2. Write to Sizov to make him aware of my letter (to Yermash).

3. On the 5th, Monday, (in the second session) refilm the remaining 6th and 7th parts.

4. Come to an agreement with T. G. about the television adaptations (if possible).

5. Organize a preview on Tuesday in order to have a stock of exploitable opinions: Surkov, Kondrashev (one of us), Simonov (seems to be a shit); Shostakovich (if he can—he is ill), Smotkunovsky, Karasik, Chukhrai (?) and so on. Felix and I must work out who should be invited of the writers, artists and poets.

6. It may be possible to write down these people's opinions and for them to sign. Then I should have something to show Yermash.

7. If the picture still does not come out, and Yermash actually makes me unemployed, then I shall write to Brezhnev.

8. If even that doesn't help, ask permission through Goskino to go abroad for two years to make a film there, without compromising myself ideologically.

18 September

It is still not clear what is going to happen to *Mirror*. Yermash won't utter, he refuses to get involved, he's scared, and waiting to see what will happen.

He has already shown the film to Demichov (because he is a fool and because he's scared of the powers that be) and Demichov apparently did not like it (hardly surprising) and expressed doubt about whether it could possibly be a success. My God! What on earth can Demichov know about art?

Today Yermash invited Evgeny Danilovich Surkov to see *Mirror*, obviously he wants his advice.

Will E. D. sell me down the river or won't he?

It will all be clear this evening.

Tomorrow I shall show the film to Dmitri Shostakovich, Nikulin, Zisya and one or two others.

Angelo has arrived from Rome, and he says that our *Solaris* was a flop in Italy because without my consent it was re-edited and cut by thirty minutes or more. I intend either to give an interview to the Moscow correspondent of *Unita*, or else write an open letter to the chief editor. I might also sue Euro International Film, the distributors—the head of the company is Lanza.

The editing and cutting were done by Dacia Maraini—Alberto Moravia's common law wife.

A company in Rome called Gold Film wants me to make *Joseph*.

The question of the West German television adaptation of *Doctor Faustus* has got to be discussed by their studio.

They want me to write a screenplay for them in Tallinn. Something German. T. Mann? Hoffmann? Have they thought about the Geneva Conference?

Read Ibsen's *Peer Gynt*. Stupendous. One of the screenplays I should like to suggest to them in Tallinn is *Peer Gynt*.

22 September

Kolya Shishlin had a talk with Yermash. The news is far from encouraging. He does not want to allow *Mirror* nor does he want to let me make *The Idiot*.

Yesterday Larissa bought an armchair and a sideboard for the country.

Armchair	– 13 roubles	
Sideboard	– 65	,,
Delivery	– 20	,,
	98 roubles	

26 September

Lara has bought a bed (mahogany)	– 110r
and a table (,,)	– 65r
	175r
Delivery	25r
	200r

22 October

We are still getting ready to go to the country. Larissa has bought a whole lot more furniture, all of it, of course, needing repair.

1. Two carved beds (pear) single	—	20r
2. 7 chairs	—	18r
3. Small carved sideboard (oak)	—	16r
4. Marble washstand	—	10r
5. Linen cupboard with mirror	—	35r
6. Carved oak table	—	10r
7. Bedside table	—	5r
8. Shelf	—	5r
9. Carved round table	—	20r
10. Ledges	—	6r
11. Two bookshelves	—	12r

	180r
Delivery	45r

Mirror—37r., wardrobe with mirror (mahogany) 65r. + del. = 122r., 3 carved oak chairs—90r. + del. 7r., 2 chairs and 2 armchairs = 8r. + del. 10r.

List of essentials to be bought for the country:

1. Ledges or rods for curtains for 11 windows (3 + 1, 3 + 3), I; one bracket each, 75 × 10 + 14
2. Venetian blinds for windows (12 not counting the veranda)
3. Extensions—2
4. Chandeliers for passage and nursery (2) and 1 for kitchen
5. Table lamps—2 for first room and one for nursery
6. Television and aerial (Felix)
7. Ledges for blinds—Tamara Georg. 295–66–88
8. Material for blinds—57m. by 1m.30 (dye)
9. Fringes
10. Puppy (Alsatian)
11. Typewriter
12. Typing and copy paper
13. Books—Dostoievsky, on Dostoievsky. Hoffmann
14. *Rublyov* poster
15. Books and 'dump lorry' for Tyapa
16. Carpet runner
17. Rugs

18. 2 oil lamps
19. 2 single mattresses
20. 3 bedspreads
21. Drying oil—40 litres
22. Tiles
23. Blankets

25 December

Andrey, the First Called!*

I liked Bagrat's film very much. The Armenians are not interested; all they care about is football. Two frames of *Mirror*
are enough for me to know about all the rest. Is there any
colour? I liked *Solaris* in black-and-white. I don't want colour!
I am sorry we did not meet in Tbilisi at Tamez's farewell
evening. I am becoming accustomed to the idea of 'isolation',
like a cosmonaut to outer space. The truth of my situation and
this set-up is that it is the pathological syndrome of the criminal
world. This is strict regime! I didn't see *The Granite Quarry*. *The
Red Snowball Bush* seems to me a series of arabesques on a theme.
The world that I was playing at—the world of fairies, poets,
story-tellers, tsars of Kievan Russia—is ridiculous in the context of a boy with 10 convictions, tattoos over 90% of his skin,
that way of speaking, the whole syndrome. What am I doing?
I'm alone. First write, then sew up a bag, at the moment I'm
the laundry-girl! When they see me they start singing, 'A thief
will never be a laundry-girl' and so on. They say I should
appeal for clemency. What's the point? I wasn't sentenced for
clemency. I could not have imagined that the 14 charges made
against me in the Ukraine would be replaced by the article . . . !
(sorry). How could I have refused that invitation to dinner
(and get drunk at Grigoriev's binge) and offend you and
Larissa. When I see Larissa I shall give her a diadem in honour
of her son. It's probably hard for her—for Larissa—to be the
wife of a genius. Andrey, don't write, my address may change.
Transfer.

Sergey Paradzhanov

Is *The Idiot* really what I want to do? Might the adaptation not
become a demonstration of my principles, which cannot be an
organic structural part of the novel itself?

*i.e. 'first of the Apostles'—Paradzhanov's way of addressing A.T.

Perhaps for me (even with knowledge of the classics to help me) *The Death of Ivan Ilych* would be better suited—it would need to be substantially 'rewritten', dug over ... Everything in it would have to be brought back to life, through being lived all over again. That would go to the very heart of things.

Of course *Dostoievsky* would be the most appropriate project for me, even though there is something rather constructivist about the idea. What I envisage is bringing together, as it were, the different layers; the present, the past, and the ideal.

At the moment I can see a film version of something by the Strugatsky brothers as being totally harmonious in form: unbroken, detailed action, but balanced by a religious action, entirely on the plane of ideas, almost transcendental, absurd, absolute.

Beckett's *Molloy*.

A diagram of the life of someone who is seeking (actively) to understand the meaning of life.

And act in it myself. Would I stand up under the weight of the two streams? Oh, how wonderful!

1. Two actors. 2. Unity of place. 3. Unity of action. 4. It would be possible to be aware of nature in the background now and again (as it grows dark or light).

(Take *Molloy* for the Strugatskys.)

In *Solaris* that problem was never solved. We only managed, with some difficulty, to organize the plot and ask one or two questions.

What I want is an explosive fusion of the emotional (imbued with the simple, valid feelings of an autobiographical account) with the aspiration to understand certain philosophical and ethical questions which touch on the meaning of life.

The success of *Mirror* has demonstrated to me yet again how well founded was my conjecture about the importance of personally experienced emotion in telling a story from the screen.

Perhaps cinema is the most personal art, the most intimate. In cinema only the author's intimate truth will be convincing enough for the audience to accept.

27 December

Krymova (the critic) telephoned Sasha. She and Efros think *Mirror* is a work of genius.

1975

How does a project mature?
It is obviously a most mysterious, imperceptible process. It carries on
independently of ourselves, in the subconscious, crystallizing on the
walls of the soul.

1975

2 January, Myasnoye

I shall finish this notebook here in Myasnoye. I have started another one for Moscow, so that it doesn't have to be endlessly carried between there and here.

We saw the New Year in here, at home. It is lovely here. We shall finish off one or two things in the summer, and being the wiser for our experience this winter, intend to start off next winter fully equipped:

1. Skylights on the veranda and in the kitchen.
2. Make the kitchen warmer.
3. Reinforce the house and render it on the outside (kitchen).
4. Acquire a dog (Alsatian).
5. Put a fence around the house, and a hedge down below.
6. Plant some flowers.
7. Lay on water.

That is the minimum plan.

8. Make a bathroom.
9. Gas stove.
10. Spare room with stove.
11. Build an attic room onto the first floor.

After the holidays, I shall go back to Moscow about the 8th or 9th—I must organize a press showing at the studio. I must ask Shklovsky and Zolotusky to write something in the papers. (Must write to both of them and to Larissa.)

Tyapa is very highly strung. (What would he be like in Moscow?) Anna Semyonovna gets terribly tired. I must find some woman to live in here and look after them, as soon as possible.

4 January

A thought—what if I were to have a female instead of a male protagonist in *Roadside Picnic*?

25 February

I have been travelling a lot over the last two months. I went to Tbilisi, where there was a première, and several previews, which were a great success. The Shengelay brothers made me extraordinarily welcome, and their friends, and Gizo. Admittedly plenty of drink flowed.

Then Larissa and I went to Leningrad (the première there was a success) and to Estonia. Success there too, and a lot of drinking. I went to see Yarvet. In Leningrad I went to see the director of the Pushkin Dramatic Theatre, Kiselyov (on 14 February). They want me to direct *Hamlet* (together with Solonitsyn, whom they are taking on to the staff of the theatre). We may have to take an Ophelia from somewhere else. I signed an agreement in Tallinn for *Hoffmanniana* (by August 1st). Yesterday and today I have been working on *The Idiot*.

I went to see Yermash, who seems to have surrendered. He began by saying that I should make a film about Lenin. I said, certainly, provided there were no control commissions from either the Central Committee or the Institute of Marxism-Leninism. He said that would be impossible. Then I told him that the whole thing would end up in a monumental scandal, and that everyone would get it in the neck, and he, Yermash, more than anyone else. He agreed in silence, and at that moment, I think, decided to give permission for *The Idiot*.

We still do not know anything about the distribution of *Mirror*.

Mr. Bessy is coming today (has already arrived). I must telephone Pozner about it this evening.

2 March

Yermash has refused point-blank (despite having given his word to Bessy last year) to let *Mirror* go to the Cannes Festival, and he won't give any reason for his refusal. Bessy is furious. Yermash has persuaded Bessy to take Bondarchuk, and Bykov, and Plissetskaya. After every showing Bessy was in a rage, but . . . The trouble is that Bessy said that he could guarantee *Mirror* the supreme prize. And that is precisely what the powers that be cannot bear, they are doing all they can to humiliate me and the film. Still nothing about *The Idiot*.

I went to see Sizov and asked him a string of questions:

—Why did Yermash not let *Mirror* go to Cannes, despite Bessy's request and the decision of the special committee (when they considered *Mirror*)?

—Why am I not told about invitations from foreign firms to make films?

—Why are they being so punctilious about arranging for the Committee to review *Mirror*? (When Khrushchov heard that his speech to the Board was going to be published, he went running off to the editorial offices to grab it back. Brilliant! When Khrushchov was in Tallinn and heard that I would soon be arriving he tried to scarper as soon as he could.)

—Why did Naumov, when he was ill, drop both his illness and his filming and dash to the Committee (in Moscow) in order to slate *Mirror*?

—Why did they make *Mirror* 2nd category?

—Why is *Mirror* not being distributed? (73 copies).

—Why is it considered ignominious to mention my festival triumphs in the press?

—Why did *Solaris* not receive a State prize when it went through every stage almost unanimously?

Sizov started muttering something and tried to answer one or two of the questions, as if I were interested in answers. By way of conversation he said—'We don't need that picture (*The Idiot*)! Perhaps you should make it in another studio?' I answered—'Perhaps I ought to leave Mosfilm altogether?' Sizov murmured something mollifying.

Something must be done about Cannes. *Mirror* must be let through. Bessy has gone, promising to make a row, and without taking a single Soviet film. He wanted *Mirror*, which everyone there is expecting and which Yermash definitely promised. A coward and a creep!

Of course if it were given the prize, *Mirror* could bring in foreign currency—but that is of no interest to Yermash. All he cares about is having his arse in a comfortable chair, and to hell with the interests of the nation!

I shall probably go to the country on Tuesday to see Tyapa, and around the 15th to Leningrad, to the Alexandrinka.

8 March

I've come to the country for ten days. For the last few days it has been misty and warm—three degrees above freezing. The snow is receding and melting, there is hardly any left on the roof.

Tyapa is misbehaving. He has grown, he is very funny and covered in freckles.

Only a month now till the real spring. Spring here will be concerted—it will all let rip at once.

21 March

Hamlet at the Alexander seems to have fallen through. According to Solonitsyn, who telephoned Kiselyov on behalf of Masha Chugunova, Kiselyov said that 'powerful opposition' has arisen to the idea of taking Solonitsyn on in the theatre. He now wants to postpone our meeting till the beginning of April, having earlier been in a great hurry to start work on *Hamlet* and having promised to give Tolya a permanent job in the theatre.

I gather this is Gorbachev's doing.

I must talk to Zakharov; perhaps the idea of doing *Hamlet* in his theatre might be revived.

Came back from the country on the 19th. Tyapa has grown. Great big fellow! He is a terrible wailer—like a kind of natural calamity. I even had to slap him two or three times.

To be done in the course of the summer in the country:

1. Water
2. Firewood
3. Shed
4. Bath-house
   and finish things off in the house.

27 March

HAMLET

Even if they were to decide to do *Hamlet* at the Alexander with Solonitsyn, it probably would not be a good thing to do it since we now know what Gorbachev's attitude is to the idea—that bandit. It would mean that one powerful lobby is ready to go to any lengths to ensure that we crash. There would be no point in working in those circumstances.

I went to see Zakharov. He wants *Hamlet* to be put on in his theatre. Of course that theatre pays very little—1000 roubles for the production (from September to January '76)—200 roubles a month.

I went to see Arkady Strugatsky. He is very pleased that I want to make a film of *The Picnic*. There are three screenplays, all equally viable.

8 April

Something odd is going on: the picture is showing in two cinemas. They say it has been released earlier than it was announced (September) in order to see how popular it is with audiences.

Rubbish! I don't believe a word they say. Not a single poster, not a single advertisement. No première! In fact—all sotto voce, as a secondary feature.

Some woman appeared today to invite me to meet *Pravda*. I don't like it. It's bound to be some kind of provocation. Felix Kuznetsov wants to help have the *Mirror* controversy published in *Literaturnaya Gazeta* and *Komsomolskaya Pravda*.

I think he said something also about *Nedelya*. I saw M. Zakharov today. He wants to see Tolya Solonitsyn performing. I must contact him quickly.

11 April

Mirror is showing in two cinemas—on the Taganka and in the Vityaz in Cheryomushki. No publicity, no posters. (Allegedly in order to find out how much interest there is going to be.)

All the same it is impossible to get hold of a ticket. And for the first time (at least, I have never heard of anything like it) the cinema audience actually applauded.

Still not a word about *The Idiot*.

20 April

One of the notes handed me when I met audiences in Zhukovsky, Fryazino, and other places: 'The impression made is tremendous. Thank you for what you are saying and for what you make one think about. Even though it is frightening.'

30 April

Still nothing clear about *The Idiot*. Yermash seems to have died. There is a rumour that everyone is fed up with him and that he is going to be dismissed. If only he were! (Whom would they appoint?)

I went to see Chernoutsan yesterday in the Central Committee, for some 'advice'. He is going to help to get things going. As for the uncertainty about Solonitsyn and the administrative complications, I agreed with Zakharov that rehearsals of *Hamlet* would start in September, with Solonitsyn if he agrees to the contract. If his part, and the production, work out, then Zakharov will take him on in his theatre.

I must talk to Tolya quickly. The Hoffmann screenplay has ground to a halt.

6 May

I went to see Chernoutsan just before the May holidays. I wanted him to help me arrange an interview with Suslov. But somehow it didn't work out. He—Chernoutsan—evidently cannot do that. All the same, he is taking steps of some kind. I shall ring him after 10 May.

Nevertheless, I would like to write either to Brezhnev or to Suslov in order to clarify my position once and for all. I shall have to ask Kolya and Lyova, to make sure that the letter does not just lie around.

In Tallinn they want to make a film of Thomas Mann's *Doctor Faustus* jointly with West Germany.

Obviously there won't be anything in that for me.

3 June

Here I am, back in Myasnoye; I arrived a few days ago. It's paradise. Larissa has sown the entire vegetable garden. Of course there is an enormous amount to be done: not only to the house, before the winter, but other things as well.

Hardly anything happened in Moscow.

Mirror is running in the Leningrad Giant with great success.

Starting rehearsals of *Hamlet* in the Lenin Komsomol Theatre. Hamlet is Solonitsyn, Ophelia—Churikova.

The Italians are going to invite *Mirror* to the Unita Festival in Rome.

I wonder if Yermash will be able to refuse the Italian Communist Party?

Still no news about *The Idiot*.

I have made an agreement with the Strugatskys about *The Picnic*. I met Boris. He is nice too, but unlike Arkady makes a point of being clever. He seems to be an ideologist. Arkady is hard-working and a nice chap. Although it is not that simple.

Soon, while I'm here, I must write a libretto for *Joan of Arc* and a script (by the end of July) for the Hoffmann for Tallinn. I can't somehow get the script right. There is no idea on which to build it.

Khamreyev, and Uzbekfilm generally, are being rather non-committal: they—or perhaps even Goskino—seem to have raised some sort of difficulties. Sasha is in Moscow and will deal with it.

2 July

I have been in Myasnoye for a month now and still have not sat down at my desk. I relaxed (relatively speaking), had a go at the vegetable garden, did things around the house—and for the moment I have done no work. Next week I must start building a shed, I shall probably have to ask V. Akimov to help.

Next week we shall start converting part of the veranda (15 out of the 45 square metres) into a room that can be lived in, in the winter.

We have fenced off the garden at the bottom; in the autumn we must plant some trees. There has been no rain for a whole month— everything is burnt up, the grass is dead, it looks like straw. We had to water the vegetable garden nearly every day.

This morning at dawn, after two days of north wind, it suddenly started to pour. A heavy sky. In the afternoon it stopped, but by evening it was drizzling again.

I have to have the Hoffmann finished by the 1st, and I still haven't written a line, it's going to be a nightmare.

Incidentally, Yermash would like an 'expanded' (8–10 pages) outline of *The Idiot*. Maybe something is happening.

Larissa held on to the letter I had written to Yermash when she realized I'd had a telegram.

3 July

How does a project mature?

It is obviously a most mysterious, imperceptible process. It carries on independently of ourselves, in the subconscious, crystallizing on the walls of the soul. It is the form of the soul that makes it unique, indeed only the soul decides the hidden 'gestation period' of that image which cannot be perceived by the conscious gaze.

Hoffmann is difficult. It is clear that one level must be the man himself, his illness, his unhappiness, his love, his death.

And the other—the world of his fantasy, of his *still unwritten works*, his musical compositions (his own, and Glück's and Haydn's).

He seems to escape into his fantasies. More than that: they are his home, his castle, his citadel. He is not made for this world, he does not need it.

There must not be too many characters (in line with Hoffmann). They must not dictate their own plot, but be there as the starting-point of the fictional characters; the cause of the condition of which those characters are born.

Я открыл её приглашенные мило и непринужденно беседовали с ней, улыбались ей... Хорошее воспитание? Лицемерие? Капитерство? Свобода? А он мне понравился. Граничкон в сапогах...

Как хорошо здесь, в меньшем У меня прекрасная комната;

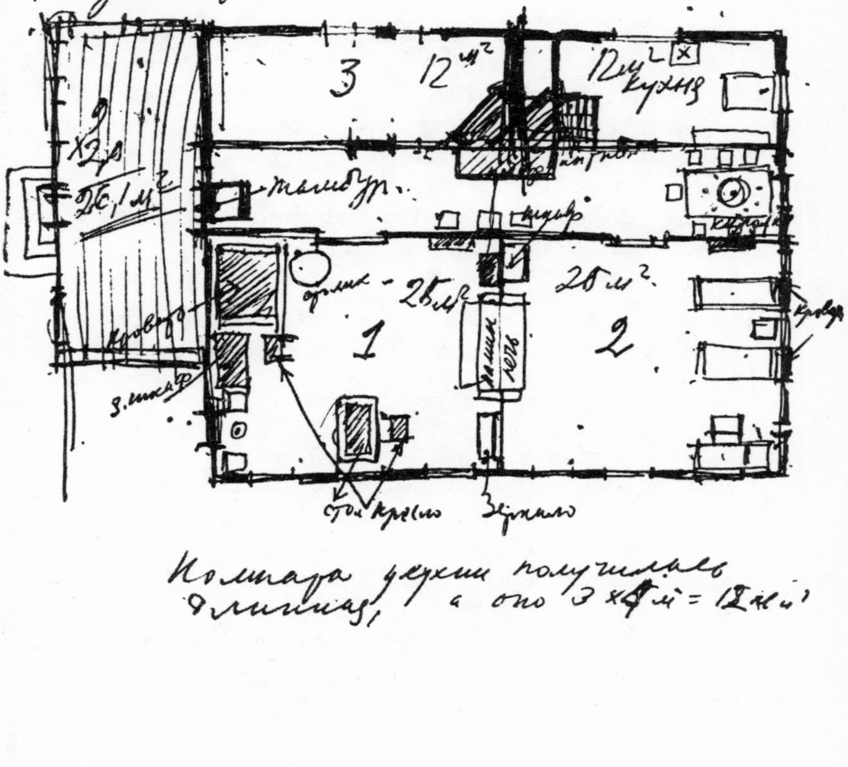

4 July

Give up private property . . . In order to give up something you have to refuse something that is actually there. And I have no experience of private property. How can I give up something I have never known in my life? That is at the root of one of the basic ideological errors.

Reading Max Frisch's *Stiller*. He is clever. Too clever for a good writer. He is precise, economical; charming. Like a tiny Japanese garden.

He is very nice, and very like his characters. That is not a plus, either. I know him. He gave Larissa and me supper near Locarno. He was with his mistress, whom everybody in Switzerland condemned just for being his mistress.

It was a delicious supper; a delightful restaurant with tables set under the oak trees (or beeches?). And all the people who condemned *her* and had been invited, were making pleasant, easy conversation with her and smiling. Is that being well brought up? Hypocrisy? Humbug? Snobbishness? Anyhow, I liked him. A real Puss-in-Boots.

How lovely it is here in Myasnoye. I have a wonderful room.

5 July

This is how the house will be by the winter. Apart from the third room and the lobby it is all done. The room beside the kitchen has turned out very long—12 square metres.

21 July

Yesterday Larissa telephoned Moscow. Sasha M. has written a treatment, apparently a very good one. According to Sasha (and he always exaggerates the things that have worked and plays down all the ones that haven't) Felix K. is delighted with the treatment for *The Idiot*. Allegedly Barabasch is equally delighted. She is the committee editor, appointed by Yermash to cut *The Idiot*, bypassing our group and Mosfilm.

I have written to Tallinn asking them to extend the deadline for the *Hoffmanniana* by a month.

Busy with building work. We are building a third 12-metre room. There is a lot to be done. By the evening I am dropping with fatigue. At this moment I am writing lying down.

25 July

Perhaps they really will let me make *The Idiot*?

Of the decent directors only Antonioni was at the Moscow Festival, and he announced that he would leave immediately if he was not shown *Mirror*. For a long time they didn't want to, but in the end they had no choice but to show it. He liked it very much. He even wanted to meet me. Our officials very nearly summoned me from the country for the meeting.

On the Voice of America they were saying that pressure was being put on me again, and that my film was not being sent to Cannes or West Germany or Locarno. That is in fact the case.

14 September

We are living quietly and peacefully in the country. We have built on a third room (only the ceiling still to be done). A shed (really good). We have heating in the kitchen and the third room. We have brought over half the firewood.

We've come to the end of the money—waiting for something from Khamreyev in Tashkent.

Again—the script for Tallinn. I still have not written a line. Towards the 1st of October I shall go to Moscow to start rehearsing *Hamlet*. I am not ready for it. It's going to be a tight schedule for putting the play together. Shall we make it?

Not a word about *The Idiot*.

Yermash obviously asked me for the synopsis during the time of the Festival in order to lull me into a sense of security, and in order to prevent me from complaining to foreigners.

Bergman has invited me four times (!) to stay with him in Sweden. I was told nothing at all about it, even verbally. It was Olga Surkova who told me; she talked to the Swedes at the festival. The festival was ludicrous. Rumour has it that Kurosawa has made a very bad film.

We've had two days of Indian summer. We must get the firewood ready as soon as we can.

21 September

The Idiot has fallen through. I've had a letter from Sasha Mishurin. I wrote to the Strugatskys to ask them to do something about it. (Can they do anything by themselves?)

I have to go to Moscow. But—Hoffmann, Hoffmann!

26 September

I've written ten pages of Hoffmann. M. Zakharov wired to say that the beginning of November will be the best time to start rehearsals of *Hamlet*.

I have not had a moment to write about something that happened here one Tuesday in August.

It was the 12th or the 13th—I don't remember. At 8.15 in the evening Larissa and Tyapa went out to the car to see off Nikolayev (district prosecutor) and the chief investigator, who had come here with some friends to have a picnic by our stream. They were standing chatting by the car when one of them noticed a strange gleam in the sky. (Incidentally, Vladimir Lipotkin, a builder from Shilovo, was with them as well.) As they watched, the patch of light came toward them; it was mushroom shaped, and around the edge was a brighter glow, like moonlight.

The light came straight on at them, enveloping everything and spreading as it advanced, and then it dissipated. By that time it was quite dark and there were stars in the sky.

Someone—I think the prosecutor—said something about a nuclear war, and observed that it would be better to die at home than somewhere on the road. Then they got into the car (three of them) and drove off.

Nothing like it happened either before or after this incident. Tyapa was very scared and for several days talked of nothing else, and kept asking the grown-ups for an explanation. But of course nobody could explain it.

The whole thing took several minutes, it was not at all instantaneous. I have written it down as Larissa, Tyapa and Vladimir Aleksandrovich Lipotkin described it.

10 October

For some reason (working on Hoffmann) I remembered Armenia. A thunderstorm, and a shepherd drives his flock of sheep into the half-ruined church. 'Marmarashen'. *A film.*

14 October

Nearing the end of the Hoffmann screenplay. I read it to Larissa, who liked it very much. Only—who is going to make the film? In fact—will anyone be able to make it?

I still have to write one major episode; I don't know what. But it is necessary in terms of structure and scale.

I shall have to send the manuscript off to Masha around the 29th. I am bound to have to stay on here in order to work on *Hamlet* and also to get the firewood ready.

16 October

I cannot see what it is that *Hoffmanniana* still needs. I feel very unwell. Backache.
Evening.
I think I have it. 'The fire at the opera-house', 17 June, 1817.
Another meeting with Glück.
The loss of his friends. The friends leave. Another meeting with his Double.

24 October

I finished Hoffmann on the 19th. Masha Ch. and Gosha Rerberg came here and took it to Moscow, to retype it and send it off.
Their visit didn't make me happy. Gosha is really not very bright, and he drinks a lot. It's a pity.

20 November

Masha came again. Yuri Semyonov promised to lend me some money.
The river froze over on November 1st. Everyone at the Tallinn studio liked the script. It is now being read by the Estonian Central Committee. Actually they don't know who could make the film apart from myself. They will ask me to go to Tallinn soon to talk it over.
The actor, Babkauskas, has hanged himself, during the shooting of a film by Zhalakyavichus.
I must make sure that I can film the Strugatsky material this summer. Otherwise it isn't going to work out. The Tolstoy anniversary is going to be upon us.
Death of Ivan Ilych?
The Flight?

10 December

Sizov liked the Strugatsky synopses. I think they want it to be *The Picnic.*
'Life is very short, and it ought not to be spent crawling at the feet of miserable scoundrels.'—Stendhal.

1976

What is love? I don't know. Not that I don't know love, but I don't know how to define it.

1976

27 January

We have already had a (first) read through. Today we had an individual rehearsal, discussing each character.

Oleg Yankovsky does not want to play Laertes. I tried to persuade him by saying that when I direct *Macbeth* he will have the part of Macbeth. But he still would not take it: he had so longed to play Hamlet, he said, that when he heard that Tarkovsky was going to direct it, but with Solonitsyn instead of him, he realized it had passed him by and that he would not have another chance. And he was upset. He refuses to have any part in the production.

I am working on the text of *Hamlet*. Morozov's literal translation is a great help. Lozinsky's version is inarticulate and clumsy, but he always pursues Shakespeare. Pasternak's is appalling, opaque; there are moments when I feel he is deliberately obfuscating the sense of the play, or at any rate of some passages.

Vysotsky put it very well when he said, 'Any critic or actor working on the part of Hamlet has to be fanatical.'

'The more inaccessible a work is to reason, the greater it is.'—Goethe.

'Son, be of good cheer, thy sins be forgiven thee.'—Matthew 9.2.

6 February

Went to see Varvara yesterday.

7 February

She is more of a collector of psi phenomena than a clairvoyante or a healer. But you can feel her power. Of course it is not clear which are the spirits whose services she uses. She does not know herself.

Yuri is right—you have to start with your own soul and moral integrity. But what she is doing is important—she is working to make parapsychology accepted as a science.

Yuri L. and two of his friends stayed with us for three days. They are nice lads.

Another example of parapsychology. In the mountains of Georgia, where they graze their flocks of sheep, there exists a special profession—that of *mtsnobari*, or diviner. His function is to carry stray lambs back to their mothers in the middle of the enormous flocks. The *mtsnobari* infallibly carries each suckling lamb to the right mother, in a flock of hundreds of animals, finding her by means of a particular 'sense of smell'. He has nothing to help him except the answering voices of ewe and lamb. However, if you take into account the fact that the entire flock is bleating, that is clearly not going to simplify things much.

About the theory of synchronicity: one example is the incident with the *Rublyov* manuscript, when I lost the only copy—I left it in a taxi, and hours later the taxi-driver saw me walking along the street, in the crowd, at the same spot, and braked and handed me the folder. An unbelievable story.

8 February

I am convinced that Time is reversible. At any rate it does not go in a straight line.

18 February

'A great man is a disaster for society.'—Chinese proverb.

19 February

Last night I had a very disturbing dream. I had been sent to prison because of some sort of petty crime. Although I knew that it was something trivial, I realized that all the same it affected my foreign contracts. The prison was somewhere on the outskirts of the city. (Not as they are today, more as in pre-war times, or immediately post-war.)

Then I somehow found myself 'on the outside'. Rather like in Chaplin's *Modern Times*. I was terribly scared, and start hunting for the prison, wandering blindly through that pre-war district of Moscow. Some very amiable young man showed me the way. Then I bumped into Marina (or maybe that was before the young man) who recognized me and followed me along the street, sobbing and saying that Mama knew exactly what had happened to me (even though I hadn't told anyone). I was furious with Marina, and ran away from her by a staircase with a bust of Lenin.

At last, to my joy, I saw the entrance to the prison, which I recognized by the bas relief emblem of the USSR. I was worried about how I was going to be received, but that was as nothing compared with the horror of being out of prison. I went towards the door, and woke up.

3 March

I've had a letter from Tallinfilm. They say that Goskino will not take the script because they do not consider that I carried out my brief.

5 March

An editor from Soloviev's script-studio suddenly demanded a synopsis for the Tolstoy. Two days ago he told me that Soloviev is afraid to have anything to do with me over the Tolstoy. What is it all about?

17 March

Last week I dreamt that I was lying on a bed, together with Seryozha Paradzhanov, and suddenly realized to my astonishment that I had not run off to get Sasha Antonenko to celebrate Seryozha's homecoming. Seryozha was sad. I started to look for my dusty boots. On the floor were Seryozha's boots and the wraps for his feet.

The wind was blowing up through the floor-boards, whistling and moaning. Outside the windows it was dusk, and for some reason the alder bushes were not moving.

It was an inferior bed with metal webbing, very uncomfortable.

18 March

Antonenko came to see me around the 15th and told me that Seryozha Paradzhanov had appealed for clemency, that the order granting clemency had allegedly been signed by Podgorny, and that a letter had already arrived from Seryozha saying that he had been officially told that he would be released in two months' time.

I find it very worrying. Why did they announce it like that, for the whole camp to know? For one thing it makes it hard for Seryozha, and for another the crooks don't like it if someone is let out early. What if the whole thing was deliberate?

Of course Yermash found out that I had written a letter to the Congress. He summoned me and 'explained' that he needed the third outline in order to show it to some foreign television producers, in order to sell *The Idiot* before it had even been made (television version, 7–9 instalments). For Kodak film and equipment.

It's time to give up cinema. I have grown up. I must start with a book about my childhood. (The screenplay of *The Bright Day* will go into it.)

Burning the pig—the initial episode of 'the biscuits'. Having my skis taken away. Being butted by a ram.

Alcohol can only be destructive. Protest is creative—protest against anything, including alcohol.

About drunkenness:

> ... This heavy-headed revel east and west
> Makes us traduc'd and tax'd of other nations:
> They clepe us drunkards, and with swinish phrase
> Soil our addition; and, indeed it takes
> From our achievements, though performed at height
> The pith and marrow of our attribute.
>
> *Hamlet*, Act I, Scene IV

16 May

Points for the Italian version of the two filmscripts:
(Introduction: Dialogue with Tonino)
1. Hail.
2. 'The Falcon' and the kitten.
3. Tyapa goes to the forester.
4. I should like to make some amateur film, in order to demonstrate that cinema ought not to be guided by the audience (the market).
5. Paris and Rome.
6. A foreigner abroad who provokes an incident in order not to feel his own loneliness and irrelevance.
7. Favourite books.
8. About *Rublyov*—six hours. About the scenes that were left out or altered.

Italo Svevo. *The Confessions of Zeno.*
Jorge-Luis Borges, *Fictions.*
Jean Genet.

27 May

Larissa and I went to Gorky where I gave three talks. Very tired. I take these occasions too seriously. In every studio I was greeted with great warmth. I would even say with enthusiasm.

I shall not be able to produce *Hamlet* as the English have always produced it: it has to be without Shakespeare the poet. Translations, particularly of well-known verses, are impossible. However regrettably, there will be no poet Shakespeare in our production. But it is better to be aware of this than to take Pasternak's very mediocre (not to say inferior) translation and pretend to oneself and the audience that here we have Shakespeare's poetry.

9 July

Angelo has taken 32 negatives of *Mirror* to Rome.

24 July

Sizov tells me that there has been no letter from Cristaldi, addressed to Sizov and Yermash, with an invitation for me. And that if I want I can let the Italians know that they should write again and send the invitations.

It's probably because Shauro had a letter from Cristaldi, in which he complained about the fact that there had been no reaction of any kind from the cinema administration.

Very odd: I had a letter, but Sizov and Yermash did not? They're talking complete rubbish.

I have had the crazy idea of setting up a theatre. I shan't be allowed to do it on my own.

I spoke to E. D. Surkov. He is experienced and has connections, and he is educated. I would have to start it somewhere new. For instance, if I could get hold of the Stanislavsky Theatre and reorganize it; it is practically free of honoured old men, which is more than can be said of the Pushkin Theatre.

Actors?

Solonitsyn	Churikova?!
Gruzsky	Terekhova
Petrenko	Demidova
Kaydanovsky	Akhedzhakova
Grinko?	Kalmykova
Lapikov	Fedosova

I think they are going to sign an agreement with me for *The Idiot*.

30 July

Now, about 9.30, on my way to see Sizov and Yermash about Italy. They are going to try to persuade me to refuse Cristaldi on the grounds that 'he's a crook' and that Yermash is rescuing me from him.

Back from the Committee.

'. . . Cristaldi of course is a "crook", and if he wants me to make a film in Italy then he has first to carry out all his previous obligations towards Goskino.'

That was all. If I were to insist I should be acting against the 'interests of the nation'. So they've got me.

I have no room to move! The last remnants of culture are disintegrating in this dead atmosphere; the first thing is to create a different atmosphere—clear away the deadweight, gnaw through the crass, bourgeois insensitivity. But how?

31 July

Nearly midnight.

Go off to the country . . . Write . . . About what? About four pictures which in your opinion will eventually be significant and famous? Pathetic.

The theatre . . . Stick around in Moscow and humiliate myself? A book? Prose? What about bread and butter? Filmscripts?

Yes, well.

Remove myself?

Surrounded by lies, cant and death . . .

Poor Russia!

4 August

For financial—budget—reasons, I've agreed to a multi-purpose shot. Going to the country tomorrow for a few days to see Tyapa.

5 August

Still have not been able to get away to the country. Too much to do. I have heard rumours—Larissa was told by N. A. Ivanov—that Yermash was against my going to Italy: all the others, basically Sizov and 'even Dobrokhotov' were in favour. We shall see. Particularly as Tonino said that Berlenguer is involved.

Enn Rekkor came here today. He suggested my taking a job as artistic director for a group of three young directors. I agreed. He suggested writing an adaptation of a Simonov. I agreed. He said he kept thinking about my idea for an adaptation of *Peer Gynt*. I told him about a piece in *Literaturnaya Gazeta*, about a collector who had been murdered by his son. He was interested. I think it should be made at Mosfilm.

Geller is worried about how little time we have left for finishing the 'Zone'.

We have no assistant director, but on Tuesday Andrey Masliukov will apparently be free. I don't know him, but everyone tells me he is very good.

For the moment I have no ideas about the 100 metres of reflections on Kafka which I promised to Tonino. I must reread the Kafka selection, perhaps something will occur to me.

Mishka Marinin has again (for the second time) failed his entrance exam for the faculty of biology. Three grades short. Really! Not even bribery could put that right.

Olga has been exempt from her school-leaving exams because of her heart condition. We've decided not to enter her for an institute this year, not only because of her illness but also because she doesn't know which one to go to. She may as well have a year to think about it.

11 August

I arrived in the country on the 7th, in time for Tyapa's birthday. It's wonderful here.

I have been here for three days and feel as rested mentally as if I had been in a sanatorium for a month. I really don't want to go to Moscow.

The Tallinn studio are going to commission some work from me. I could do it quickly here, and I could write *The Idiot* at the same time. Tyapa has grown, and of course he's being naughty. It's extraordinary to think that in a year's time he'll be going to school, poor little Tyapka.

17 August

From Dostoievsky's notebooks:

'Strength lies only where blood can be squeezed. Only the blackguards have forgotten that this is not the strength of those who let blood, but of those whose blood is let. Such is the blood law of this world.'

'. . . Germans, Poles, and Jews are corporations, and they help themselves . . . Only in Russia are there no corporations, only Russia is splintered. But over and above those corporations stands the most important one of all: old, rigid administrative practice. People say that our society is not conservative. True, our historic progress (since Peter) has precluded its being conservative. But the point is that it cannot see what to preserve. Everything has been taken away, including legitimate initiative. All the rights enjoyed by the individual Russian are negative. If you were to give him something positive you would see that he too can be conservative, for then he would have something to preserve. *The only reason he is not conservative is because he has nothing to preserve.* The worse things are—the better. That is not merely an empty phrase in this country, unfortunately it is actual fact.'

'Even if they had the whole of Russia at their feet with their *kahal* and their scheming, even if they were sucking the Russian peasant dry—but of course, by all means, we shall not say a word: otherwise we might have an anti-liberal calamity on our hands, people might start thinking that we consider our religion superior to that of the Jews, and that we have a down on them because of our religious intolerance—and then where should we be? Just think—wherever should we be then?'

'. . . The Paris Commune and Western socialism do not want the best people, they want equality, and would chop off the head of a Shakespeare or a Raphael.'

18 August

From Dostoievsky's notebooks:

'. . . How bookish and superior it all is. They do not know how to write simply. They are so proud of themselves, their tone is always wrong, they patronize, teach, behave like guardians, wrap themselves about in the cloud of their own fame . . .' ('Vindictive Novelists'.)

'*To the critics*—I ask for nothing and I shall accept nothing. Nor do I seek glittering acclaim for my way of thinking.'

'Nobility of soul can be measured in part according to how much, and to what, it is capable of showing respect and reverence (tenderness).'

20 August

Last night I dreamt that Misha Romadin's wife had died. But somehow Misha was not particularly upset. Either he was expecting it, or else he was in a state of shock.

Then there was a run-of-the-mill Tovstonogov première. An adaptation of some classical prose work or other. Dreadfully boring, sequential, cynical and portentious.

21 August

My back is terribly painful. Yesterday the big toe on my right foot went numb. It must be somehow connected with my back. Lara is still not back. She went away around the 15th.

22 August

If we can start making *Stalker* in the autumn (it doesn't seem to be definite that we can) we shall start with the scenes in the studio. Then—outdoor locations (Moscow in winter) and starting with April '77—the Zone (Isfara). It's a pity, of course, since spring in Asia is not autumn.

On the other hand by November or December I shall be completely finished with *Hamlet*.

I must finish the film by the end of September. Only I can't imagine what will happen to *The Italian Journey*.

Lara still has not come. Apparently Larissa Nikolaevna's daughter did not get in. If that is true, then there's no point in expecting any help from them.

26 August

My back is very painful. Admittedly I am doing a lot of work in the house. Today I dug a trench by the front garden so that the damp would not get into the foundations. Larissa may be coming on Saturday. How are things in the team, I wonder.

Remind Geller:
  I.   Room for the team, and for me (furniture)
  II. Assistant director
  III. Assistant props manager
  IV. Let the actors know their new working dates.

29 August

I had a very unpleasant dream last night. For some reason I was in prison. A.M. was in the same cell, and he was boss of all the criminal element. Leva Kocharian was there as well, busy writing a shooting-script. Then they killed him with an iron bar, but despite that he collected his things together into a chamois hold-all which I wanted to have myself since its owner was dead.

The dream began with a station, full of people spending the night after escaping back home from abroad: people who had emigrated and were coming back. They and their children lay there outside, asleep, and the clothes they were wearing—some of them—looked like clothes on corpses which had been left lying around for several years.

Larissa is supposed to be coming back on Tuesday. *Her* protégé, Lena, from Shilovo, has been given a place in the Institute.

I must reread Kafka for those 100 metres for Tonino.

7 September

Larissa arrived on Wednesday. The agreement for *The Idiot* has been signed. They've paid an advance.

Between the 10th and the 15th Larissa and I shall evidently have to go to Moscow. I must talk to the production manager. Then Tonino and Antonioni will be arriving from Yerevan. Maybe something will be decided about the Italian trip.

10 September

Yesterday at zero hours something, in other words, during the night of the 8th, Mao Tse Tung died. Not that it matters, but it's good to know.

12 September

Yesterday I received the agreement from Tallinn, about the artistic directorship, for my signature, and also a screenplay (three novellas). Not very good. Before I sign it and send it back I ought to find out about the legal rights involved. I think an artistic director is entitled to some percentage of the royalties. I shall have to ring Moscow from Shilovo. I may even have to go there.

13 September

We all either underestimate each other, or else exaggerate each other's virtues. Very few people are capable of assessing others as they deserve. It is a particular gift. In fact I would even say that only the great are capable of it.

14 September

Letters to be written without fail:
1. Strugatsky (First scene with the wife. The row. He had pro-

mised he wouldn't go to the Zone. Slips out quietly).

2. Laguzhkin (if Lara wants).
3. Sedov (to the theatre).
4. Solonitsyn (theatre).
5. Surkova (at home, or to her father).

How lovely it is here in Myasnoye! What a wonderful house we have! Of course Tonino would think it was a hovel, but I find it beautiful.

Mustn't forget Anna's birthday (30 September).

6. Write to father.

15 September

At 11.30 at night we went out into the meadow to watch the moon through the mist. (I, Lara, A.S. and Olga). It was unbelievably beautiful!

An episode:

Several people gazing at the moon, in the mist, enjoying it. They stand in silence; move around. Delighted faces; all have the same sort of expression; the look in their eyes almost one of pain.

NB: Must read through my will.

I must learn to use a cine-camera, and do some filming here.
It is possible to attain immortality.

Dostoievsky:

1. Text, read by a character.
2. Different scene. Pause.
3. Abstraction—from the lives of characters imitating the characters of Dostoievsky.
4. Piercing music, something very simple (Bach or earlier).

Dearest Larochka! How grateful I am to you for this house. For understanding what matters to us.

We need peace; but not only peace.

A flock of rooks came flying over, and was attacked by a hawk, which brought one of them down. We rescued him, and now he's living with us. He tries to peck you; and eats very little. What is love? I don't know. Not that I don't know love, but I don't know how to define it.

Милая Лариса, как
благодарю тебя за
твой дом. Зч понимаю
того, що наше Дни
парико.?
Нам плохой путем. Ч
не разумеешь!

Лариса брат грачей.
Я сперва палецем на все.
Сам отнго! Обыли!
линвер у нас. кусаешь.
Мало остане любовь
що ранее не знаю. не потому
що не знакоми, я
не знаю, чостпреде
любов

16 September

Unless I can put off starting the *Hamlet* rehearsals till November I shall not have time to do the script for the Estonians.

I have written a letter to Zakharov.

Hoffmann is not going well: there is no unifying idea.

17 September

Grishka the rook is recovering. He is flying better. But he is longing for freedom and keeps on trying to escape. I'm keeping him in the shed. I've written the letters. Must send them.

Reread Kafka's *Metamorphosis*. Somehow it does not affect me.

25 September

Grishka flew away a few days ago. I am going to Moscow to see Alik B. and Gosha.

And then on to Tallinn. I sent off the agreement. They're expecting me. Kafka doesn't get through to me. I hope I shan't be away from here more than ten days.

It is cooler now, but dry. The trees are as green as in summer.

I dreamt about Lyova Kocharian. We were celebrating his birthday in Georgia.

20/21 October

A lot has happened since I returned from the country. I've signed an agreement for the *Idiot* script. *Hoffmanniana* has been published in the eighth issue of *Iskusstvo Kino*. I went to Tallinn; unfortunately, still no agreement for a screenplay—we still have not found a subject.

I shall start making *Stalker* on 26 January. The date for *Hamlet* is 24 December. On the 1st I am going to Isfara. About the 10th—back to Tallinn. Tonino G. is convinced that I shall be able to make *Italian Journey*. We have nearly finished the script. There will be some Russian scenes in it as well. Tyapa and Anna Semyonovna are in the country; they will apparently be back by New Year. I must find some woman to look after the house.

Arkady S. came here yesterday. We have worked out the script almost to the end.

10 November

Lara, Tolya Solonitsyn and I have come here for the holidays.

Everything here is exactly as it was: Kotlikova hasn't done any of the things she promised.

Tolya and I chopped some wood. Tolya was pretending he had a stomach ulcer (he was late back from his trip and missed some of the rehearsals for *Hamlet*) but he has stopped now. He is drinking rather a lot.

Things to be done in Moscow:
1. Write a plan of the screenplay and send it to the Strugatskys in Leningrad. Letter from Arkady; I had the feeling he was being idle.
2. Go through the synopsis for the Italians.
3. Transcribe the interview for Tonino.
4. Write a letter to Tallinn.

We are doing repairs in Moscow. There is a lot to be done, and we don't have enough money for the materials. We are doing the work ourselves. Tolya S. is working very hard, and Volodya Sedov is a great help. For Tyapa and A.S. to be able to come to Moscow we shall have to find a woman to live in here and look after the house. It is not safe to leave it. Tyapa and I are reading *Gulliver's Travels*.

13 November

Tomorrow, 14th, I have to go to Moscow. Volodya Ivanov will take me as far as Shilovo. I am unwell. Yesterday I felt really ill. Aching limbs and a high temperature—Tyapa has broken the thermometer so I don't know how high. I shall have to go: there is so much to be done in Moscow.

A bit of income, at least.

No word for the moment from Tashkent. I shall obviously have to sue them. Whatever happens I have plenty of work and plans.

Tonino Guerra was here recently from Italy. They want me to make a film there. (Our authorities are against it.) Or else a television production (a journey through Italy). That would mean an invitation to Italy for two months (between *Hamlet* and *The Picnic*) for me to get to know the country. However, man proposes, as they say . . .

The editorial board of Tallinfilm are discussing the Hoffmann.

14 December

It's only two days since Lara, Tyapa and Anna Semyonovna arrived from the country. They were met by total chaos—there's

※ Остервенело репетирую «Гамлета», сдача которого намечена на 21 ое. В дня было порядно — поу Солоницына что-го с полов, то Инка Чурикова на концерте, то Терехова не пришла на репетицию.

Костюмы поначалу очень неудачно — работа Кати — понемногу исправляет Тегин. Он молодец.

Со светом еще полб не вяжся. Придумал очень хороший финал для спектакля:

после триумфа (4 капитана) смерть Гамлета через затемление — возникает гора трупов (внизу) из нее подниматся (после крика петуха) тень погибшего. Гамлета и поднимися по очереди — марта короля, королеву (воскресшая, т.е. хотел бы воскресить).

Постепенно разгорается свет на сцене и зал. Положение апофеоза при. ходит к поклон.

II Этаж

I Этаж

1. Клавдий
2. Гертруда
3. Лаэрт
4. Гамлет
5. Горацио
6. Офелия
7. Полоний
8. Фортальдо
9. Розенкранц
10. Гильденстерн
11. тень отца Г.
12. 1 актёр
13. Озрик
14. Вольтиманд
15. I могильщик
16. II могильщик

no room, the repairs are still not finished, there's nothing to sleep on. However, none of it matters, at least we are all together.

The country house has been left in the care of Matryona Ivanovna, she is living in the small room. Lara says she feels quite happy about her. Anna Semyonovna and Tyapa will go back there in the spring, in April.

Frantically rehearsing *Hamlet*, which has now got to be ready by the 21st. Three days have been lost—either with Solonitsyn having something wrong with his foot, or Inna Churikova being at a concert, or Terekhova not turning up for rehearsal.

The costumes, which to start with were pretty bad—Katya's work—are being put right bit by bit by Tenghis. He's a good man.

For the moment nothing at all has been done about the lighting. I have thought of a really good ending for the play: after the triumph (the four Captains) of Hamlet's death, there rises through the darkness a mound of corpses (below) from which arises (after the crowing of the cock) the shade of the dead Hamlet who raises in turn Laertes, the King, the Queen (resurrects them—that is, he would have wished to resurrect them). The house lights come on gradually. The actors move into a bow.

If only I could have another eight rehearsals!

Stalker:

Assistant director: Kolya Dostal.

No sound operator so far.

Stalker is from the word 'to stalk'—to creep.

29 December

On the 22nd Management saw *Hamlet*. They discussed it the day before yesterday. On the 22nd there was a small audience. On the 24th there was a dress rehearsal in front of an audience. A run-through. General opinion, or rather, generalized opinion, has it that the production is interesting, and the actors are bad.

That tallies with my view. But what could they hope to see after only two run-throughs? The production is not ready but I shall pull it together. The acting will be better.

No one is acting well yet, not even Churikova. The costumes are not finished; some scenes must be shortened, made lighter (Polonius, Laertes, Ophelia in Act I), others must be made more precise, with music (ghost, Act I).

The Gravediggers scene must be shortened. Work to be done on the scene with Gertrude, Hamlet, Ghost—Act II.

1977

Our lives are all wrong. A person has no need of society, it is society that needs him. Society is a defence mechanism, a form of self-protection. Unlike a gregarious animal, a person must live in isolation, close to nature, to animals and plants, and be in contact with them.

1977

7 January

We have done some tests for *Stalker*: Solonitsyn, Grinko, Kaydanovsky. I haven't seen them yet. I am ill. The *Hamlet* première is being postponed until the 28th (instead of the 21st) because Churikova has gone off on holiday with Panfilov. She was not even gracious enough to inform me.

Where else could that happen? In what other country? In what other theatre? What other actress could behave like that?

Of course it is Gleb's influence, and it is going to be Churikova's undoing. That is what I prophesy. And God will punish him. What a spiteful, envious man he is. It really is true that GENIUS and WICKEDNESS are not compatible.*

8 January

I have received a strange note from a young man accompanied by a girl who hides her face:

Dear Andrey Arsenevich,

We have opted out of all the possible ways of living within society and envisage a different kind of life for ourselves. That is actually why we can quite naturally approach you, bypassing the usual conventions. We are approaching you on the grounds of certain considerations which are difficult to put into words, but really, if we had not seen *Mirror* we probably would not be doing this. For a relatively short time, perhaps for a month or two, we need to have an empty flat to live in, or a house in the country, all by ourselves, in order to recover from our past lives, and generally get it together.

But we don't know exactly what we should do. Can you possibly help us? All we need is some empty accommodation for

*A quotation from Pushkin's *Mozart and Salieri*.

that time, nothing else. Of course we don't know what your own situation is practically speaking, it may be you don't have anything at your disposal. We shall come and see you tomorrow at 8.0 p.m. and if you are not there at that time please will you leave us a note.

Volodya, Marina

Olga Surkova told me about some young woman who asked to come and see her, and a young man hiding on the landing outside her flat.

Today we find that the door on our letter-box has been broken. In a way it's not surprising—one more case of vandalism. On the other hand could it be the KGB—to justify the 'disappearance' of the letters?

9 January

I have decided to write a letter to Shauro. It's time the question of *Mirror* was settled.

1. Why, when the picture has been accepted (2nd category)

(*a*) is it not being shown?

(*b*) was it taken off and not brought back despite official promises?

(*c*) Why am I assured that this is because the distributors do not want the film, when everywhere I go all the distributors ask me to help them to get hold of it?

(*d*) Why is the film not being sold abroad despite the fact that the USSR needs foreign currency and despite all the publicity in Sovexportfilm? They are even putting up special obstacles in the form of an exorbitantly high price.

2. Would you kindly tell me—

Is *Mirror* not a patriotic and highly moral picture?

Is it inhumane, or—perish the thought—anti-Soviet?

3. I have received an enormous number of letters from cinemagoers, thanking me for *Mirror*, and others wanting to know why they cannot go and see it at the cinema.

Why is *Mirror* nowhere to be seen? Why was it forcibly removed from our screens? (At the Taganka and elsewhere.) Why are articles analysing *Mirror* not being printed? There were plenty of them.

I am tired of being the butt of suspicion, dirty looks, insulting comments behind my back—on the part of the cinema authorities.

Would you kindly answer these questions; and re-establish my name as a Soviet director and my title of Honoured Artist of the RSFSR, by putting *Mirror* on general release in this country and abroad.

Otherwise I shall take the liberty of deciding that Soviet culture, Soviet society and its masters consider me to be either redundant or actually a harmful influence.

27 January

Things are pretty bad at the theatre. Zakharov seems to want to replace Solonitsyn and Terekhova in *Hamlet*. I want them to be there for the entire run.

They are not considering my needs at all, they have arranged for performances on Saturday, when we shall be filming in Isfara. They don't raise a finger to help me.

'. . . And I gave my heart to seek and search out by wisdom concerning all things that are done under heaven: this sore travail hath God given to the sons of man, to be exercised therewith. I have seen all the works that are done under the sun; and behold, all is vanity and vexation of spirit . . . For in much wisdom is much grief; and he that increaseth knowledge increaseth sorrow.' (Ecclesiastes, I, 13–14, 18.)

'. . . For there is no remembrance of the wise more than of the fool for ever; seeing that which now is, in the days to come shall all be forgotten. And how dies the wise man? as the fool.

'Yea, I hated all my labour which I had taken under the sun; because I should leave it unto the man that shall be after me. And who knoweth whether he shall be a wise man or a fool? Yet shall he have rule over all my labour wherein I have laboured, and wherein I have showed myself wise under the sun. This is also vanity!' (II, 16, 18–19.)

'. . . All the labour of man is for his mouth, and yet the appetite is not filled.' (VI, 7.)

'. . . That which has been is named already, and it is known that it is man: neither may he contend with him that is mightier than he.' (VI, 10.)

'. . . Sorrow is better than laughter: for by the sadness of the countenance the heart is made better.' (VII, 3.)

'. . . Then I beheld all the work of God, that a man cannot find out the work that is done under the sun: because though a man labour to seek it out, yet he shall not find it; yea, farther, though a wise man think to know it, yet shall he not be able to find it.' (VIII, 17.)

'. . . for to him that is joined to all the living there is hope . . .'
(IX, 4.)

4 February

From Chekhov's letter to Suvorin, 9 December 1890, Moscow.

'. . . God's world is good. Only one thing is bad; us. How little sense of justice we have, how little humility, what a poor sense of patriotism. A seedy, worn-out rake of a husband loves his wife and children, and what good does that do? According to the newspapers we love our country, but how does that love express itself? Instead of knowledge—an excessive degree of arrogance and self-opinion; instead of hard work—idleness and swinish behaviour; no sense of justice; the notion of honour goes no further than "the honour of the uniform", the uniform that serves daily to decorate the benches of the accused. What matters is work, and to hell with the rest of it. The most important is to be just, and everything else will be added.'

To M. P. Chekhov, 17 March 1891, Petersburg.

About Duse:
'. . . I don't understand Italian, but she acted so well that I felt I was understanding every word. A remarkable actress. I have never seen anything like it. I watched Duse and I was consumed with sadness at the thought that we have to develop our sensibilities and taste with our wooden actresses, such as Yermolova and her like, whom we call great because we have seen nothing better. Looking at Duse I understood why the Russian theatre is boring.'

5 February

Yesterday Dmitriev told Larissa P. on the telephone that the French had bought *Mirror* from the Germans (Gambaroff) for 500,000 francs! No one anywhere has ever bought any of our films for that sort of money.

I should like to make one or two changes to the editing. Particularly in the penultimate part.

24 February

Shooting on location in Isfara? Postponed because of the earthquake in Shuraba, just where we should have been filming.

We have just filmed Stalker's flat. We must go and look for some new landscapes. A month's extension. Things are going better now at the theatre. The première on the 18th, and for the first time I felt that the play might work. Tolya has started to act.

There is a performance today, but with Matiushina as Gertrude. That's bad, she didn't cope with it last time (on the 15th).

After today's performance two extracts are going to be filmed for television (the mad Ophelia and Polonius' murder) plus an interview with me, Terekhova and Solonitsyn.

This bottle was broken on the first day of shooting *Stalker* (15.02.77).

5 May, Tallinn

On location in Estonia. Signed two agreements for scripts. One for 6000, the other for 8000—two series, one for Tallinfilm and the other for Tashkent.

Sidelnikov's mother died yesterday.

On the 7th I am going to Tallinn.

Villy does not work well at all; he is helpless.

15 May, Tallinn

Write a book about a man of fifty in love with an eighteen or twenty year old. He suffers from an inferiority complex. She loves him, but he is not aware of that. She won't tell him (too shy? or proud?). He is a man who all his life made people around him unhappy (out of pride? or weakness?); he wanted to lord it . . .

And then—he dies, not from frustration, but because he was not able to 'give himself', . . . 'no one took him' . . . or as a 'statement'.

A tale of jealousy.

28 May, Tallinn

From Chaadayev's philosophical letters, quoted in A. Lebedev, *Chaadayev*.

'We must free ourselves from all the trivial curiosity that destroys and disfigures our lives; first of all we must root out the stubborn tendency to let our hearts be carried away by anything new, to chase after the topical and as a result to be always on tenterhooks, waiting to see what will happen tomorrow.

'Otherwise you cannot attain peace or well-being, but only disappointment and revulsion. Do you want worldly vice to be

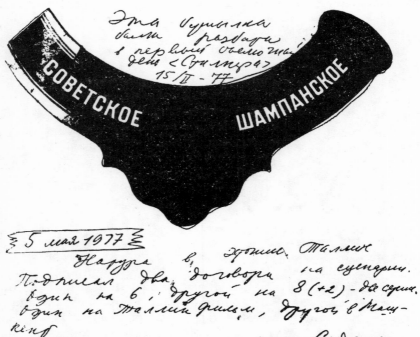

Эта бутылка
была разбита
в первый съёмочный
день «Сталкера»
15/II - 77

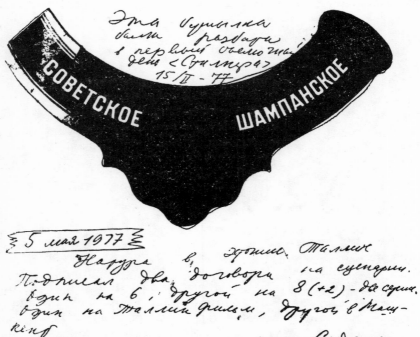

§ 5 мая 1977 §

Наружа в гостин. Таллин
Подписал два договора на сценарии.
один на 6; другой на 8 (+2) — за сцен.
один на Таллинфильм, другой в Мос-
кино
Вчера умерла жена Сидельни-
кова.
7го еду в Таллин.
Вилли очень плохо работает;
беспомощен.

shattered on the threshold of your peaceful dwelling? If you do, then banish from your soul all those restless passions that are aroused by worldly events, all those latest pieces of news. Bolt your door against all noise, all echoes of what is going on outside. If you have sufficient resolution, eschew even light literature, for it too, essentially, is nothing but that same noise in written form.'

Mama is gravely ill, she has had a stroke. She has very little control over her left side. It is my fault. It is the result of our conversation about Marina and how she treats Larissa.

But Marina is not perfect, either. She will never accept that she can be wrong. Mama is a little better now, Larissa told me on the telephone.

Filming is fraught with problems, I don't know how it will work out. Boim is drinking a lot. If I don't part company with him before the end of the film, I shall certainly never see him again.

And Gosha, too. Lightweight, shallow people, with no self-respect. Childish degenerates. Cretins.

23 June, Tallinn

Our lives are all wrong. A person has no need of society, it is society that needs him. Society is a defence mechanism, a form of self-protection. Unlike a gregarious animal, a person must live in isolation, close to nature, to animals and plants, and be in contact with them. I can see more and more clearly that it is essential to change our way of life, to revise it. We have to start living differently. But how? First of all we have to feel free and independent, to believe and love; we have to reject this insignificant world and live for something else—but how, where? That is the first misapprehension, the first stumbling-block.

21 July

A book: fantastic plot with parallel actions—one on the earth, the other somewhere else. Contrast: not an analogy but a contrast.

It's all awful. We have had to retake practically everything. In fact everything—1400 metres. No money. No energy. Rerberg is to blame.

26 August, Tallinn

'Precision is the soul of the artist's work.' (Gustav Mahler, quoted by Anna Mildenburg.)

'What our contemporaries say about great art not being necessary for the creation of a work of art is utterly senseless. It would be nearer the truth to say that a huge investment of artistic means into everything from the first, general outline to the last detail, is a necessary condition for the creation of the kind of perfect work that could not be imagined in the wildest dreams of our naturalist friends—those impotent creatures!

'And anything that is not imbued with that supreme craftsmanship is doomed to die before it even sees the light of day!' (Mahler, quoted by Natalia Bayer-Lekhner, July 1896.)

'In Bach all the vital seeds of music are brought together, like the world in God. Nowhere else has there ever been such polyphony!'

'Such polyphony is an unheard-of miracle not merely for his time, but for all times.'

'Schumann is one of the greatest composers to have written songs, he can be mentioned in the same breath as Schubert. No one else has been such a great master of the perfect song form.' (Mahler, quoted by Natalia Bayer-Lekhner, summer 1901.)

A lot has been happening. Total disaster, so conclusive that one actually has the sense of a fresh stage, a new step to be taken—and that gives one hope.

Everything we shot in Tallinn, with Rerberg, had to be scrapped twice over. First, technically; for a start the Mosfilm laboratory processing of the negative (the last of the Kodak). Then the state of instruments and the gear.

Konoplyov, the chief engineer, is responsible for that.

Rerberg is responsible as well, but for other reasons—he has made a mockery of the principles of art, of talent. He decided that talent was tantamount to himself—and therefore he degraded and destroyed it, as he did himself; through drink, lack of faith, baseness and vulgarity. He's a disreputable whore.

As far as I am concerned, in other words, he is a corpse.

I have come to an agreement with L. I. Kalashnikov. He is a conscientious professional, potentially capable of far greater things than Rerberg because he wants tasks for the sake of finding solutions. For him the failure to find a solution would be a kind of artistic impotence. The important thing is to have tasks; and he certainly is going to have those.

We stopped dead for an entire month, the day before we were due to start work on *Stalker*. That being so, now everything is going to be different; cameraman, set designer (I'll risk using Shavkat), script. (Arkady and Boris are trying to rewrite it at the moment, because of the new Stalker, who, instead of being some kind of drug dealer or poacher, has to be a slave, a believer, a pagan of the Zone.)

So we're starting all over again. Have I the energy?

I must write an article about Mosfilm for *Pravda*.

'The primacy of matter and the secondariness of our consciousness.' Not bad! I must tell Sizov about the idea in my letter.

28 December

'Weakness is great, strength is insignificant. When man is born he is weak and malleable. When he dies he is strong and callused.

'When a tree is still growing it is flexible and tender, and when it is dry and hard, it dies. Callosity and strength are the companions of death.

'Pliancy and weakness are signs of the freshness of being. What has grown hard will therefore never triumph.'—Lao-Tzu, taken by Leskov as the epigraph to *Pamphalon the Buffoon*.

1978

Man has existed for such a long time and yet he is still uncertain about the most important thing of all—about the meaning of his existence; that is what is puzzling.

1978

7 April

I have not written anything for a long time. Lots of things have happened. Lara and I went to Paris for the première of *Mirror*, arranged by Gaumont. Great success, which (to judge from their reaction) came as a total surprise to our 'bosses'. Tremendous notices in the press.

Hamlet has been laid to rest. Zakharov wanted to bring in three new actors to take the place of Churikova, Terekhova and Solonitsyn. I thought it better to take the play off altogether.

V. Sedov put on *Dear Liar* in Tallinn. I refused the job of his artistic director, because Slonimsky has not kept his promises. Chermenev is pretty despicable.

Kalashnikov refused to work with me on *Stalker*. His wife (and he too, for that matter) behaved monstrously. She telephoned around all the relevant offices and announced that 'they did not intend to work'. He didn't have the guts to say anything. I was warned about him at one point by Tito Kalatozov.

I do hope I shall be able to make *Italian Journey* with Tonino Guerra. In mid-May we shall start—for the umpteenth time—to film *Stalker*. Cameraman: Kniazhinsky; production manager: A. Demidova.

I must make the film, and take measures against Konoplyov. (Letters to the Central Committee and State Control Commission.)

The day before yesterday I had trouble with my heart. (Electrocardiogram). They had to call the emergency service. Poor Larissa was petrified. It has begun.

I forgot to say that I am designing the sets for my picture. Half-price, needless to say.

Rublyov has been listed as one of the world's hundred best films. Not a single Soviet one figures since *Chapayev*; only *Rublyov*.

9 April

Yesterday V. I. Burakovsky came here.

I have had a coronary.

Now I shall have to spend two months recovering. *Stalker* is bewitched.

Volodya sends doctors and makes cardiograms.

It is natural for a person not to think about death. But why does he not believe in immortality?

The whole question of assessing a person at first sight seems to me terribly difficult, even painful. Is such an assessment actually possible? Anyhow, I am wrong about people all too often.

I must change my life. Stop and start afresh.

Reading Hesse. Beautiful!

I have never tried to work according to a preconceived plan; or rather, even with an aim and a strategy. I have never employed tactics. A lot of time has gone as a result. Is this not the moment to make a policy decision always to have—first and foremost—a plan of action that will take me to my goal?

Obviously it is. I do not have so much time left that I can afford to throw it around.

11 April

'Nobody writes as badly as the protagonists of outworn ideologies, nobody displays less care or less conscientiousness in the exercise of their craft than they.' (Hesse, *The Steppenwolf*.)

CRYING IN THE WILDERNESS
   A wilderness.
   A voice: God! God! (*several times*) Answer!
      The camera pulls back to reveal a portal; the door is very slightly ajar. Voices inside are whispering.
   1st Voice: Answer him! Call to him! You can see that he is in agony!
   He: How could I answer him here and now? What would he think? He surely would not start believing that I am God. I cannot make my involvement obvious.

13 April

Actually—why don't I make a film of *The Master and Margarita*? Because it is a novel of genius? But it is not a question of prose, nor of treatment of subject matter, nor of plot, nor of language!

All the painting and music of the Middle Ages and the Renaissance has, in the end, one and the same subject. Dürer, Cranach, Brueghel, Bach, Händel, Leonardo, Michelangelo, etc. . . .

It has nothing to do with obscuring the primary sources. It is a question of mastery, and of material. And an artist is a master above all when he knows what he can make out of what.

14 April

Larissa is feeling very ill as well. God forbid that anything should happen to me. The children would have a rough time without me. Actually I am convinced that it's going to be all right.

What an astonishingly clear relationship there is between Hoffmann, Hesse and Bulgakov. And what children they are—pure, possessed of faith, tormented, unspoilt by fame, punctilious, naive; passionate and noble.

The Golden Pot—Steppenwolf—Master and Margarita.

At least I have plans for work that I could do abroad:
1. *The Horde*
2. *Doctor Faustus*
3. *Hamlet* (film) write a second version
4. *Hamlet* (stage production)
5. *Crime and Punishment*
6. *The Renunciation*
7. A latterday *Joan of Arc*
8. *Two Saw the Fox*
9. *Joseph and His Brothers*
10. *Hoffmanniana*
11. *Italian Journey*

Very mediocre translations of Japanese haiku by Markova, particularly of Bascho. I shall have to find the Japanese originals and get hold of Arkady Strugatsky. I think I am right. She certainly does not know Russian. All the same—how I admire them.

Bascho: 'A wise monk said, "The teaching of Zen, improperly understood, cripples the soul." I agree with him. It takes an extraordinary degree of nobility to remain unmoved by superficial glitter, not to say, "There, that is our life." '

I should like to know which improperly understood doctrine does not cripple the soul.

Bascho to his disciples: 'Do not emulate me too much. Look, what is the use of such imitation? Two halves of a melon.'

15 April

I have been prostrate for the last nine days. The doctors say that perhaps today they might let me sit up in bed. I never imagined that I would have a heart attack at forty-six. On the other hand it would have been surprising had it not happened. Oh, well . . . I have had a few telegrams from France and Italy. From Martine, Mastroianni, Tonino, Davou, Daniel Plantier, Sergio Leone.

Incidentally if Leone has not given up his idea of Westerns, it would be worth writing a Western for him about Kuzenchik.

I must talk to Tonino.

What am I to make of it all?

1. Faulty film three times running. 2700 metres. (Rerberg)

2. After the cameraman and the production manager were replaced Kalashnikov refused to go on working and walked out, having taken 250 metres.

3. I sacked Boim for being drunk.

4. I sacked Abdusalimov for behaving like a bastard.

5. No money forthcoming for a two-part picture.

6. Shooting has to begin (or rather, carry on) in May—and on the 5th–6th I have a *coronary*.

7. Olga Surkova and I submitted our manuscript to *Art*, and were given a mass of comments which boil down to a rejection.

Of course it is miraculous, but in a negative sense.

22 April

'Whether your soul is unscathed or broken in two . . . I beg you to be logical—and may I be forgiven this cry from the heart!— logical in plan and structure, in syntax . . . be a master architect in detail as in the whole . . . let there be story in narrative and action in drama, keep lyricism for verses, love words as Flaubert did, be economical with your means and parsimonious with words, precise and genuine; then you will discover the secret of something wonderful— that exquisite lucidity which I would call—*clarism*.'—Mikhail Kuzmin.

23 April

'The fact that time flows the same way in all heads proves more conclusively than anything else that we are all dreaming the same dream; more than that: all who dream that dream are one and the same being.' (Schopenhauer)

28 April

Tonino telephones from Rome almost daily. I am up and about in the flat. My heart is improving. Tonino wants to read my book. (*Art* gave it a lousy report.)

'If you would understand the poet, you must go to the poet's land.' (Goethe)

16 May

Tonino has sent me his book, which consists of sixty-eight short, poetic stories, with occasional poems. He suggests that I write a reply to each of them, the result of which would be a duel in 136 shots.

Next week I am going into the sanatorium.

1. Lily-of-the-valley for the landlady's daughter.
2. War. The encounter on the main road.
3. Snow in July.

28 May

I am going to the sanatorium on the 1st. Kolya Shishlin got me a pass for the 'Podmoskovye'.

Larissa is in the country. She has been very ill. She is going to stay there while I am in the sanatorium. I shall certainly cure her. I myself have started on a diet and a regime. (I must get hold of Bregg.)

For the sanatorium: books, paper, pen, pencil, underwear, shirts, socks, trousers, leather jacket, eau-de-Cologne, cream, razor, nail-file, cotton wool, soap, alarm clock, tennis shoes, trainers—41, dressing-gown, medicines, handkerchiefs, towels, swimming-trunks.

28 June, Tallinn–Merrivale

We have arrived in Tallinn. We are staying—Larissa and I—in the suburbs, by the sea. It seems all right, but this is only the first day . . .

I spent a month in the sanatorium. Miserably depressing. Average age of incumbents—sixty. All servants of the people.

I hope to goodness this 'expedition' is going to sort itself out. It's the second time we've been here!

Arkady Strugatsky has shown himself to be petty and calculating. To hell with him.

I am going to owe him 1200 roubles for our shared expenses.

14 July

Must see *Youth Technology* no. 6 for 1973—V. I. Zemtsov, 'The Future in the Mirror of the Past'.

Vladimir Lossky: 'Essay on Mystical Theology' in *Journal of Theology*, no. 8, Moscow 1972.

16 July

– Food taken before sleep is digested better than during the day.
– Young plants grow at night.
– So do children and young animals.
– 41 per cent of men and 37 per cent of women talk in their sleep.

22 July

Nekhoroshev was here. He vowed his love for me and his determination to shield me from the bullet, should occasion arise.

Mosfilm have brought out a publication which includes an article by Bakhrin on *Mirror*, in which he quotes several of my father's poems and compares the film to *The Glass Bead Game*.

Lyona is going to Moscow today. I have asked him to do what he can on the question of the flat, and about permission to film in Italy.

6 September

Books:
Rudolf Steiner (the theosophist), *Knowledge of the Spirit* (1930).
  Knowledge of the Supernatural in our Time (1930).
Ed. Tennemann, *The Immortality of the Soul.*
K. Kaups, O. O. Rozenberg
Sarvepalli Radhakrishnan, *Indian Philosophy.*

20 September

This film is terribly difficult to make. Nothing is turning out as it should. I don't think Kniazhinsky's work is up to much. The smoke scene has not come off. There is no sense of place. And no atmosphere. I am afraid it may be a disaster. I just cannot see how to shoot the *dream*. It has to be utterly simple.

We are failing to achieve the most important thing of all: consistently developed sense of place.

  L. N. Tolstoy on karma:
    '...Just as in our lives we dream thousands of dreams, so too

this life of ours is one of thousands of other such lives, which we enter from that real, genuine, true life which we leave in order to come into this one and to which we return when we die. Our life is one of the dreams of that other, real life, and so on to infinity, to the one, last, true life—the life of God.

'Birth and our earliest perceptions of the world are a falling asleep and the sweetest of dreams: death is an awakening. Dying early is like waking a man up when he has not had enough sleep. Dying old is when a man has slept his fill, and starts to sleep fitfully, and wakes up of his own accord. Suicide is a nightmare which finishes because you remember that you are asleep, and deliberately wake yourself up.'

From a letter about karma:

'Karma is a buddhistic belief according to which not only a person's character, but all that happens to him in this life is the consequence of his behaviour in a previous life, and that the good or evil of our future lives will equally depend upon our efforts to avoid evil and do good in this world.'

And it is a fact that only two opposing concepts worry us more than anything else: life—death, good—evil. Around these we build up all the philosophy that a person needs. Why? Clearly because the essence of our existence lies in those concepts; the meaning, the secret, the principle of our inner drive. And this has been known for so long that it is surprising that good remains unattainable. On the other hand, it makes perfect sense. Human existence demands constant moral effort to do good in order to realize our own lives, and at the same time bring our own positive contribution to the universal human process.

The concept of good and evil (and the conflict between them) is as crucial to eternal life as the opposing forces which are a necessary precondition for electricity; or the differing barometric pressures which produce wind. And so the struggle between good and evil will go on for as long as man continues to exist on earth. Man has to make his way across to the opposite shore. The sea water is evil, the oars and the boat—good. Row for all you are worth and you will make it. Leave your oars and you will perish.

Man has existed for such a long time and yet he is still uncertain about the most important thing of all—about the meaning of his existence; that is what is puzzling.

29 October

Enn Rekkor said that a writer friend of his asked an acquaintance who was high up in the Estonian Central Committee why the statistics relating to our achievements in agriculture did not correspond with fact. The answer was: 'These days even statistics are an ideological weapon.'

7 November

Lara was worried about Myasnoye and went to the country yesterday evening with Rashid and Arayk.

I have demoted Arayk. Larissa is now officially assistant director. Salary 160 roubles, and 260 for writing out the editing pages.

Today I went to see Tito; he had a slight heart attack this summer.

9 November

On the set today (in the 1st Mosfilm Studio) Grinko suddenly asked me, 'Andrey Arsenevich, do you know someone called Zaruba?'

I told him that I did, and that he was a friend of mine.

Apparently somebody told Grinko that they had read my letters to the—now late—Zaruba (of course, his papers are there in the Security Committee, where there is an official from the Ukrainian Ministry for Foreign Affairs) and that my letters were remarkable for their vividness and the graphic way in which they express ideas. What on earth did I write? I don't think there was anything essentially negative. No doubt I complained about life generally.

17 November

7 a.m. I don't remember whether I wrote that when I asked the Cinema Union for an ex-gratia payment to cover my time in the sanatorium (when I was ill) they only gave me part of what I asked for. Yet it was only a question of a couple of hundred roubles or so (which were to be paid back). For some reason I've just thought of it.

Why do people so often dream about things that have never happened to them? That they are flying, for instance? That is very much a recurring childhood dream. 'Be ye as children'—Gospel.

23 December

For some time now I have had the feeling, which is becoming more and more acute, of being on the brink of a period of tragic trials, of foundering hopes. And this is at a moment when I am possessed as never before by the urge to create.

I am working on the soundtrack, I hope the music will be done soon ... It is turning out rather long, but I think in the end the length will be modified as it needs to be.

The picture is coming together. It is new for me in two ways—for one thing it is simple in form, for another it breaks with the traditional approach to the functions of film as such.

What I am trying to do in it is tear apart the way we look at the present day, and turn to the past, during which mankind made so many mistakes that today we are obliged to live in a kind of fog. The film is about the existence of God in man, and about the death of spirituality as a result of our possessing false knowledge.

After *Stalker* I hope to be able to make *Italian Journey*, provided there is no row over *Stalker*.

Actually, I feel there will be.

One might reasonably hope that Yermash will not want to make a fool of himself after the way he behaved over *Mirror*. But can one rely on it?

I am afraid of the future: of the Chinese, of cataclysms, of apocalyptic disasters. I am afraid for the children and for Larissa. God, give me strength and faith for the future, give a future in which to glorify you. To me! For I too want to have a part in it!

On the 21st I gave a talk at the Institute of World Economics before a showing of *Mirror*. The Kochevrins work there. Senka and Irma came. There were several notes. Here are three of them:

'Andrey Arsenevich! Our deepest gratitude to you for your superb art, and for raising Russian culture up to the level of Tolstoy and Gogol. There are a great many of your admirers in the hall, and we all wish you success in your work, good health, strength.'

'This is not a question. I simply want to take this opportunity to thank you for your outstanding talent and for the tremendous humanity which runs through your films. They are a source of aesthetic delight and a stimulus to serious reflection.'

'Andrey Arsenevich! For several years I have wanted to be able to thank you for *Mirror*, which for me is a deeply feminine film. I take this opportunity. Thank you!'

In the light of the past few months I want to look again at possible plans.

1. *The Master and Margarita.*
2. Documentary film of reflections: *The Country.* (16mm)
3. *Italian Journey.*
4. *The Horde.*
5. A film based principally on Castaneda.

And books:
1. On cinema
2. Biography—work at Mosfilm.
3. Essay.

I must have a camera, 16mm with sound, and a good tape recorder.

Letter from the distributors of *Mirror* in Italy (brought by Tonino, with another one for me).

To the Executive of Mosfilm. Moscow.

As the distributors in Italy of Tarkovsky's film *Mirror*, we have decided to present the film to the critics and the Italian press on the occasion of the première in San Vicente (Valle d'Aosta) in the presence of the author, Signor Tarkovsky. In the hope that this invitation will not interfere with Signor Tarkovsky's work schedule, we should be most grateful if you would be kind enough to decide on a date with him, in March, in order that preparations for the showing of the film may go ahead.

We thank you in advance. It is a great honour for us to show one of your films to Italian audiences, who have always had the keenest interest in the work of Soviet cinematographers.

We look forward to hearing from you, and send you our warmest wishes.

And to me:

To the esteemed Signor Andrey Tarkovsky, Moscow.

As the distributors of your film, *Mirror*, on Italian territory, we hasten to inform you of our intention to present your work to the critics and the cinematographic press at the première in San Vicente (Valle d'Aosta) in the course of March 1979.

Your presence at this showing would be greatly appreciated. We look forward to hearing from you so that we may decide on a definite date. It is a great honour for us to show your film in Italy.

We send you our warmest good wishes.

(Signature)

I shall hand this letter to Sizov on Monday.

31 December

Another New Year. And one more appalling year has gone by. There is nothing in the shops on New Year's Eve. In Ryazan meat is rationed; 300 grammes per head per month. Life is becoming impossible.

Sasha Mishurin telephoned. His mother has just died. He said that on the radio yesterday, on programme 1, they announced that in France *Mirror* had been named the best film of '78, and Terekhova best actress. And this is a year that included Fellini and Bergman. The Americans have bought *Mirror* for distribution in the USA. So there could easily be an Oscar. Not that I want it, but it would be one in the eye for that idiot Yermash.

Tonino and I have had the idea that I should make a 16mm film about the country. It is to be a confession, based on Myasnoye. A storm in a teacup. The story of how the front garden was improved to the point where it became an eyesore. Sasha Kaydanovsky is to play me. If he agrees, that is. The opening scene will be Sasha's arrival and the explanation of why he has to take my part, and not I myself. Self-portraits: Fellini's *Clowns*, *Mirror*, *The Hand and the Bird*.

At the end, when Sasha is looking through the window and seeing it all again as it had been originally, Sasha turns into me. Kuzya. The invalid house. The black stream. The shop. A quarrel in the house. The wife in tears, as if someone in the family had died, when in fact it is the usual sort of conversation about the washing-up not being done. Rain. Water on the veranda. Take some episodes of the Italian journey. But who will be the traveller?

1979

I want to preserve the level of quality. Like Atlas holding the earth on his shoulders.

1979

Lord, let this cup . . . !

1 January

Lora and Tonino arrived last night after one a.m. We spent a quiet, peaceful evening together; Tonino and I talked a lot. I think he realizes the situation I am in here; and I think he would help if anything were to happen.

Our first project is the amateur film—16mm—about the country.

5 January

Larissa and I have been thinking very seriously about Tonino. I cannot go on like this. I don't know how I am to pay off my debts. Nor how I am to make *Stalker*. They obviously won't accept it (unless I make significant changes, which, whatever happens, I am not prepared to do) unless of course a miracle happens!

Or perhaps I have to believe that they will accept it, without any difficulty, and that everything will be all right?

All that I am left with is faith and hope . . . against all common sense.

And then what?

Yermash won't want to let me go to Italy to make *Italian Journey* unless I mutilate the film. He will even say that it's entirely up to me whether I go or not.

And I shall be stuck here unable to do anything.

Let's say I make my 'amateur' film. It will then have to be edited. Where? Here? Then I shall have to have a cutting copy and a work track. And that won't be possible either: Mosfilm will stick by their rights. And nobody is going to give me permission to leave before I have made the alterations to *Stalker*.

So that amounts to two years of misery; with Andriushka at school; and Marina, and Mother, and Father. It is going to be hell

Это значит года два мук:
а Андрюшки в школе, а
Маринка, мама, отец.
Их же замучат.
Что делать?!
Только молчать! и верить.

Самое важное — эфемерной, которой
не дано понять, а лишь чувствовать.
Верить, вопреки всему — верить..

Мы распяты в одной плоскости,
а мир — многомерен. Мы это
чувствуем и страдаем от
всего этого поэтому нельзя..
А знать не нужно!
Нужно любить. И верить. Вера — это
знание при помощи
любви

Может быть чудная картина
о памятнике!
Надо только, чтобы всё было:
И аппаратура и плёнка.
Надо думать о том как её
снимать. Полагаю снимать
её надо видимо в апреле и мае.
Надо думать и думать...

NB!

Паня

Дождь на траве

магазин

Ущелка

встреча С.С. сон <обмен му...>

расчистка садика

Слова обмен слова садик

«трагические» слёзы

обед

дом пирамидов Кузя

ледник

трактории Сергей

история покупки дома Забудкины

— где религиозная идея?

В чём? В тщетности действия? В характере творчества? Пока неясно.

for them. What can I do? Only pray! And believe.

The most important thing of all is this symbol, which it is not given to us to understand, only to feel. To have faith in spite of everything, to have faith.

We are crucified on one plane, while the world is many-dimensional. We are aware of that and are tormented by our inability to know the truth.

But there is no need to know it! We need to love. And to believe. Faith is knowledge with the help of love.

The garden could make a wonderful film! Provided we have all the necessary stuff: all the equipment and film. I must think about how to make it. Because it probably has to be shot in April and May. I really have to think and think.

What about the religious idea? Where is it? In the futility of action? In the creative instinct? For the moment it's not clear.

21 January

Read Gorenstein's *Psalm*. It is a stunning book. Of course he is a genius. He writes of a man and of his God with such passion, such persistence; pain finally overcome by purification, by an understanding of the divine role. It is a book that has to be read.

The first three parts are less successful: there are moments when it is not quite self-sufficient, and clumsily expressed; and stylistically the string of prophecies is artificial and contrived. However, the closer we go to the end, the more remarkable it becomes.

The idea of the five passions of the Lord, the hunger for faith and the hunger for knowledge of God, were all treated by Dostoievsky.

Seryozha Naydenov telephoned. (He came here yesterday.) Someone is selling a portable typewriter for 200 roubles—nowadays that is cheap. I must buy it.

I had a dream about someone dying unexpectedly.

I am unwell—37° during the daytime, but I always have a low temperature with 'flu. It goes up in the evening.

If God takes me to himself I am to have a church funeral and be buried in the cemetery of the Donskoy Monastery. It will be difficult to get permission. And no one is to mourn! They must believe that I am better off where I am. The picture is to be finished according to the pattern we decided for the music and sound. Lucia must try and tidy up the end of the bar scene. 'The Room' should include the new text from the notebook (the sick child) plus the old one, written for the scene after the 'Dream'. If it works out without the

'Bar', at the end of the 'Dream', after the hand, the scene with the little girl on crutches by the bar should stay. Remove the fish. Cut from the last shot of the 'Room' to the little girl (in colour) on her father's shoulders.

Sound of breathing.

Important to have all speech as it is on the track. In the final scene on the bed, Sasha should be more restrained, not wail as he does on the cutting copy. Synchronize the little girl in the last shot. Sasha Kaydanovsky can help with the sound, he has a good ear. Sharun must not direct, he must check it by ear. No other alterations are to be made. That is my last wish.

Tyapa is to be baptized.

An elm is to be planted over my grave.

Nothing is to be kept secret from Tyapa.

That's all.

27 January

Just reread my last entry: what awful rubbish. I clearly had a high temperature. I remember I really did think at that moment that I might easily die.

I must recover as quickly as possible and finish the picture. I am becoming more and more convinced that there is something wrong with the way I live. Something false about everything I do. Even when I want to do something good, I feel that it's only in order to seem a better person.

Reread Castaneda's *The Lessons of Don Juan*. A marvellous book! And very true, because—

1. the world is not at all as it appears to us.
2. under certain conditions it could well become different.

28 January

How about developing *Stalker* in a subsequent film—still with the same actors?

Stalker starts forcibly to drag people to the Room and turns into a 'votary' a 'fascist'. 'Bullying them into happiness'.

Can it be done that way? Bullying them into happiness. Vl[adimir] Ul[yanov]? Sharik*? Those who shatter the very foundations—how are they engendered? There is something in all this, without any doubt. I must think about it.

*Protagonist of Mikhail Bulgakov's *The Heart of a Dog*.

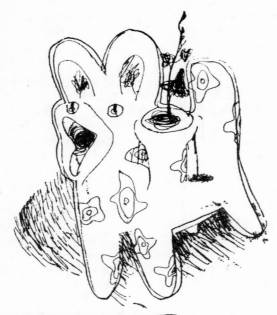

21 января 1929

Прочел «Псалом» Ф. Горенштейн
Это потрясающее сочинение!
Вне сомнения — он гений.
С какой скорбью, последователь-
ностью и страданием, в фина-
ле, преодолевая очищением,
пониманием В.Рози он рассказы-
вает о человеке, и его Боге.
Это надо читать!

Первые 3 части менее удачны,
иногда несоразмерны и
косноязычны.
И манера — чередование прозы
— казутная, прирученная за уши.
Но чем ближе к концу, тем
удивительнее.

Цель же Vстрадцей Господних — между
Вам. между Помощь Бога —
Пред'Восхищил Достоевский. —

Позвонил Серёша Койденов
(Вчера приходил) Кто-ро продаёт
порраневшую, пишущую машинку
за 200р. — Лепезъ ужо дешево. —
Надо купить.

Приснилось так неожидан
Забол — 37 дней. но ушла
жить всегда с нежностью теме
Карутюдъ.

Вечер — t° —

Если Бог меня прибережет, отпевав
меня в Церкви и хоронить
на кладбище Донскогомонаст.
Трудно вдоль добится разрешить.
Не грустить!! Верить, что мне
лучше там. Картину закончить
по схеме последнего разговора

6 February

I went to see Tonino. We had supper with some very important official from Italian television, a writer and playwright. He likes Tonino.

He said that Lapin—!?—is not against my being sent to Italy to make *Italian Journey*. (I would go to Italy and some Italian would come here to the USSR.)

That's an unexpected move on Lapin's part! Entirely independently of Yermash. The point is that the two of them are at loggerheads. So it could well happen.

I saw Sizov. He said that the Italian trip would be all right. And the Italian première of *Mirror*. And even that *Stalker* would have to be shown at the Moscow Festival. Only the picture must be finished as quickly as possible. I feel that what is going on is this:

1. The picture is not to be sent to Cannes.

2. They are going to insist on corrections (Sizov has already asked me if it's quite clear where the action takes place).

3. And as a result—I shall not be allowed to go to Italy (unless now it can be done through Lapin?).

I have established (through Kniazhinsky) that Gambaroff-Chamier, Interalliance GmbH (West Germany) are 'buying the film'. That information is from Surikov, a Sovinfilm official. So that's clear! The film has already been sold!

A story (or an episode):

Some people arrive in a new place and start to live in houses built close to one another. Suddenly one of them dies. There are no graveyards. You can't just bury a person in the middle of a field! And you can't have a graveyard with just one grave! The corpse can't just be dumped all by himself, with no other dead around him, but all alone. So they bury the dead person close to the house, in the front garden, under the windows.

10 February

Lord! I feel You drawing near, I can feel Your hand upon the back of my head. Because I want to see Your world as You made it, and Your people as You would have them be. I love You, Lord, and want nothing else from You. I accept all that is Yours, and only the weight of my malice and my sins, the darkness of my base soul, prevent me from being Your worthy slave, O Lord!

* Образ — это впечатление от Истины,
на которую Господь позволил
взглянуть нам своими слепыми
глазами.

Кажется, действительно по <Сталкер>
будет моим лучшим фильмом.
Это приятно, не более верно, это
придает уверенности. Это вовсе не
значит, что я ... высокого мне-
ния о своих картинах. Мне они
не нравятся — в них много
суетливого, преходящего, ложного
(В <Сталкере> этого меньше всего)
Пройдут другие делают картины
во много раз хуже.
Может быть это гордыня?
Может быть. Но раньше это приятно.

Я должен лично откуда-то по-
звонить с Тошико. В понедель-
ник я с утра отправлю
кого-нибудь в Переделать

Help me, Lord, and forgive me!

An image is an impression of the Truth, which God has allowed us to glimpse with our sightless eyes.

I think *Stalker* really is going to be my best film. That is good to know, but nothing more. Or rather, it makes for greater confidence. It does not for a moment mean that I have a high opinion of my films. I don't like them—there is so much in them that is fussy, ephemeral, false. (Less in *Stalker* than in others.) Which is merely because other people's films are so much worse. Is that pride on my part? Perhaps it is. But it is also the truth.

I must introduce my father to Tonino. I shall send someone to Peredelkino early on Monday morning.

What a great joy it is to feel the presence of the Lord.

Doctor Faustus may not be such a bad subject.

Leverkuhn is a character one can so well understand. The music will present some difficulty.

Is there an affinity between Thomas Mann and Dostoievsky? Atheism? Maybe . . . but it is different for each of them.

12 February

Mann 'understands too much' about God, whereas Dostoievsky wants to believe in God but cannot—the relevant organ is atrophied.

I went to see Tonino and told him an idea for a plot:

A writer, a man of great spiritual depths, prepared for death, an honest, virtuous, solitary man who despises success and the fuss that goes with it, glances one day at the mirror and sees on his face signs of a terrible illness—leprosy. For a year he waits, expecting the stark effects of the disease to manifest themselves at any moment. And at the end of the year he is told—by doctors or experts—that he has recovered. He returns home, where everything is covered in dust.

There is a pad of mildewed paper and his pencil goes right through it when he tries to write something down.

'Never mind!' he says huskily.

'Never mind!' he repeats aloud to his living reflection in the mirror, as he affirms that he is indeed alive. But he is empty. As empty as a chrysalis from which the butterfly has emerged.

And he realizes that the greatest sin of all is pride. For he had imagined, at one time, that he had attained great spiritual stature,

Великое старче — очередное
прикуривание Господа.

«Добрая фигура», может быть не
такая уж плохая тема
Либерхоп — фигура очень и очень
понятная.
Спутники с музыкой
Роднит — ли Т.Манна с Достоевским
уж много? Безбожие" М.б...
Только оно у них разное.
12.II. — Манн слишком с много
помышляет о боге, а Достоевский почему
не может верить в бога, орган оттра-
фированная.

whereas now he is nothing: through his illness the knowledge of death has laid him waste.

He opens the Bible and reads:

'And out of the ground the Lord God formed every beast of the field, and every fowl of the air; and he brought them unto Adam to see what he would call them . . .'

'At the beginning was the word,' said the unhappy man.

18 February

I came across Prishvin's *Diaries*, written in the '30s. He was a clever man. He has some wonderful things to say about cinema. He slates Roshal's *Petersburg Night* and Petrov's *Thunderstorm*.

'. . . In film, as in a photograph, you have to make use of the specific means of the art. If there are no ideas in the material, then it is better to have a film empty of ideas, like the American ones, rather than putting in ideas culled from literature. Cinema must have document as its starting-point.' (31 March '34.)

'. . . I think that the basic thing about a screenplay has to be the fact that it can only be realized by using cinematographic means.' (3 April '34.)

'. . . As I watch films in the cinema, I realize for the first time the great virtue of the theatre, its humanity. It is rather like gazing at an aeroplane and seeing for the first time how delightful is a bird's flight, a bird's feather.' (4 April '34.)

22 February

A few days ago I met Vladimir Safronov (through Naumov). He is the author of *Ariadne's Thread*—not published—he promised to let me have a copy. He is a diagnostician (he also uses photographs) and a healer.

From photographs he diagnosed that Larissa has trouble in:
1. The right side of the head.
2. The urological zone (the 'Bermuda Triangle' as he called it).
3. The right hip (I didn't know about that).

and for Olga
1. The front part of the head (we knew nothing about it).
2. The heart area.

and Dak
1. Hind legs (we knew).
2. Liver (we didn't know. All because of his distemper?).

5 March

Gave a talk yesterday at the cinema lecture hall (Propaganda Office), on acting: Terekhova and I appeared together. I think I must have said more than I should. Anyhow the director (a colonel in the KGB) warned me not to behave like that in any future talks— no taking the name of the Moscow Party Committee in vain, and no slating the critics.

Someone in the audience: 'Please tell us something about yourself. You are a great artist. *Andrey Rublyov* is incomparable. Thank you.'

14 March

There was a lecture in the Ballbearing Factory Club before they showed *Mirror*. It almost led to a furore.

Some typical questions:

'Andrey Arsenevich!

In *Mirror* we hear poems by your father, Arseniy Tarkovsky. What beautiful poems! Will this brilliant collaboration be continued in your future films? May I say how deeply I admire your exquisite films.'

'Andrey Arsenevich!

Will *Mirror* be shown more widely?

Please tell us something about your father and his poetry.'

'Andrey Arsenevich!

Please would you tell us what your father thinks of your films. And please tell us something about how *Stalker* was made.

Warmest wishes for your future success. Yu. Lapin.'

'Andrey Arsenevich!

I feel that your work has something in common with the paintings of Ilya Glazunov. If I have understood you correctly, you are pre-occupied with the same question: "Man and history". What do you think of Ilya Glazunov?'

'Why is it that in this film in particular audiences try to find some kind of sub-text?

'Is there any point in chewing everything over and over when virtually 90% of the audience only want to spend a couple of hours in the warmth and away from the daily round? You said yourself (and I agree with you) that in one fragment of *Mirror* can be seen almost everything that surrounds us, and that no episode contains an answer to questions about some "secret meaning".

'I was stunned by your film. I couldn't wait for this evening—to see *Mirror* for the second time. I am so enormously grateful to you! N. I. Astashkina, engineer.'

'Dear Andrey Arsenevich!

I am happy to be alive at the same time as yourself and consider you to be amongst the best directors of the century. My warm good wishes.'

24 March

Someone asked my father, 'What do you think of Pasternak?' He said, 'I have always felt as I might of a woman—adoration one moment, hatred the next, now admiration, now contempt.'

9 April

I returned to Moscow from Italy to find everything in a foul state. My room at home full of guests, smoking, loud music, wine and brandy spilt on the table. Quite revolting.

Italy is beautiful, Rome is powerful and courageous.

Clean air, even in town, no factories—they are all concentrated on the outskirts.

The streets are full of wistaria, and prunus, and judas trees in flower. Wonderful light.

On my birthday Tonino and his friend Franco took me to the provinces: Perugia—marvellous square in the centre of the city; Pienza—built by one architect, and all at one time, in honour of Pope Pius V; Assisi—where St. Francis of Assisi is buried. A double cathedral, built on two levels—amazing frescoes by Giotto. Wonderful Montepulciano.

The landscape, with ancient towns on the rocks, is astounding. I have not been so impressed by anything for ages.

I saw Antonioni, Rosi, Fellini. With Rosi I met Trombadori, a Communist and Member of Parliament, who delivered a thundering speech berating us and explaining the differences between Italian Communists and ours.

We stayed in San Vicente, for the press conference; after that we went by coach to Turin, and from Turin by train to Rome.

This is Dakhus.

10 April

The Italians offered to enter *Mirror* for the Donatello prize

Это Бакус

(Academy Award) with assurances that it would be selected. Our people refused, and suggested some film by Lotyanu instead of *Mirror*. Everyone in Rome is staggered.

Tonino and I have thought of a wonderful idea (in my view) for a screenplay—The End of the World.

A man incarcerates himself and his family (father, mother, daughter and son) in his own house, because he is expecting the end of the world. The wife has another son. The father is a religious man. They spend some forty years shut up together. In the end they are taken away by the police and ambulance service, who somehow found out about their existence. They are in an appalling state. The elder son tells his father that it was a crime to have hidden the real world from him for so many years.

When they are taken away the little boy looks around him and asks, 'Dad, is it the end of the world?'

Tonino telephoned yesterday evening. He says everyone is very anxious to help me with *Italian Journey*.

Today I asked Larissa to tell Shkalikov that I intend to write to Zimyanin and complain about the Donatello business.

13 April

During an argument about the submission of *Stalker* Pavlyonok remarked: 'Why use the word "vodka"? It's too Russian. In fact vodka is the symbol of Russia.'

I said, 'What d'you mean, the symbol of Russia? For heaven's sake, Boris Vladimirovich, what an idea!'

He's an idiot.

In fact altogether the level of discussion is abysmal—cut out 'vodka', 'one for the road', 'carrying their medals' (as they do in this country?). 'This whole world cannot help you' (but we live in the land of developed socialism). Pretty grim.

The Voice of America has apparently announced that American doctors are on their way to the USSR to treat Brezhnev, and are bringing equipment for the investigation of brain tumours.

My God! What happens when he dies? What will take over? Where shall we be heading? God only knows. Only one thing is certain, and that is that it won't get any better, in fact it can only be worse.

Very little chance of *Stalker* making it to any of the festivals.

15 April

Evening. Friedrich Gorenstein was here today. In two or three years' time (if he goes abroad as he hopes to) he will be famous.

What about making a film of Castaneda's *Don Juan*?

Stalker seems to have turned out the best of all my films.

16 April

2 a.m. All the Russian geniuses thought their greatness could not have grown out of soil that was flat and senseless, and so they called their country great and its future messianic.

They felt themselves to be the 'voice of the people' and did not want to be 'voices crying in the wilderness'; if they were to carry within themselves the essence of a people, then it had to be a great people, and the country had to have a great future.

Pushkin is more modest than the others: in *Monument*, and in his letters to Chaadayev in which he speaks of Russia's destiny merely as a protective buffer for Europe. And that is only because Pushkin's genius is harmonious.

There is nothing comfortable, nothing harmonious, in the genius of Tolstoy, Dostoievsky, or Gogol: it is the genius of discomfort, full of disharmony because it is embodied in the conflict between the author and the vision to which he aspires.

Dostoievsky did not believe in God, but he wanted to. He lacked the means of believing. And yet he wrote about faith. Pushkin is superior to the rest because he did not give Russia an absolute meaning.

Yermash telephoned the publishing committee, and Art Publishers, to tell them not to be too hard on *Juxtapositions*. Maybe it was just for the sake of swearing at them? I must tell Olga Surkova.

Enn Rekkor has sent a manuscript by Cross for a screenplay. And before doing so he altered the contract from 6000r. to 4000r.

I must ask Larissa to telephone. How maddening they are. I did not actually realize that the last script agreement specified contemporary Estonian writing. How can they suddenly cut the agreed sum? It's not how things are done. I shall have to have another go. Perhaps there is some point in doing the Estonian script? It is money, after all.

Yermash is insisting on *The Idiot*. Whatever happens, I have got to do the *Journey* in Italy.

19 April

There have been a great many cases of very serious side effects after children's immunizations: because of poor quality vaccines, or dirt. Doctors themselves are advising their friends and relations not to have their children immunized.

The film has been submitted, despite Bondarchuk's efforts.

20 April

Yet again Olga is coming home at one in the morning. Oh, Larissa is going to rue the day, and it will be too late. She has spoilt the girl.

21 April

A telephone call yesterday from the Union of Cinematographers: the Czechs are going to publish the script of *Mirror* in one of their literary journals.

23 April

This is a personal letter to Neya Zorkaya, in response to her article about me in *Kinopanorama* (sometime last autumn):

Dear Neya Markovna,
    Having read your article in the latest edition of *Kinopanorama*, I feel I must write to you.
    I do not know Tarkovsky personally. Like many people I have merely heard stories about what a hard time he has had, about his courage, his uncompromising loyalty to his principles, and the difficulties encountered by almost all of his films. (For which you and your fellow critics are in part to blame, as you yourself admit.)
    I am merely a viewer of his films. And those films do not seem to me to be mysterious hieroglyphs. I understand Tarkovsky's ideas, his sense of history, his concern for the fate of Russia. His films are perhaps sometimes complex in form, and it may well be that some people, as they emerge from their working men's club, as you say, fail to understand what a particular Tarkovsky film is about. Perhaps that is a danger signal. But the blame lies not with Tarkovsky but with the ignorance of our audiences who are fed on abusive claptrap in place of criticism, by illiterate reviewers.

Neya Markovna, may I follow your example and give you a piece of advice: cast a veil of modesty over your lips when you utter the name of a great artist.

Yours sincerely,
Rena Lenko

27 April

Andriusha Smirnov and Sergey Solovyov telephoned *Iskusstvo Kino* to congratulate them on the extract from *Juxtapositions*.

Rostotsky and Bondarchuk are very indignant. I must get the book finished as soon as possible and bring it out. It will be published immediately.

12 May

No question of any festivals. Yermash refused Cannes, saying the film is so good that he wants to show it at Moscow (?!)

It is only being printed now. The first showing will be on 14 May, I shall go to the Studio to see it.

I had a talk with Sizov yesterday about the letter from the Italian TV about making a film. He said no letters had come yet, but that when they do (he will have to be sent one as well) then the thing can go ahead straightaway. God grant it can! Is it really possible?

The fact of no Cannes is in itself a blow to my plans. Does it mean they have all collapsed?

The Italians sent the letter on 27 April.

I simply cannot make up my mind.

Larissa is going to the country in a few days' time to put the house in order. She is going with Rashid.

22 May

Went to Riga (Office for the Propaganda of Soviet Films). I earned 400 roubles in four days (seven 20 minute appearances on television).

I am tired and fed up. How I dislike those 'meetings with the audience'. If it weren't for necessity I should never agree to them.

Larissa talked to Lora, and today I established that four days ago letters from Italian TV (registered) were handed to Sizov, Yermash and Shauro.

I shall go and see Sizov tomorrow.

Larissa has gone to the country with Arayk and Rashid. I sent her 200 roubles. Oh, if only Italy really happens.

пятница 24 IV

Антоша Спирин и Серг. Соловьев звонили вчера. Никогда поздравляли со среднеч и «Соприкасением».

Ростоцкий и Бондарчук возмущены. Надо скорее делать книгу и выпустить её. Сейчас не напечатают.

Суббота 12 V

О фестивалях не может быть и речи. Отказали Канну, сказав, что картина настолько хороша, что он хочет её исправить на Московском фестивале. (!?)

Сейчас еще только печатается копия. Как будет черная — пойду в лабораторию смотреть.

Вчера разговаривал с Сизовым о письме с Английского TV по поводу постановки.

Он говорит, что писем еще не было.

А как будут (он даже должен получить их), то сразу будет дан ход этому делу Фау-то би.

Неужели это возможно?

У моих планов нарушилась уже то, что нет Китая.

Не рухнули ли они все тем самым?

Письмо Апрельянову послали 29 Апреля.

Никак не могу решиться окончательно.

Two-year-old Andrey with his father Arseniy, 1934.

With his mother, Maria Ivanovna, 1935.

As a schoolboy in Moscow.

Father and son: Arseniy and Andrey, Moscow, 1948.

Andrey with his son, Andriushka.

Andrey on the sets of a student film at VGIK, Moscow, 1956.

(*Below*) Explaining, defending, clarifying:
Andrey with Goskino officials, Moscow.

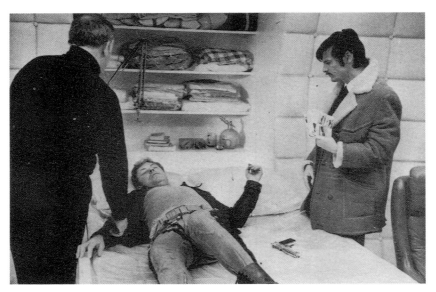

(*Above*) At work on *Solaris*.

Shooting *Mirror* in Tuchkovo: Andrey with his mother.

Working with actors : Andrey directing Kaydanovsky (*above*)
and Alissa Freindlich (*below*) in *Stalker*.

Nostalgia : at the baths in Bagno-Vignoni.

During the shooting of *Sacrifice*, his last film.

(*Below*) Conferring with cameraman Sven Nykvist.

His *Hamlet*: a scene from the play.

Scenes from the created works: *Ivan's Childhood* (1962).

Andrey Rublyov.

Natasha Bondarchuk in *Solaris* (*above*);
and (*below*) Margarita Terekhova in *Mirror* (1973).

Another scene from *Mirror*.

The child in *Stalker*.

From *Sacrifice* (1986).

One or two of the studio staff saw the film today in room 3. They were all stupefied.

A retrospective season of Yoseliani started yesterday at the Tbilisi cinema in Moscow. I introduced him, and *Pastorale*.

I have invitations to take *Stalker* to Kiev, Leningrad, Siberia, Tallinn, etc.

2 June

I saw Sasha Mishurin, having completely failed to meet him yesterday—I slept through the time of our rendezvous; then today I forgot all about him and only remembered too late. I hurried to get there on time, despite various delays, and eventually arrived half an hour late, but at least I found him there. There is something second-hand about him. He isn't drinking.

I met a couple of nice young people. He is Kolya, from Leningrad; she is Tanya, from Moscow. She is a Christian.

'. . . I am convinced that extraordinary surprises await us. It's a pity one can't imagine what one can't compare to anything.

'A genius is a negro who dreams of snow . . .' (Nabokov, *The Gift*.)

As for how I see my own vocation, it is to achieve the absolute, seeking to push higher and higher the level of my skill.

Dignity of the craftsman. Level of quality. Lost because nobody has any need of it, and in its place is an appearance of quality, its imitation.

I want to preserve the level of quality. Like Atlas holding the earth on his shoulders. He could, after all, have thrown it off when he got tired. But he didn't; for some reason he went on holding it up.

That, incidentally, is the most remarkable point of the legend: not the fact that he held it up for so long, but the fact that he did not become disillusioned and throw it down.

'. . . *Traviata* made Lenin break down, sobbing . . .' (Nabokov, *The Gift*.)

5 June

I want to ask Friedrich to write a script for Enn: I can't possibly do it myself. I shall have to pay him.

15 June

    Sea salt—2 tablespoons
    Pine needle extract—1 teaspoon
    Aubergine skin—1 teaspoon
    Sweet sedge root—1 teaspoon
    Mix with vegetable oil, and rub on gums.

    Propolis—5 gr. Put into a dark earthenware bowl.
    150 gr. spirit, leave for a week or ten days.
    Sieve—mix deposit with boracic vaseline.
    Boil up the solution:
    Mix 360 gr. of oak bark decoction with 150 gr. of the infusion.
Gargle.

17 June

    330 roubles received from the Bureau of Propaganda, and (a long time before) 170 roubles salary, mine and Larissa's.

    Kolya Shishlin says Yermash told him that I really am going to go and work in Italy, but that there's no point in hoping to make money, as I shall have to give a huge proportion of what I earn to the Embassy.

24 June

    Abasha (region)
    Mingrelia
    Collective farm—vines, sweet corn, vegetables.

    An experiment at kolkhoz level. 150% goes to the State, 50% the State buys up at an inflated purchase price, anything over 150% belongs to the kolkhoz. They've all grown very rich. (There is a similar kolkhoz in the Crimea.) The government is not too happy: 'That is not socialism.'

    Obviously there are those who support it. There seems to be a kind of balance, for the moment, in official attitudes to the idea.

7 July

    The day before yesterday Larissa Shepitko was buried, and so were five members of her team. A car accident. All killed instantly. It was so sudden that no adrenalin was found in their blood. The driver seems to have fallen asleep at the wheel. Early in the morning; between Ostashkov and Kalinin.

And today K. Shishlin telephoned to say that Volodya Bura-kovsky's younger daughter, Marina, was killed the day before yesterday in a car crash in Jordan. After all that happened to his elder one—she very nearly died from an abcess. Extraordinary. Shepitko, Volodya Burakovsky.

I am waiting for my documents for the journey to Italy. The Italians are worried, it puts out all their plans—hotels, cars. Or per-haps Lora is imagining it all.

8 July

I was not given any outright payment last year when I was ill. They gave me 250 roubles which I paid back a few days ago.

9 July

Oh, God, what a beautiful dream I had! It was one of the two dreams which have recurred all through my life but which I had not had for a very long time.

It was summer, not far from the house (which I don't remember).

It was sunny, with a little breeze. I was out walking, and walking somehow rather fast, as if heading somewhere specific. But I was following a path I had never been along before. And immediately I came to a most beautiful, wonderful place, a paradise. Overgrown with all sorts of different, untended flowers. In the dis-tance I could hear screams, as if someone was struggling in the grass—fighting, moaning. It sounded almost like a battle to the death.

I went on along the wonderful forest path, round a corner, and into a field, and came upon children fighting at the roadside. Village children. A young woman, or girl, was sitting at the side of the road busy with something. I said to her, 'They're going to kill each other.' 'You don't have to worry! You don't have to worry about the girl, go on, go on, never mind, they won't kill each other.' Or something in that vein.

Someone came out of the bushes, I think an elderly woman, and poured a whole lot of berries—large ones, not quite ripe, they looked like raspberries—into the cupped skirt of the younger one.

I went on. It was not at all a long walk. I glanced to the right, and stopped—at my feet was a precipice.

Down below was a broad, clean, beautiful river, its surface covered in ripples, and on the far bank grass, and a leafy, cosy wood. It was peaceful and silent! How was it that I had never been to this place before! I lay down in the grass at the very edge of the precipice.

In front of my eyes—along the path—was fresh grass, a little meadow covered in blue flowers, perhaps hemp; and beyond that the picture rounded off in a darkish area—partly of pine?—while at the far end of the meadow grew two enormous flowers (in the background, but looking as if they were right in front of my eyes, and resembling the violets that grow on my windowsill); at the edge of the wood was an old, dead fir tree, which stood out but somehow did not spoil the landscape. A little to the right, through the trees, I glimpsed the convex brick wall of some ancient building, not very obvious, either a tower or a rounded wall.

Silence. Sunshine; flowers; breeze; cool; peace! I lay there, looking in front of me at that amazing scene, my whole being filled with a sense of happiness attained . . .

*17 July**

Arrived in Rome yesterday. I am tired. We touched down in Milan. There was a delay.

Panorama of the *town*? At different times—through time (weather, time of day, precipitations, light).

The hero—a translator. (Could he be an architect?)

Loneliness.

Giotto, Assisi. He doesn't notice anything and doesn't look at anything.

It is terribly hot; difficult to think. I shall have to acclimatize. Only now do I realize how tired I am, after Moscow, all I had to do, the film, being penniless. And how are they getting on—my Larochka and Tyapus and Dakus?

Title: *Nostalgia*.

Should the hero marry? An Italian woman? No.

A town with baths. A man puts his feet in, and tells a blind man the story of the film. This sets off the hero's imagination, and he pictures to himself a conversation between God and Mary.

*The Italian entries that follow were written in an Italian engagement diary which A.T. referred to as his 'Italian notebook'.

18 July

I have to be up at 6.0. Ilyin is coming at 8.0 to take me to see the Ambassador.

Agostini—the Italian firm that wants to buy *Stalker*. NB: I must have a press conference to make it clear that if cuts are made there will be a row. The press conference will be the right moment to issue a warning.

Tonino and I are struggling to discover *the reason* (in a poetic sense, in terms of images) for our hero's journey.

The film can start with a dream in which the hero is arguing with his wife.

Larissa telephoned from Moscow. Bad news:

1. Mama's tests are not good. Lara has invited M.A.
2. Yermash doesn't want Larissa to go to Rome.
3. Yermash does not like my title for the film. He wants the film to include titles (jokes—advertisements, posters).
4. Lizzani was not shown *Stalker* when he was in Moscow—and he is the director of the Venice Festival.

Rosi said he would make a fuss. Refuse the Moscow Festival for the sake of Venice.

19 July, Rome—Amalfi

We left Rome at 8.20 (Lora, Toni, myself, Franco—who is also the leader of our team, a cameraman with two assistants, the sound mixer—an amazing character).

We filmed Tonino leaving his house—as the 'Companion'.

We travelled in Franco's Mercedes. Terribly hot.

We did some shooting. The 'goat pass' in Pozzo d'Antullo, next to Collepardo, and a little in the monastery, the church at Dituralti, and the chemist's shop, which is old and astonishingly beautiful.

Stopped at a wonderful hotel near Amalfi, the Saracen. The situation and the view are unbelievable.

20 July

We are on our way to Sorrento. We paused in Furore and shot a sequence (smugglers).

1. Pan. Close-up of Toni and me, then pan shot of the bypass bridge.

2. Conversation on the bridge. Landscape.
3. Close-up of Tonino.

Made a sequence (not very satisfactorily) about the history of Princess Gorchakov's villa in Sorrento. Went out in a boat, briefly, and did a little filming. Made a detour to Ravella in order to film an inner courtyard overgrown with hydrangeas.

I have had two swims. Wonderful! So sad that Tyapus and Larissa are not with me. I miss them so much.

21 July

From Amalfi to Ostuni.
A marvellous journey, but I am tired.
Later I shall show where it all is on the map. So tired I am falling asleep. 300 kilometres in the heat, with the scenery changing every 30 minutes.
I wanted to write some letters.

Next morning:
We went right across Italy from the Tyrrhenian Sea to the Adriatic. Alberobello is a lovely town!
Amalfi—Salerno—Potenza—Metanonto—Taranto—Martina Franca—Locorotondo—Alberobello—Ostuni (*Trulli*!*).

22 July, Ostuni. Incanto Hotel

This morning we went to Lecce and Otranto. The baroque in Lecce!
Did some shooting. I am not happy about Giancarlo (the cameraman).
We had a swim in the evening. Franco, me, Tonino, Lora, Evgeny (Eugenio), Giancarlo and the two assistants.
A young man on the roadside. Hitchhiking. He puts up his hand, nobody stops. Sad looking, with fair hair. I was reminded of Tyapa. He will grow up as well, become an adult, and will feel lonely.
Eugenio Rondini is the sound mixer. He is very good.
(A red wilderness . . .)

Trullo: conical, primitive dwelling, originally mudbuilt, found in this part of Italy.

The guitar-playing tram worker in the cathedral.
The vow: climbing uphill with the woman.

23 July

We left Ostuni, and went through Fasano, with its wonderful centre and two cathedrals. The sea is to our right all the time. *Trulli* on either side of the road. The roads are superb.

In Trani.
The cathedral is right beside the sea (on a street). We bathed. Cooked spaghetti, and fish and shrimps. It was the best meal of the lot. I swam. We took two long shots, with the cathedral. Going back to Rome. Harvested corn fields with burnt stubble. Black hills, with trees scattered over the black fields. Olive trees. Straw burning on the fields.
The hero refuses to look at beautiful places. 'Penance'.

'What have I forgotten?' He had forgotten about death. 'What was it I dreamt about?'—and he had dreamed about death.
He doesn't want to look at Giotto, and weeps.
Solonitsyn's hands.

Rome. Back in the Leonardo Hotel.

24 July, Rome. Leonardo da Vinci

I must write letters tomorrow. Telephone Ilyin and the Consul.
I have been travelling around: Bomarso (the Monsters and the Orania Castle)—Civita (dream). Dying town—next to Banbreggia—Bagno-Vignoni (baths) and back to Rome via Chianciano.

A man wets his feet, with his shoes on (the blind man, who is being told the story of the film). A room looking out onto the well, where the hero has his heart attack. The hero is a writer, who is advised to visit N., where either the father or the son of *The End of the World* is in hospital. His hobby is architecture, which turns out to be not as one has always known it.
A glove covered in lime.
Solonitsyn's hands. A woman looking at his hands.
1. Subjective angle shot of the hands in action.
2. Objective camera shot simply of the hands.
Tuscan landscapes.

25 July

Nothing today.

I went to see Toni. Franco brought the contract. I asked him about the timing for the film. Apparently it will be three months of preparation, two of shooting and two of editing. Perhaps if Tonino and I were to write a screenplay of *The End of the World* the producer might add a couple of months for shooting and editing it?

Tonino and I worked together. We could not settle on a job for the hero. We decided to give him interpreters, with a view to distribution: there has to be very little text in Russian.

26 July, Rome

T. and I have been working, and have settled lots of things; in fact almost everything. The finale will be the hero's death from a chance terrorist bullet. I must write or telephone to Sizov and Mossin.

The death must be justified by the logic of the whole story. He is wandering along the street, close to the wooden house. He sees in front of him a crumpled Italian newspaper; and perhaps in the final frame—a pavement, with the ashes of the newspaper.

He forgets that he dreamt of his death.

The girl is his interpreter. The contract has to be translated into Russian.

5,000,000 each for Toni and me—8500 dollars in all, that is 6630 roubles in foreign currency.

27 July, Rome

We have made a plan of two-fifths of the screenplay. For the moment the first draft is going well.

Tomorrow we are flying to Sardinia to Antonioni.

28 July, Sardinia

We did not fly here this morning: there is a strike. We sailed by steamer for eight-and-a-half hours. We finished the journey by car (hired). Antonioni's house.

We arrived late, at night. A round house. White interior. Tomorrow I shall look around more thoroughly. It's a bit bourgeois. Modernistic.

I'm tired. I slept in the car. My heart is giving the odd twinge. Tomorrow we shall have a day off, Toni announced.

We lack a basic idea. A concept.
Nostalgia.

The impossibility of being alone in beautiful Italy does not amount to an idea.

NB: We are very close to the idea, it is a question of looking for it.

29 July, Sardinia

In Michelangelo's villa, Costa Paradiso. This morning I got up at 7.0. The villa stands above the sea, with the sea all around it. Tamarisk, thuja, shrubs, cliffs—granite.

The beach is amazing. Weathered cliffs. The granite has taken on astonishing shapes. Silence. Sunshine. The sea is azure. It's a fairy-tale place. Heaven. Paradiso.

Only where are my Tyapochka and Larissa!

We've been swimming and sunbathing—I'm as red as a lobster.

Michelangelo is very nice. Enrica is kind and a wonderful hostess. My room is delightful, with the sound of the sea down below.

Tonino and I made this a day off. Could one ever become used to this sort of life? (Of course I don't mean work.)

According to Tonino this house is worth about 2,000,000,000 lire = 170,000 dollars.

The house: Michelangelo has excessively 'good taste'.

30 July, Costa Paradiso

Worked. We have made a plan. It will have to be simplified for Yermash, made more schematic; more like any other feature or documentary.

This evening I saw in the paper that *Que Viva Mexico* and a film by Danelia are coming to Venice. *Stalker*, which Lizzani (the Festival director) and Moravia asked Yermash to let them have, has been refused. In any case they didn't want it shown. The reasons given were:

1. Venice is a decadent festival. (So what is Danelia doing there?)

2. Tarkovsky must not be shown in Venice because that might make it 'more important' than the Moscow Festival.

Very upsetting. The bastards.

31 July, Costa Paradiso

The outline has been altered, and made more precise. NOSTAL-GIA.

Tomorrow we shall discuss the scenes—dialogue, characters, etc. Tonino and I really like it.

Tomorrow, or the day after at the latest, I shall start writing the scenes—there are about 14 of them—and give them to Lora to translate for Toni. Then Toni will rewrite them, Lora will retranslate them and send them back to me. Then finally I shall edit the definitive Russian version.

Today I had a first session with Enrica—*transcendental meditation*. Tomorrow I shall have a solo session. There are four altogether. At the first one the pupil has to give the teacher (as thanks) a little bunch of flowers, two sweet fruits, and a white cloth—a napkin or a handkerchief.

Tomorrow I shall have to go to the shop with Michelangelo.

1st Meditation
Mantra.

1 August, Costa Paradiso

Worked. The character of the interpreter. Beautiful but flawed. Her husband. The formal dinner. She keeps on mistranslating.

First meditation lesson. It seems to be working. In the evening (now) less well. I think I fell asleep and failed to notice my blue vibrations.

2 August, Costa Paradiso

Meditation in the morning. It was deeper, but occasionally I fell asleep. It is a pity the fast day coincided with the first day of meditation. No blue vibrations.

Worked. We have worked out the interpreter's character. She is hysterical, *à la* Galya Shabanova. The plan is shaking down into something really good.

Meditation was better in the evening. Enrica and Lora and I worked on it together. And again there was the blue shimmer.

We looked at the moon through Michelangelo's telescope.

3 August, Costa Paradiso

Meditation in the morning—quite good. In the evening it was not good at all, I almost gave up. I was struggling against all the things that got in the way. My hopes are set on tomorrow morning.

T. and I worked. We have thought out the dinner scene. The screenplay is going to be very good.

This evening there was a row: Michelangelo yelled at Tonino because the 'Special'* was not properly prepared and was slipshod. He accused him of not consulting anybody. It may be true, but Tonino is an angel and wanted it all to be as good as possible.

We must write the screenplay immediately, not for ourselves (all we need is the '*scaletta*'†) but for Moscow and Italian TV, who don't mind in the least which scene is finished. They are reckoning on the names, not on the script.

4 August, Costa Paradiso

Worked. The plan of the film is finished. Only the scene with the psychiatrist has to be polished.

My last day staying with Michelangelo.

Meditation is quite good. Eight states:

1. waking
2. sleep
3. hypnosis
4. transcendental state
5. cosmic
6. unity
7. divine
8. absolute

All these states are attainable through meditation.

5 August, Rome. Leonardo da Vinci

The draft screenplay is finished. We are leaving Antonioni.

(Meditation quite good. Not so good in the evening. New place.) The journey to the airport (Sardinia) was terribly tiring, I felt sick. It was the heat and all the bends in the road. Back in the Leonardo da Vinci.

Telephoned Moscow yesterday evening. Olga frightened me with an account of Larissa's conversation with Sizov about *Stalker*.

I left my razor behind at Michelangelo's. He rang and promised to send it on.

Pleased with how work is going.

Missing Larochka and Tyapa and Dak.

*Provisional title for *Tempo di Viaggio*.
†shooting-script.

6 August, Rome

Telephoned Olga again this morning. My anxiety was un-necessary: it was simply that Sizov or someone didn't like the trailer. (Let them remake it without me. Though actually Larissa said they wouldn't do it unless I was there.)

Worked till lunchtime, slowly. Telephoned the Consulate and the Embassy and Ilyin.

Tried to get through to Sizov.

Saw Tovoli, the cameraman who is filming with Antonioni at the moment. He is going to do the 'Special'. We talked together, and I think he was pleased.

This evening Toni, Lora, N., Fr. and I had supper together.

7 August, Rome

Tyapus' birthday—he is 9!

(Must telephone Bobylev in the Consulate, and Ilyin.) Telephone Gambarov. Telegram to Franco Rosi in Moscow.

No work. This afternoon there was a terribly silly film about Frankenstein.

Rang Olga and Sizov (about the title).

8 August, Rome—Bagno-Vignoni

To Bagno-Vignoni in the morning: the Tovolis, Eugenio, Franco and two others.

On the way we filmed:
1. The ruined church in Formello
2. The landscape around Bagno-Vignoni (Tuscany)
3. Sheep that we passed, grouped around a tree, in the shade.

Luciano is a nice, gentle person, he looks like Shtepsel, and his wife Laetitia reminds me of Valya, the production manager of *Stalker*.

9 August, Bagno-Vignoni

Early this morning there was a thunderstorm, very beautiful. Rain. This morning we looked at the hot water baths—St. Katherine. It's a fantastic place for a film.

Tovoli showed me the stream, and the room with no windows for the 'Companion' and for the film. *Madonna del Parto*.

We filmed Piero della Francesca's *Madonna of Childbirth* in Monterchi. No reproduction can give any idea of how beautiful it is.

A cemetery on the borders of Tuscany and Umbria.

When they wanted to transfer the Madonna to a museum, the local women protested and insisted on her staying.

This evening—Siena!!! It is the best of all the cities I have seen. The square is astonishing, like a shell, and in wet weather the rain runs over it; the buildings around it are unbelievably beautiful.

I went to see a heart specialist. He examined me and said there was nothing wrong. My heart is fine and there are no signs of a coronary.

10 August, Bagno-Vignoni

Filmed St. Katherine's baths this morning. Drove about in the countryside. This afternoon—the Church (Abbey) of Sant' Antimo. The living quarters of the Abbey are inside the church, by papal decree.

Had a meeting with a religious order. They sang a Gregorian chant specially for us in the church, when they heard that it was me! They had seen *Rublyov*. Eugenio Rondini recorded it all.

This evening it was raining, we did not film the hot stream. They have all gone to Rome—Tovoli and his wife, Eugenio and Franco. Toni and Lora and I have stayed here to work.

11 August, Bagno-Vignoni

Massage in the morning, like yesterday. We didn't work. Walked a little. In the afternoon an orchestra arrived, the musicians are Americans from Siena. They are giving a concert.

This afternoon I had a sleep and was woken by the sound of instruments being tuned. They have brought a piano with them. It is going to take place beside the baths and the spring, in the gallery under the roof, and instead of stalls there will be steaming water.

I was sorry I couldn't film the rehearsal.

The evening concert was ghastly.

12 August, Bagno-Vignoni

No work today, the last day of the holiday. Tomorrow we shall fling ourselves into the script.

T. and I discussed the screenplay, and talked more about the producer. He says he is a decent, honest man. T. explained the question of taxes, percentages of royalties, and so on.

I telephoned Moscow. Olga has written an essay, according to her quite a good one. It will be clear tomorrow when it is marked.

Larissa hasn't rung from the country. I asked Olga to send her a telegram.

I am missing home terribly.

13 August, Bagno-Vignoni

Worked quite satisfactorily. It's nice here, very cosy. There are lots of snakes in the woods, and blackberries which nobody picks.

Yesterday we went to the upper part of Bagno-Vignoni. A 'village' consisting of a few houses, a fortress wall, a tower, a church. It'll be very cheap to live there while we are filming. It will cost us practically nothing. In fact one could evidently even buy a house there for very little. It is an amazing place, a kilometre from Bagno-Vignoni. About an hour and a half from Rome by car.

Gave Lora one scene to be translated for Tonino—'The Palm Hotel'.

Wrote to Gambarov. Shall telephone him tomorrow.

Gorchakov forgets that he had a dream about death.

14 August, Bagno-Vignoni

Worked quite satisfactorily on the second outline. I have written out one page of the first one.

We rang Tonino to ask him to buy me a Polaroid. I want to take a few photographs.

Tomorrow is the start of the harvest festival—the end of summer.

I want to take a few pictures from the window at different times of day. The morning landscape at dawn.

I think the Moscow Festival started today.

15 August, Bagno-Vignoni, Hotel Le Terme

Worked successfully on the outline for the Russians.

I looked round the wonderful abandoned house on the square by the baths in Bagno-Vignoni, opposite my windows.

Iolanda, our masseuse, took us to San Cirico and Montequello, where there is a folk theatre. The director is a locksmith and plumber. Every year there is a play about life in the town. The whole team are the authors. The town is fabulous.

16 August, Bagno-Vignoni

Federico—the nephew of Franco Terilli—arrived early this morning and we visited the nearby towns: it was a fairy-tale journey.

Monte Oliveto Maggiore—a monastery. Volterra. San Gimignano. Breathtaking places, astounding. I can't take it in any more. My perception is becoming blunted.

17 August, Bagno-Vignoni

Worked quite well. Tomorrow we shall finish working out the second—Russian—outline.

I telephoned Moscow at 12.10 at night (Moscow time) and Olga was not at home. Rang Tosia, and no one answered. Very worrying.

Francesco Rosi is going to Moscow for four days. He must meet Larissa and introduce her to Marnesono. I shall ring tomorrow morning.

18 August, Bagno-Vignoni

I spent all day trying to get through to Moscow. The Russian version of the outline is all decided. We shall write it tomorrow. Then I shall finish the Italian version.

19 August, Bagno-Vignoni

It has all started to go well: we have thought of a new finale, the scene with the 'madman'. We haven't finished writing it out. We'll do that tomorrow, on our last day here. In Rome I shall write the 'telegraph': the outline of the 1st version, and the Russian scenes in detail.

Must think about the 'Companion'.

20 August, Bagno-Vignoni

Spoke to Tosia this morning. She had only just arrived and could not get hold of Olga either. Seryozha told her that Olga had failed her exams. She must have panicked and gone off to the country.

Oh, Lord, help me . . .

We finished the 2nd outline for Moscow. Not bad at all. The screenplay is going to be all right. There is a lot in it that ought to be put into the film.

Evening.
Franco Terilli has arrived and tomorrow we are returning to Rome, via Florence. I shall telephone Tosia from there. She promised to wire Larissa in the country.

Now I have to pack.

21 August, Bagno-Vignoni—Rome

Back in the Leonardo da Vinci, again in room 511. We left B.V. for Florence this morning. After Florence, the Uffizi, (Leonardo's *Adoration of the Magi*) and the Ponte Vecchio—I collapsed. Quite ill. I am writing now lying down.

The city is amazing, fruit of the Renaissance, with no trees. Trees here would look ridiculous. A rich, noble city, with wonderful shops, full of marvellous things. I want to buy two or three rings.

I must try and sleep it off, in order to work tomorrow: I shan't leave the hotel until I have finished the 1st outline.

Ring Moscow tomorrow.

22 August, Rome, Leonardo da Vinci

Civilization on the wrong road. But there is no possibility of turning back. Crossroads. In conversation with mathematician in the film.

Finished the *scaletta*. Still have to write 'Dostoievsky'. I've booked a conversation with Tosia (11–1 a.m.) No answer either to my call or to Tonino's. It's vital that I ring and find out what is going on. Terribly worried.

23 August, Rome

Went with Lora to the Vatican Museum and St. Peter's. The Sistine Chapel is in the museum. Above all—the Leonardos. In the museum: *St. Jeronimus*; Giotto, Perugino, Botticelli. Appalling modern religious art. Buffet is a disaster.

We had supper with Franco in the evening. He is very nice, that Franco, and so is Julia.

Saw the first part of Antonioni's *China* on television. Very poor.

24 August, Rome

Seeing Samokhvalov this evening (must ring).

Saw Carlo di Carlo. He is going to Venice to the Biennale, as a journalist.

I wrote an answer to an invitation from Lizzani to go to Venice (as if he had invited me). It will be published if Lizzani sends an invitation.

Interview with Carlo di Carlo (as if he were telephoning me from Venice).

Saw Samokhvalov and his wife. Had a chat with Ilyin and his

wife. My contacts seem to be falling into place.

Went to church. Father Victor—a grenadier in Wrangel's army. The church is simple. The altar has copies of Catholic paintings. Very odd. He went from Constantinople to Belgium to Rome.

Sunday is the Feast of the Transfiguration.

Moravia, who was in Moscow, is full of praise for *Stalker* in the *Espresso*.

25 August, Rome

No work. Saw Sokolov, who is full of hopes for Australia, with his wife. I saw on television that Godunov (some dancer with the Bolshoi) has asked for political asylum in the U.S. His wife was grabbed and taken to the plane, on the grounds that she doesn't share her husband's views. The American authorities won't let the plane take off until she has said so herself.

Saw a monstrous film called *Fontagni*. Moravia's article has been translated—he did not understand the film at all. Obviously they did not give him a translator. I must find out. Tonino wants to write to him. He is in Venice at the moment.

26 August, Rome

Transfiguration. I went to the service at Fr. Victor's church in Via Palestro. A poor church, and poor parishioners (in appearance at least) and very few, despite the great feast.

In the afternoon went with Tonino and his friend Gete Stranio to Palestrina, to see the triangular villa (15th century), belonging to the Princes Barberini. A wonderful place!

Then we went on to the Villa Adriana (1st century B.C.). Grandiose ruins, and the remains of beautiful columns, floors, halls, baths. The impression is absurd and strange.

10 p.m. Tired. I must try and get through to Tosia.

27 August, Rome

Went to the editing studio. The 'Special' may be quite successful. But there's rather too little material. We need an hour and ten minutes. Then there'll be more money. I shall wait for the coloured negative before starting to splice.

We went to see Cao to try to sort out the question of the contract. In the evening met a man from television—the one who decided it all. Cao makes a lot of fuss in order to prove that she does actually earn her bread and butter.

The editor is someone called Frico who edited Antonioni's *The Passenger*.

I rang Tosia this morning, no, last night: Olga failed her French.

28 August, Rome

Editing the 'Special'. Luciano Tovoli is ill with an asthma attack.

29 August, Rome

Editing. Luciano is ill. Postponing filming on Tonino's veranda for two days.

Earlier Franco gave me	+ 210,000 +?	
Today	+ 1 million	
Did my first shopping today:— purse	8,500	
Eau-de-Cologne (lavender)	13,500	
	22,000 l.	

30 August, Rome

Wrote the Dostoievsky scene.
The script is finished.
Talked to Tovoli about the 'Special'. Up at 5 a.m. tomorrow for filming.

Went to see Rosi, who was given the Grand Prix in Moscow. Lots of impressions. Conversations with Trombadori. Shouting, arguing. Rosi has a nice wife, Giancarla. Wealthy, with a fashion shop.

There is an article in a (right-wing, Milan) newspaper condemning Rosi for not protesting about the fact that Tarkovsky, one of the world's three greatest directors, was excluded from the festival, and for the fact that he took—i.e. accepted—the prize.

31 August, Rome

With Toni from early morning on, filming the 'Special'. It was so early that after getting back last night from Rosi at 2.0 in the morning I didn't have time to do my exercises, for the first time in eighteen months.

We filmed about forty minutes (!) of good time. Well done, Andrey! And Tovoli doesn't miss a trick either. He understands everything, and is very nice and easy to work with.

While we were shooting the scene with the burning candle

Larissa telephoned! I was so happy. They've had a lot of trouble: Tyapus was ill and now will not be coming before 10 September, Lara was ill (still the same furunculosis), and Dakhus was ill for four days and nearly died, Lara said. They are going to the country again. Lord, give them happiness! Tomorrow I must be up at 3 a.m.

Gambarov telephoned: he really did buy the rights of *Stalker* when work on the film was just starting. But he says he was not given the film by Mikheyev, the engineer from the print lab. with whom Konoplyov discussed the possibility of high quality print direct from the negative, in order to prove what good quality Rerberg's stuff was.

1 September, Rome

Ring Larissa this evening.

Up at 3.15 a.m. We finished shooting. Once it is edited the whole film could be 1 hour 20 minutes (!!). Toni and I are thinking of negotiating with TV. Perhaps (if the film really happens) we shall make another film while we are shooting, and yet another, while preparations are going on. Well, 200 metres in two days! Not bad— *no male*, as the Italians say.

I didn't talk to Larissa, the lines were busy. They have booked it for tomorrow morning at 7 a.m.

2 September, Rome

No call from Larissa, she must have been unable to get through. I couldn't get Moscow late last night. I shall try tomorrow morning (early). It worries me to think of her there all alone, poor Larissa, I do so wonder how she is.

Yesterday I saw *The Last Wave*, science fiction. Not up to much, of course, just a story.

In today's *L'Unita* there's an article by Greco about *Stalker* which he saw in Moscow. It's a brilliant article; I've bought a copy of the paper.

Tomorrow Toni will finish the Dostoievsky scene, and the script will be ready.

3 September, Rome

The script is finished and typed.

Editing. Franco helped me do some shopping. I bought:

1. A radio with a dictaphone and a clock, batteries and cassettes —140,000.

2. A Braun electric razor.
3. An American electric razor.
4. T-shirts for Tyapa and the grown-ups.
   Total—200,000.

I have four razors and a dictaphone.

Visited Samokhvalov. Our Embassy has an absolutely beautiful villa.

4 September, Rome

Went to the television studios. A clause has been written into the agreement. We are going to give the script tomorrow.

The script will leave for Moscow tomorrow for Volchich to translate it.

I have bought Larissa a gorgeous present. Of course she deserves far more.

1. A gold cross, Italian or English, with rubies and a star (130,000/158 dollars, beginning of this century, Art Nouveau).
2. A handmade Italian gold chain (mid-19th century, 180,000/ 98 dollars).
3. A seventeenth century Italian ring (293 dollars/240,000).
   Total—550,000/400,000.

I think Lara will be very pleased. I have never given her a present.

I talked to her: my impression was that she was a little bit woozy. Sizov is interested in the timing of the Italian picture. So perhaps there will be a picture? He said that Solonitsyn is a 'non-traveller'— is that because of Bulgaria?

5 September, Rome

Tried to do some editing, after taking a look at the material, which I didn't much like. But I only had a brief look. Tomorrow.

Went to the cinema with Franco this evening. We saw *Zombie II* —science fiction horror film. Ghastly; repulsive trash.

6 September, Rome

Spent all day in the cutting room. This evening went to see Antonioni and Enrica who are back from the Venice Festival.

We watched *China* on TV.

7 September, Rome

Edited the material to be shown on TV. It is turning out really well. I shall have to finish editing it before I leave, and do the credits.

I've been paid 4,600,000 for the 'special edition'.

Saw Bertolucci's *La luna*. Monstrous, cheap, vulgar rubbish.

8 September, Rome

Shopping:	Larissa: sheepskin coat	370,000
	Tyapa	90,000
	Leather coat (1)	570,000
		1,030,000
	Light boots (for me)	25,000
	Tyapa: trainers	8,000
	Tyapa: shoes	15,000

This evening we went to see Francesco Rosi. Giancarla wants to be producer of my next film. Gilo Pontecorvo appeared towards the end of the evening. I remember him from 1962 when we were introduced in Venice. He has aged a lot. Both Franco and Giancarla are terribly nice, and extraordinarily well disposed towards me.

Several producers are interested in *The Italian Journey*.

Since Bagno-Vignoni I haven't got anywhere at all with meditation.

9 September, Rome

We have drawn up a contingency plan just in case I am not able to return for the filming.

Saw Michelangelo and Enrica. We did some meditation. I was on the right wavelength straightaway and for the first time I saw Soma—green and yellow radiance.

We had supper all together. Michelangelo is a stiff, cold person. And a frightful egoist, judging by his business relationship with Tonino.

I telephoned home, and talked to Olga. Tomorrow I shall ring Sizov about the contracts and the information.

10 September, Rome

Prepared the material for showing tomorrow, in order to increase the budget for the 'Special'.

I am flying to Moscow on the 17th at 9.30 a.m.

Went to Rinascente—I didn't buy anything and I'm dog tired.

11 September, Rome

A crazy day. In the morning I showed Fichera and the RAI team *The Journey* with the aim of developing the 'Special' into a full length film. *Everyone was wildly enthusiastic!*

One eminent critic called *that* a masterpiece (!!?). It's their problem. Anyhow, the great thing is that Tonino is delighted.

I have written a *scaletta* for 1 hour 20 minutes. We are short of time—it is not possible to make a full length film in one week's shooting and three days' editing! All the same, I shall do it. Tonino is very proud and pleased.

Giancarla Rosi invited me and gave me fantastic presents for myself and Larissa. (Misspelt Larissa's name—brilliant!)

What it amounts to is that in less than two months we have written a screenplay, done a *scaletta* of the second draft, worked out how we are going to work on *The End of the World*, and filmed the 'Special'. Unbelievable! That's the way to live! Working with sheer delight.

Lora telephoned Olga.

12 September, Rome

TV have extended the 'Special'. F. Terilli has added 40 million plus, with 30% of the sale for me and Toni.

The press conference went quite well.

I received the money—4 million, and 1 million I paid in tax (= 5).

I'll have to take 50% to the Embassy.

Spent the evening with Franco and Giancarla Rosi. Scorsese and Rossellini are a very nice pair.

13 September, Rome

Went running round the shops, and did some work in between. Came back twice to check how Franco Letti was getting on with the editing of the 'Special'.

Went to the dentist for the second time; he has made me a protective plate. He tells me there is no paradontosis. I should not traumatize my teeth, they should be left to recover, and have an operation at some time in the future (pockets and loose teeth).

14 September, Rome

I was not in the editing studio much. All day I was running around shopping and of course didn't buy anything worthwhile, apart, naturally, from things for Larissa. And I am terribly tired. I looked at myself in the mirror and gasped.

I took two million to the embassy.

Today several papers carry reports of the press conference.

Tonino is clamouring that Moravia wants to interview me, but I do not have time.

15 September

Until midday I was dragging around the shops and didn't manage to do it all. I went up and down Via Sannio several times. Tired as a dog.

Did some editing of the 'Special'; not enough time.

In the evening had supper with Tonino together with the Samokhvalovs.

Tried unsuccessfully to ring Moscow at night.

16 September

Tired as a dog, tired as a son of a bitch! Can hardly stand.

All day editing 'Special'. It's now 3.15 in the morning. I have to be up at 5 a.m. Didn't get through to Larissa. I wonder whether they will be there to meet me?

17 September

Flying to Moscow! The plane leaves at 9.30 this morning. Alitalia.

5 October

Mama died today at about one in the afternoon.

She suffered a lot. The last two days she was on Promedol, and I hope did not have so much pain. But what do we know about death, when we know nothing about life? And when we do know something we do our best to forget it again.

Lord! Grant her eternal rest.

8 October

Mama's funeral is today.

(Apart from *Ivan's Childhood* not one of my films was included in the exhibition of sixty years of Soviet film.)

Mama's funeral. It was in Vostryakovsky Cemetery. Now I feel quite defenceless; and no one in the world is ever going to love me

глаза старинного здания, то ли башни,
то ли закругления сферы.

Тишина, солнце, уют, ветер,
прохлада и покой! Я сижу,
гляжу вперёд на этот удивительный
пейзаж и на душе у меня блаженное чувство огромного счастья...

5 октября 1979 г

Сегодня около часа дня умерла мама.
А до этого 2 месяца была Италия
об этом в (дневнике путешествий)
и о «Подземелье» и о Эрколе
А сегодня умерла мама
Она очень страдала последние дни
дни на пределе и надеюсь, не слишком страдала Хотя, что мы знаем о
смерти, когда о жизни то не знаем
ничего А если живём, то справимся
завтра
В мир! Упокой душу её. ✝

as she did. She did not look at all like herself in her coffin. Darling, darling mama! You will see, God willing, I shall do so much more. I must begin all over again! Goodbye, no, not goodbye, because we shall meet again, I am convinced of that.

12 October

A momentous day: I gave Olga a hiding yesterday with a dog's leash. Really hard. I couldn't bear her insolent, sluttish behaviour any longer.

What is more—I'm very glad I did. She's been driving everyone mad for the last three years.

16 October

Friedrich G[orenstein] was telling me about Afanasy Trishkin— apparently a very interesting actor who played in a film made by an Armenian director (Babayan?) from his—Friedrich's—screenplay.

Enn has read *The Imperial Madman* and says it could never be put on. But I think he would be willing to pay me, if I refuse to make any changes to the screenplay. If it's possible, I must take the money and call it a day.

Mossin told me that Andin Genti told him, Mossin, that Tonino Guerra tried to persuade me, Tarkovsky, to stay in Italy. What is that about? Is it true, or is it a way of indicating what they think of me? A hint at the actual situation? What does it mean? Are they preparing the way for refusing to let me go to Italy?

Arkady Strugatsky telephoned today. His mother died as well, two weeks before mama. He was drunk. He is coming to see me on Saturday at 4 o'clock.

Still living in railway stations or out of suitcases, as unsettled as ever. Lara is in the country, ill, with a temperature. Oh, God! We cannot go on like this.

22 October

God! how utterly wretched I feel! To the point of nausea, to the point of hanging myself. I am so lonely . . . and that feeling becomes even worse when you begin to realize that loneliness is death. Everyone has betrayed me or will betray me. I am alone. Every pore of my soul is opening up, and my soul has no defence, because what is starting to seep in is death. I am afraid to be alone. I do not want to live. I am frightened. My life has become intolerable.

30 October

In this world everything is possible.

3 November

100 roubles lent to Valya.

21 November

Spoke at the Moscow Institute of Physics and Technology today.
(+ 150r.) I was introduced to the Rector, Oleg Mikhailovich
Belotserkovsky. We talked about Arseniy.

22 November

A few days ago I had a talk with Seryozha Mitrofanov, we
arranged for him to come here to me. He told me a lot about yoga.
He has one and the same explanation for clairvoyancy and spiri-
tualism and all those things—he says it is a question of gathering
information by means of concentration. He has twice made prog-
nostications for me, once before and now:

1. *Question* (on the first occasion): Ought I to change my life
decisively, almost starting it again from scratch, or at any rate in
new circumstances?

Answer: Yes, I ought. If everything remains as it is, he told me, I
shall be bogged down in money problems and have a great many
enemies. If I change my life, then fame will come to me. (Fame can
only mean work, that is all-important.)

2. *Question* (on this occasion): Do I have the moral right to make
such changes?

Answer: Yes, I do.

3. *Question* (on this occasion): Should I believe what Boris Pasternak told me about making four films?

Answer: No, I should not, it is not true.

4. *Question* (on this occasion): Shall I be able to take Andriusha
with me?

Answer: Yes. And it will depend on a woman. (Larissa? Giancarla? The Ambassador's wife?)

I don't like the scenario Tonino and I wrote. It lacks the most
important thing. There are no real scenes. Never mind, we can
rewrite it. I am waiting now for letters from the TV in Rome.

I spoke at the Electronic Scientific Research Institute. (+ 100r.)

1 December

Masha and I went to Kharkov. I saw Oleg and Lyuda Tochilin. Black Sea coast. I gave four talks (+ 550r.). Then Tbilisi (+ 70). Paradzhanov. I felt terribly sorry for him. He is not being given any work. No income at all. He is obviously frightened of what happened before.

Eldar Shengelay and Temiko Cherkadze were so kind, and took so much trouble. I went to see Gia Konchely. Was introduced to Robert Sturua, and saw his *Richard*; not much impressed. I saw Chubchik, what a delightful man he is.

I have started to pay back my debts.

1. Paid back to Chubchik—130r.
2. Paid back to Alyosha Artemiev—1500r.

3 December

The other day, before Kharkov, Sizov talked to me about what I was going to work on after Italy. He was all for a topical theme, for something on the dissidents. I told him I could make a film about a kolkhoz. He understood that it was no good giving me a topical theme and asked for a list of possible classical subjects.

I gave him one as follows (allegedly Grishin has been pestering him):

Projected work by A. A. Tarkovsky, director, Mosfilm Studios. Moscow, December 1979.

1. *Nostalgia*, screenplay by A. Tarkovsky and T. Guerra. Italy, RAI (State Radio and Television).
2. *The Idiot*, from the novel by F. M. Dostoievsky. Two films, each of two hours, screenplay by A. Tarkovsky.
3. *The Escape*, a film on the last years of Lev Tolstoy. Screenplay by A. Tarkovsky.
4. *The Death of Ivan Ilych* from the novella by L. N. Tolstoy.
5. *The Master and Margarita* from the novel by Bulgakov.
6. *The Double*—a film about Fyodor Dostoievsky based on his biography and his writing.

I went to Poland—to Warsaw, Katowice, Poznan. I saw Beata, and Wajda. Beata wants me to help her with some scenes from Julio Cortazar (Cora). A sensational subject.

It was a ghastly trip. To be formally ticked in Yermash's report. 'An expeditionary force', he called it at one of the dinners. The Poles shuddered. Thirty (!!) Soviet cineastes.

The day before yesterday I gave a talk at the Institute of World Economics (+ 100r.).

I have heard a rumour that *Stalker* is going to be shown on third category screens, and with no publicity—like *Mirror*. N. Zorkaya told me yesterday, in the House of Cinematography—she was to write the publicity. I asked Arkady Strugatsky who is going to write to Zimyanin.

4 December

Evdokia Aleksandrovna's address is apparently Malakhovka (Kazan Line) Fevralskaya Street, 6 (must discover her surname).

(Must return the 2000 and take back Larissa's IOU.)

Volodya Sedov was here. He asked me to tot up our debts to him, they seem to be pretty close to 5000.

Seeing Volchich tomorrow. Must tell him (for the letter to the TV):

1. How long Larissa and I are going for (a year)
2. How much money or salary we shall be getting
3. What actors we need and for how long
4. What sort of set-up. Any services? What?

Pay back debts. Manuscripts. Photographs. Records. Clothes. Dishes, etc.

Religion and art are two sides of a coin.

12 December

Went to Kazan for three days with Masha, and gave 7 talks. Saw Rashid. Masses of people in the hall. Very poor projection, but the interest was evidently tremendous. (I got + 1000r.)

Some of the notes from the audience:

'What philosophical premise underlies your films? *Mirror*, *Andrey Rublyov*? If there is one, what is it? Is it linked with the modern concept of time?'

'Thank you for the fact that you and your films exist. What are you going to be working on now?'

'Why, in Soviet films, do you allow pornographic scenes?'

This was in the museum in Kazan.

'Andrey Arsenevich, in the best possible sense I consider you to be in the tradition of the great Eisenstein. What do you think about that? You said that you do not aim to please people, more or less as the case may be, that that is the least of your concerns. Does the audience's opinion really not concern you? In that case who do you make your films for? Why is there so much water, literally, in all your films? What is it that makes you make films "differently" from everyone else? Please give an answer that goes to the heart of the question. Do you believe in an after-life? It seems to me that you prefer black-and-white film. If that is the case, what makes it superior to colour? What is your opinion? Gafiatullin, engineer.'

'Andrey Arsenevich! If you can, please would you answer the question: What is the worst thing about our Soviet society? Respectfully yours, I. Bork.'

'What brought you to Kazan? The urge to make the essence of your work accessible to the dull-witted audience, or some other aim?'

'Is *Andrey Rublyov* an attempt to penetrate into Russian meta-history, and *Mirror*—into world metahistory? I use the term here in the sense of what lies beyond history.'

'It seems to me that *Mirror* is based on your father's poetry. If it is not, then why, both in the poems and in your film, is there so much water? Are you a Baptist?'

'How for your part do you explain the ban on Tarkovsky films (in other words why are they not on general release?)—Students of Kazan University.'

'Forgive me for asking a question which concerns you only indirectly: will there be another edition of Arseniy Tarkovsky's poems? Thank you for your beautiful, masterly films.'

'This question is from my friend, who was not able to get a ticket for your talk: do you consider yourself *odd*?'

'*Mirror* in my view is your best film, it is a film about life, the most truthful and realistic film about life that we have ever seen. How is it that you have such an amazingly subtle understanding of all the confusion, complexity and splendour of life?'

'A number of actors would love to take part in your films. For many it is the dream of their lives. Most of them probably try not to think about it too much, in order not to live with that constant yearning. What does the actor mean to you? What actually do you want of him?'

'Please tell us about your father. What does his poetry mean to you? What do you think of him as a poet? Is he your favourite poet?'

'Just as boldly as you say Arseniy Aleksandrovich Tarkovsky is the greatest Russian poet, we say that you are a film director of genius. And we shall always be proud to be alive at the same time as you.'

'How do you envisage the cinema of the future?'

'Andrey Arsenevich! Thank you for your films! They force one to think—that of course is the main thing. That is the first point. 2. What do you think of the reaction to your work in the socialist countries and abroad? 3. What do you think of Nikita Mikhalkov? 4. Do you like Shukshin? We wish you every success and thank you in advance for answering our questions—University Students.'

'Comrade Tarkovsky! Several people are still outside the door—your passionate admirers. We hope you will be able to help us.'

'The struggle with officials and bureaucrats involved with the arts is very hard. Does it help you personally in your work or does it merely get in the way?'

'You once said you were waiting for the discovery of a new way of recording reality in a work of art. (X + the author). Does that mean that modern technology does not provide you with the means for complete self-expression?'

'Andrey Arsenevich, my deepest thanks to you for your wonderful films. May you live for a hundred years.'

'To what extent is *Mirror* autobiographical? Was your father in a prison camp under Stalin?'

'Andrey Arsenevich, what nationality are you?'

'Why do you think it is that they are so unwilling to show your films despite the number of people who want to see them?'

'Andrey Arsenevich! The people present here are very well disposed towards you and hope that your visit to us will be easy and relaxed. Please try and talk with this hall full of people as you would with an old friend who has loved you for a long time, fully understands you and shares your views on the art of cinematography.'

'Dear Andrey Arsenevich! Your father is known to have been born in a family associated with the People's Will*. What does that signify? How do you define its *place*? Are you aware of your responsibility in the development of Russian (Soviet) culture? How would you define it? How do you explain the *attraction* of your films for many people? They are intimate, chamber works. Does that fact not put you on your guard? Do you not detect a certain snobbishness

*Revolutionary extremists responsible for the murder of Alexander II.

among your audience (or sections of it)? Going with the fashion and all that.'

'Andrey Arsenevich! Do you and your father always collaborate? If so, what form does the collaboration take? How does he influence your work?'

'Why did you stop working with Vadim Yussov?'

'Is the first episode in *Mirror* (the boy with the stammer) about the fact that you *were not allowed to speak* or that for some *endogenous reason* you were not able to speak?'

'Is the episode in *Mirror* where the boy reads Pushkin's letter to Chaadayev *partly* for the benefit of the people who did not approve of your attitude to Russia?'

'1. What would you have done in life with no cinema? 2. Do you have any affection for your admirers amongst your audience? 3. What do you feel about the view that your films are elitist?'

'Several years after they are completed, your films look as if they have just been made. How do you do it?'

'Andrey Arsenevich, judging by your views on Russian painting, you regard the last few centuries of history with some scepticism. Is this the case?'

'Kolya Burylaev when he came here said that, because some of your audiences fail to appreciate *Mirror*, you were revising your attitude to film narrative. Do you not think that such a revision would be to the detriment of your artistic individuality?'

'Dear Andrey Arsenevich! For those of us who await your every new work, *Mirror* has turned out to be quite different from all your previous films, in its image structure and in its style. What is the explanation: a natural process of development, the maturing of your artistic manner, or the content of the film, which demands that form and no other? It would be very interesting if you would tell in detail how the film was conceived and made.'

'Do you realize the influence which your style has on the development of cinematography in this country as a whole? (In particular your perfect editing of colour and your sound images.)'

'What do you mean, you don't understand why you get slated, when every film you make is about the conflict between people with talent and people without.'

'Andrey Arsenevich! Are you satisfied with your professional life?'

'Andrey Arsenevich, we were expecting a lot from our meeting with you, but what we have had exceeds all our expectations. Thank you for your films and for all you have said today.'

'In your films you champion human values—both on the screen and in the auditorium. Have you ever thought of making a film version of Petrarch's *Book of Conversations*? In terms of the number of actors it is a chamber piece, on the other hand, what scope it allows for ideas!'

'You are a great and truthful artist. I am very grateful to you.'

'Andrey Arsenevich, among contemporary Soviet and foreign writers and poets, who is most important to you? Is there any book which you always have by you? What helps you to find peace at difficult moments of your life?'

'It is extraordinary how you managed to reproduce on screen—so convincingly—the remote fifteenth century. What helped you to achieve this?'

'What is the link between you and Mikhalkov-Konchalovsky? (I am thinking of the film you made together—*Andrey Rublyov*.) What do you think of his films?'

'Your version of *Hamlet* is the most modern production I have ever seen on stage. What prompted you to turn to a radically different art form? Do you intend to work in theatre again? What makes your *Hamlet* so different? What has happened to Solonitsyn? Could that production be put on again?'

'Dear Andrey Arsenevich! Please may we ask you to do something about all your admirers who have been left standing outside the door. There are still some empty seats in the hall, it is a shame for them to be wasted. Please?'

'What is your view of the function of humour in art and the importance of self-irony in the professional life of the artist?'

'What are we to make of the fact that representatives of Soviet culture are leaving the country? And do you know anything about Saveliy Kramarov?'

'Andrey Arsenevich! When and how did you conceive the idea of collaborating with the Strugatsky brothers? What is it that you see in their work for you, as a film director? Lastly, was Rerberg right when he said that the Strugatskys were not capable of producing prose worthy of Andrey Tarkovsky? What is your view of science fiction?—A group of students from Kazan University.'

'Are you interested in philosophy, in its classical form? Which philosophers do you like best? Which of their works?'

'Andrey Arsenevich! Are you ever in conflict with yourself?'

'Do you consider that an artist needs to be approached with a carrot and stick? How do you see the future of our club?'

'Please would you tell me *how old you are*?'

'Tell us a little about your life. Are you happy?'

'When is your book *Juxtapositions* coming out? Is it already being published?'

'Andrey Arsenevich, if it is no trouble for you, could you briefly say what you think of one or two aspects of culture: (*a*) what is your view of decadent poetry, in particular of Russian decadent poetry? (*b*) your attitude to Dostoievsky, Leonid Andreyev, and the other "great humanists" of Russia? (*c*) Have you read Vladimir Solovyov, Florensky, Berdyaev? Have you heard of Dmitri Andreyev? What are your views on Russian philosophy generally? (*d*) What is your attitude to religion?'

'You once wrote in *Foreign Literature* that you do not consider poetry merely to be a genre, and that everything around us is infused with poetry. Does that mean that you do not consider words to be capable of expressing the essence of things; it often strikes me that your films are silent and poetic—which would seem to confirm that view.'

'I have seen all the plays at Lensoviet with Solonitsyn, and all the films in which he acts. I am puzzled to know what it is that you admire in this actor, you use him in so many of your films.'

'In *Andrey Rublyov* you have the Tartars slit-eyed, and talking with a Kazakh accent. You now have the opportunity to look at some Tartars, so that in future you won't make mistakes about our ancestors.'

'It would be interesting to know how long an interval there was between your completing the filming of *Mirror* and its being shown. Why is it, do you think, that many people are so utterly against your films? It surely can't be because audiences are limited in their perceptions, or lack aesthetic training?'

21 December

My God! Time is such a simple, almost primitive idea. It is just a means of material differentiation, a way of uniting us all; for in our external, material lives we value the synchronized efforts of individual people.

Time is just a means of communication. We are swaddled in it, cocooned, and there is nothing to stop us tearing off the wadding of centuries that envelops us so that all our awareness should be common, one, simultaneous.

'. . . Lord, master of my life, take away from me the spirit of idleness, despondency, arrogance, empty talk—grant me the spirit of chastity, humility, forbearance and love . . .'—Prayer.

24 December

'. . . Harrison writes that your picture is unlikely to have any success, because the fiasco of the Vereshchagin exhibition has put people off Russians . . .' (L. N. Tolstoy, Letter to N. N. Gey, August 1890.)

'. . . A work of art will be good or bad because of what the artist says, how he says it, and to what extent he speaks from the heart.' (L. N. Tolstoy, Letter to V. A. Goltsev, September 1889.)

'. . . If I can accept that it is permissible to shut up a madman, I have to accept that it is permissible to kill him.' (L. N. Tolstoy, in a letter to K., 1890.)

' . . . Christian teaching differs from all other religious and social teachings in that it offers people happiness not by means of general rules for the lives of all, but by explaining to each individual the meaning of his life and showing him what constitutes evil in his life and wherein lies his own true happiness.' (L. N. Tolstoy in a letter to the editor of an English newspaper, 15 December 1894.)

'. . . the arguments against patriotism are so clear and obvious that it is impossible to refute them, all one can do is ignore them in silence, pretending that there exist universally accepted, irrefutable proofs, and of course there do not.' (Tolstoy, letter to Grot, 1895.)

'. . . In the last issue I read some reflections on patriotism, suggesting that it can be a good thing. That is sad . . .' (Tolstoy, letter to A. F. Maude, 12 December 1898.)

'. . . Everything I have written in recent years on social questions has expressed, as clearly as I can, the idea that the principal evils besetting people, and the disorder of their lives, stem from government action. One striking illustration of this premise is the fact that the government not only condones, but actually encourages the production and distribution of wine, that lethal poison, just because its sale brings in a third of the budget.' (Tolstoy, from a letter to A. M. Kuzminsky, 1896.)

25 December

'. . . If a feeling of hatred is sent out from one person to another, a diviner will see it as a fine cloud of light of a particular colour, and such a diviner will be able to protect himself from this feeling of hatred, just as a person might protect himself from a physical blow that is aimed at him.' (Rudolf Steiner, *Attaining Knowledge of the Higher Worlds.*)

'...Vainglory entwines itself around everything: I am vainglorious when I fast; but when I break my fast in order to hide my abstinence from others, again I am vainglorious, thinking myself wise; I am overcome with vainglory when I dress in fine clothes; but when I put on poor clothes, I am vainglorious too; if I start to speak, I am overcome with vainglory; but if I am silent again, it overcomes me once more. However this trident is cast, its points will always be uppermost.' (St. John of the Ladder, *Philokalia*, vol. I, p. 573.)

Up to today, debts repaid: 10,510r. I don't know what to do about the remaining debts.

Sizov's people rang. He wants me to go and see him tomorrow. Some sort of 'difficulties' have arisen (obviously to do with Andriushka. God help us!). I think I have to write to someone and go and see Yermash.

'Evil has no nature, nor is anyone naturally evil; for God did not create anything evil. But when, through a desire of his heart, a person gives form to what has no substance, that which he desires comes into being.' (St. Diadochus, Bishop of Photica, *Philokalia III*, p. 9.)

I know that I am a long way from perfection, in fact that I am submerged in imperfection and sin; I don't know how to come to grips with my own worthlessness; I find it hard to see how my life is going to develop. I have become too enmeshed in my life as it is now.

I am sure only of one thing: that I can no longer go on living as I have up till now, working ridiculously little, and at least some of the time going through endless negative emotions which, far from helping, actually destroy that sense of the wholeness of life which is essential for work. I am afraid of living like that. I do not have enough life left to be able to squander my time.

26 December

Lara went to Myasnoye on Sunday to 'wind things up'. Well, things seem to be moving: Sizov advised me to go and see Yermash, who pretended to be amazed that I should want to go abroad with my son. If he receives me tomorrow I shall have to make a row.

27 December

I tried to get an interview with Yermash. Today he is busy. I shall telephone him towards the end of today, in the hope of making it this evening, but I am very doubtful.

I rang, but with no success. I shall try again at 7.0.

At 7.0 I was told that the 2nd secretary would telephone me at 11 o'clock tomorrow, 28th, to tell me when to come, and that Yermash intends to see me before the New Year.

28 December

I telephoned myself, without waiting for a call from the secretary, at 12 o'clock. She (Z.G.) knew nothing about it, no one had given her any message for me. Z.G. promised to find out and to telephone me at home. We shall see.

If I go on living and working as I have been up to now, being carried downstream, I am not going to make it to the shore. The way things are at present in my life (and in my work as well), the less I do the better off I am—the safer for me and the more acceptable to the authorities.

Arayk and Larissa should have come back yesterday, but of course they haven't appeared yet. Katya telephoned, delighted about the bath and the house at Myasnoye. But I was upset, and so was Anna Semyonovna.

It's certain to be burnt down.

Z.G. telephoned from the Committee and told me to ring the Committee at 10 a.m. to be told when to go and see Yermash.

'. . . If all a man's faculties can be concentrated on one point, it will be like a spike; a blunt object cannot penetrate an obstacle, it has to be sharpened, and then it can easily thrust its way through anything.' (From the sayings of the Indian sage, Patanjali.)

29 December

I have been told to report to the Committee at 15.30. Lord, help me! I slept very badly last night; woke up three times. I dreamt of a dead woman being carried along the platform to a train.

The Moscow Committee of the Communist Party have sent some sort of half-open letter to the Mosfilm Studios criticizing the low standard of their films. As examples it quotes *Cat in a Bag*, *Youth on Our Side*, and *Stalker*.

I saw Yermash. He is categorically against Andriushka's coming with us. Of course. I demanded my rights. I said I would fight for my rights by appealing to the highest authority. We 'considered' the screenplay. Not enough Soviet 'reminiscences'. (They can be dragged in.) The problems should be more pointed. (Very well, then, we'll point them.)

I said what I thought of the film directors on the Goskino board. I said I wouldn't be a member of the board even if I were to be asked; and that they had had more than their share and had no right to condemn my films or to be party to the destruction of my life. It was a significant meeting, and very unpleasant. Sizov was there as well as Yermash, I was very glad of that.

I went to Oleg K. on his birthday, and asked him to find out all he can about my (civil) rights in connection with being entitled to travel with my son.

31 December

Lara and Arayk have come back from the country. It's not ready yet. The fireplace still has to be finished and the plumbing in the bath-house.

I do not understand at all how I ought to behave with Yermash. I keep thinking about it all the time.

Life seems to be slipping onto another plane, not a good one. Who is this mysterious woman who is responsible for helping to obtain permission for Andrey to be allowed out? The year is finishing, full of unresolved anxieties, unrealized dreams, and plans which are leading no one knows where.

1980

We have forgotten how to observe. *Instead of observing, we do things according to patterns.*

1980

1 January

We saw the New Year in at home. Everyone is ill, especially Tyapa and Lara. The only person who celebrated with us was Naumov. Not a very cheerful New Year's Eve.

Everybody assures me that this Year of the Monkey is going to be lucky for me. But it has started off unluckily enough for Andriushka. The poor little thing is lying there in his bed in his woollen cap (because of the draught from the window), ill and unhappy.

Lord preserve him!

3 January

Yesterday I went to see Sizov. He said that Yermash's problem is not that he is afraid I might not come back—on the contrary, apparently, he told Sizov that I was reliable in that respect—but that he was afraid of difficulties along the way, new demands on me and on Goskino: travelling, having to go on working trips with the family, which up till now has not happened.

So I pointed out to Sizov that it was a new situation, and as such had to be considered in the context of the national policy towards professional trips abroad of that kind.

Sizov said that in any case Shauro had to be approached first, and that if he was unwilling to be involved, then it would have to be Zimyanin.

I got through to Shauro on the telephone. Or rather, he heard that I was trying to contact him, and rang me himself—he was in such a hurry to dissociate himself from the question of our family departure. He announced that it was nothing to do with him, and a question for Goskino, and those who are in charge of me.

I passed that on to Sizov; he said it was unfortunate that Shauro had got out of taking any decision, and that I must put in a request to see Zimyanin. If he doesn't receive me I ought to write to him.

Tomorrow I shall find out Zimyanin's public number, and ask if he will receive me. Or maybe it would be better to write. Yes, in any case, I'll write a letter.

I have made up my mind to go and see Shkalikov tomorrow, and find out from him why Yermash is pushing me into fighting for rights that have been given me by the Soviet State and of which he is depriving me, when fighting for them could push me into making categorical and extreme demands just because the legitimate ones are not being met. I shall ask him if Yermash actually wants me to demand permission to leave the USSR as a result of the pressure *he* is putting on me.

4 January

I went to see Shkalikov this morning. I told him about my confrontation with Yermash, and complained about how he was treating me.

To cut a long story short: Shkalikov said that we had both over-reacted, in Yermash's case because it was unheard of for Goskino to send people to work abroad taking their children with them; it was all quite new, and that was why Yermash had over-reacted. All the same I said that I was not going to leave it like that, and that I was not going to let Yermash infringe my rights as a *Soviet* citizen. We shall have to wait and see. Shauro is right: it is all up to Goskino. Lora telephoned from Rome. I asked her to tell the TV that the thirteen months for making the film remains unchanged.

5 January

Apparently Afghan patriots have said they will terrorize Soviet citizens abroad in retaliation for the Soviet invasion of Afghanistan. If that is the case, we really have chosen the right moment to go to Italy! Of course, it is not myself that I am worried about.

8 January

Night. I went to see Volchich and told him of the difficulties surrounding our departure. He is writing a letter on behalf of the TV to get Yermash to send me to Rome as soon as possible because of the deadline.

'. . . In Thee do I place all my trust, Mother of God, hide me in the shelter of Thy protection.' (Dostoievsky's prayer, taught him as a child by his nanny.)

'. . . I believe, oh Lord, and profess that Thou art truly the Christ, Son of the living God.' (Prayer before Holy Communion.)

I forgot to write that I gave a talk in the hostel of the Scientific Research Institute, who paid me 100r. And I spent 60r. on the telephone.

Talk at the 'Sakharov' Institute on Lenin Prospekt (+ 90r.)—

'Please can you tell us if this film will be on a wide screen?'

'Are you thinking of having Alissa Freindlich in the leading role of a film based on *The Idiot*?'

'Is there any prospect of *this* film being released without first being cut?'

'How do you explain the growth of general interest in your films?'

The formalities for our journey are being arranged at the Studios: two months for Larissa and me (on orders from Goskino). I rang Shkalikov to ask; he said he knew nothing about it. I said that if that was how things were, I would demand permission to leave the USSR in order to work in Italy. Shkalikov was alarmed by that and said he would find out. We shall see.

I am not going to give in. It's quite on the cards that Yermash could force me to leave home.

10 January

I gave a talk yesterday (+ 80r.) and went to see Sizov, where I made the position clear. He is going to summon me now.

Sizov has been landed with the problem of our Italian assignment and travel permits. We both found that funny. He wants (or rather, he wanted) to designate the trip as being for the purpose of drawing up the contract—just for Larissa and me. But I am scared that after that they will simply extend the assignment and we shall be left without Andriushka. And if we go back to Moscow they'll find an excuse not to allow us to collect Andriushka. If I go alone to draw up the contract, I shall not start work until I've got Larissa and Andrey out of here.

I am going to consult Volchich tomorrow, and Dobrokhotov on the 12th.

Toni telephoned from Rome.

They have sent me a text to revise and translate as subtitles for the Cannes Festival (?!). It's simply a copy of the editing script. I shall have to explain that I have no intention of doing their work for them.

Volchich told me that *Rublyov* has been listed among the world's ten best films.

11 January

I had a dream last night.

First of all I was at the North Pole, and a polar bear was warming me in the snow.

Then, some peasants were giving me a very good book. It was morning, we were in a vegetable garden and it had been raining all night.

And in the end I was in Rome with a film team, and I said it was a miracle, because I hadn't believed it possible that I would be in Italy again in order to make the film.

I am editing the subtitles, because formally speaking they are right, in terms of the content and length of the titles.

12 January

On Monday Sizov will be sent a letter from Rome saying that I have to go there immediately in order to draw up the draft contract. Then I shall come back here together with a representative of RAI who will sign the contract on behalf of the Italians (once it has been agreed).

Tonechka telephoned from Rome. I told him how things stand with the contract.

15 January

Arayk has brought four silver belts (295or.) from Yerevan. Very pretty.

A Georgian one for—600
Persian (from Daghestan)—600
Bulgarian — 500
Armenian —1250
_____

295or.

They are issuing the papers for me to go to Rome to draw up the contract (for some reason, together with Larissa). I shall go by myself and try to be back as quickly as possible.

18 January

Talk at the Moscow Physical Institute (+ 100r.). They gave me a holograph.

'An enormous number of people in this hall admire Arseniy Aleksandrovich Tarkovsky as a great Russian poet. Please convey our respects to him.'

'Why do you make so few films? In twenty years (since 1961) you have made only five films, whereas E. Ryazanov, for example, has made about fifteen.'

'What for you is the hardest part of making a film? To what extent are you satisfied with the results of your work? Which of your films do you like best, which is dearest to you? What do you see as the goal of your work?'

24 January

'. . . Poets are above other people because they understand about people. It goes without saying that many poets write in prose—for instance Rabelais or Dickens. Snobs are above other people because they don't want to understand them. For them people's tastes and attitudes are merely vulgar prejudices. Snobs make people feel stupid; poets make them feel more intelligent than they ever dared imagine. However, the conclusions people draw from this are not entirely logical. Poets admire people and open their arms to embrace them, and in return they are crucified and stoned. Snobs despise people, and the latter crown them with laurel wreaths.'

Questions from the audience.

'Unfortunately we—that is, the majority of cinema-goers—are accustomed to having ideas dished up to us ready-made. Are you not afraid that many people will fail to understand your films?'

'How do you explain Efros' walking out of *Rublyov*? What are the ideas you express in *Rublyov*? You are referred to as a neo-Fascist, how would you counter that accusation?'

26 January

Night. I went to see Aaron. He is nice, and in many ways naive.

A few days ago Academician Sakharov was exiled to Gorky. (Shcherbitsky?) Protests are being lodged all over the world. The U.S. are mobilizing. So are we.

I think they are graciously awarding me a *kammerjunker's* uniform* (i.e. People's Artist of the RSFSR).

*A reference to Pushkin, who was made *kammerjunker*, or gentleman of the chamber, by Nicholas I, a distinction he deeply resented.

Daytime. I have received 1500r. from Arayk's brother in Yerevan. At last the militia station are promising to issue us with a passport.

Goskino got in touch with me to tell me to ring Yermash. I did so. He congratulated me on my new title. (Wonderful manners: I have to telephone the minister in order for him to congratulate me.) He expressed interest in Djuna when we talked of Mossin, and said 'we really ought to meet.' What can he have to say to me? Does he want to assure me that the authorities are well disposed to me? To hell with that.

Lena Nekhoroshev telephoned. Because of the Italian assignment we shall have to write him a request for an extension of the deadline of the *Idiot* script.

This morning someone called Lesovoy burst into our flat. He had given me some of his short stories to read and wanted me to tell him what I thought of them. I had promised to do so in writing, because I didn't want to waste time with him. He had read my letter, and come bursting into the house (when Larissa and I were not even dressed) and flung the letter down on the table, announcing—without bothering to take his hat off his head—that I have to be a man. The poor chap had clearly decided that I was afraid to tell him my opinion of his work, and that I had masses of time for him to use as he feels inclined. Yet another schizophrenic. Great.

The *kammerjunker's* uniform. And in what sort of company!

Evening Moscow, 26 January 1980—'For their contribution to the development of Soviet cinematography, the Praesidium of the Supreme Soviet of the RSFSR has awarded the title of People's Artist of the RSFSR to the following directors of Mosfilm Studios: Lotyanu, Emil Vladimirovich; Mikhalkov (Konchalovsky), Andrey Sergeich; Saltykov, Alexey Alexandrovich; Tarkovsky, Andrey Arsenevich.'

'What film are you working on at the moment? Thank you for all you do. Every film you make is a joy!'

29 January

Yesterday I gave a talk at the club of Moscow Aeronautical Institute. (They have promised to transfer 100r. to my account.)

Larissa and I decided today that she would go to see her Tartar doctor in Kazan, and I would wait for my passport for Rome. (Sizov said I would be leaving sometime in the first ten days of

February.) That will give Larissa time for her treatment. After all, ten days in our terms will mean two weeks.

It is clearly worth my going to Rome to prepare the contract there; then Italian television will ask Surikov to come out and sign the contract, and I shall be able to stay there and wait for Larissa and Andriushka without coming back to Moscow.

Larissa says she will be able to press here for them to be allowed out, and I shall be more useful there for putting on pressure at that end.

I spoke at the Central Scientific Research Institute (+ 100r.).

Tomorrow I shall telephone Yermash, and in the evening Tyapa and I are going to the 'Illusion'.

30/31 January

Lara and Arayk have gone to Kazan to see the doctor. I gave her 1000r. (She took two of my old suits and a sheepskin coat with her to sell.)

I do hope that the Tartar doctor, whom for some reason I trust, will really help her. God grant it!

31 January

Lara telephoned. She arrived safely and has taken the room that I stayed in; she liked it.

Suffering . . .
The story of a lonely man who suffers from his loneliness and then suddenly finds that he is not alone after all (unexpected relatives) and is more unhappy than ever.

The problem of communication—of distorted communication. The problem of good and evil.

2/3 February

Night. Yesterday I gave a talk at the Progress publishing house (+ 100r.).

It was a good audience. Solonitsyn was there, he came to see the film for the first time.

Lara is in Kazan. Tyapa has gone off with his aunt for Saturday and Sunday.

I am worn out by all this fruitless, exhausting waiting.

The night of February 3rd.
I went to see my father today in Peredelkino; Garik P. was with

him and took a lot of photographs. I taped an interview with my father about our family history.

4 February

This morning I telephoned Lara. She is just as she was, only today she's feeling better. (I want to send Kochevrin's friend—Sasha—to Kazan with his diabetes.)

As for my trip, I simply don't understand what is going on. The news on the radio is appalling. I shall have to talk to Sizov.

5 February

I rang Lara, everything is fine, except that she is not feeling well. I spoke to Sizov: still no news about Italy.

Giving a talk somewhere on the Berezhkovsky embankment through friends of the Kostins (+ 150r.).

6 February

Sent a letter to *Art*:

> To B. V. Vishnyakov, Director,
> Art Publishing House,
> from A. A. Tarkovsky

Dear Boris Vladimirovich!

First of all I should like to express my consternation at the fact that having returned our manuscript (to Olga Surkova and myself) for revision, the publishers have for two years (!) not taken the trouble to find out whether I agree to the comments made, what my views are on this matter, or whether I intend to do further work on the manuscript. This leads me to conclude that the publishers are in no particular hurry to have a revised version of the book. A further clear sign of prejudice against our manuscript lies in the choice of readers: neither D. Orlov nor V. Murian could be considered the kind of serious film critics who should, in my view, have been asked to read this work. Their attitude to my work was clear before they started, and the extraordinarily low level of their comments fails to provide any basis for constructive professional discussion.

Essentially I wish to make the following points:

First, the only criticism I am willing to accept relates to that section of the book where there is a discussion of different categories of cinema viewer: I now consider that the division between them is not very satisfactory. I am therefore ready to make cuts in that section, at the same time going deeper and more broadly into the question of the relationship between artist and people.

Second, I absolutely reject the editors' view that I ought to cut out the general reflections on aesthetics, the philosophy of art, and other general questions, in order to devote more space to professional issues. I find the suggestion entirely unacceptable.

Nor can I undertake to include in my book 'more about the Soviet cinema' and its protagonists: those names which occur in the course of my exposition are the ones that are essential to the development of my ideas. I reserve the right to quote those works which I regard as necessary references in the context of my exposition. Incidentally, the accusation of 'subjectivism' levelled at me by the publishers, echoing the view of the two readers, leaves me completely bewildered. Since I am writing about my *own* experience in filmmaking, how can I express any ideas other than subjective ones? I am not writing some textbook as required reading, but offering my own thoughts and reflections, and inviting the reader to share in them. Indeed, as the reviewers rightly point out, the reader is at liberty to compare my concept of the art of cinematography with the dozens of others published in this country, some of which support my ideas while others contradict them; in fact, that is precisely what I suggest—that is why our book is called *Juxtapositions*, with its open-ended structure and its avoidance of precise formulations: conclusions are to be drawn from the juxtaposition of different theses. The terms of reference include a series of other points of view; clearly some people are going to agree with me and others not. In any case I did not see it as part of my task to please everyone.

In the light of all that I have said, I would ask you to let me know at your earliest convenience what possibilities you envisage for further collaboration between us. If it is acceptable to you, the publishers, Olga Surkova and I are willing to return the manuscript within a month, having made a number of—largely editorial—corrections.

5.2.80

People's Artist of the RSFSR
(A. Tarkovsky)

Earlier I received the following from them:

State Committee of the Council of Ministers of the USSR for
Publishing, Printing and the Book Trade
Art Publishers, 103009, Moscow, Sobinovsky Street, 6.
Tel. 203.56.05; 203.58.72

> Comrade Tarkovsky, A. A.
> Comrade Surkova-Shushkalova, O. E.

Dear Andrey Arsenevich,
  On the 30th March 1978 the manuscript of *Juxtapositions* was
returned to you for revision together with our comments
on the book. Up till now we have received no reply from you.
We should be interested to know what your intentions are
with regard to further work on the manuscript and when you
propose to let us have it back duly revised.
  We would ask you to answer promptly as at the present
moment we are finalizing our plans for 1981–2.

> Yours sincerely,
> E. M. Efimov,
> Deputy Chief Editor

This letter was sent by courier marked 'Urgent, 4.2.80 by
courier.'
They don't want the book at all. That is clear. I shall have to
edit the manuscript and have it published in I[taly].

Larissa is in Kazan, having treatment; I am sitting waiting for
a fair wind. Sizov still knows nothing about when I am going.
Depressing . . .
Should I work on the book?
I am beginning to have thoughts about living in the country . . .
Tonino telephoned today. The Italians are nonplussed, as far
as I can judge. God knows how it is all going to end. These are uncertain times, nothing is stable. What lies ahead? What lies ahead
for Russia? Lord, save us . . .

8 February
  I spoke to Larissa. She needs medicines.

1. Phosphotiomin
2. Festal (tabl.) (W. Ger.)
3. Pansinorm-forte (Yug., W. Ger.)
4. Folin-Floride
5. L. I. V. –52.

Prescriptions have to be got for all these medicines. (Sasha B).
And V. Sedov will have to be asked to get them from the 'chemist'.

Not a single word about the Italian business.

I telephoned the hospital to thank Mossin for his congratulations
on my *kammerjunkerdom*.

When we talked on the telephone Tonino wanted to know
whether I was thinking about *Nostalgia* ... No, I am not thinking
about it: I can't work when I am not sure of anything. And I
should have been working long ago! Long ago!

But I do believe! I do believe that God will not abandon me.

10 February

Two Fridays ago Lara and Arayk and I went to the House of
Cinema and saw one and a half films by Jancsó: *Hungarian Rhap-
sody* and *Allegro Barbaro*. We didn't stay to the end. Monstrous
rubbish. Tasteless, pretentious, and portentious; inferior and vulgar.
He is some kind of crazed pupil of Paradzhanov, without any kind
of talent.

Today Tyapus and I went to the cinema to see some Japanese
cartoons; and to the planetarium to a lecture on civilizations on
other planets. Tyapus was very much impressed by the idea of our
possible isolation in space, and the reason for life starting on earth.
He and I must go to the Pushkin Museum on a weekday, we didn't
get in today. There was such a long queue outside that I could not
face it in the frost.

Stanislav Kondrashev had a party. He is a nice fellow, I must say.

12 February

I telephoned Larissa, she said that all sorts of things were wrong,
and that she ought to stay on in Kazan for at least a month. Her
liver is not right, her cardiogram was bad, and so on. Poor Larochka! She was very upset, and so was I. Oh, Lord! Will our troubles
ever end!

19 February

Today Bogomolov telephoned, chief editor of Goskino. There is going to be a meeting on Saturday between the editorial board and representatives of the Goskino of different republics. There will be a discussion. I don't want to go. It somehow smacks of provocation. Still nothing about Italy. I shall have to go and see Yermash.

Telephoned Lara. She is having treatment and feeling ill. And I am missing her dreadfully.

25 February, Kazan

On Friday I came down here to Lara. We are staying at the Youth Centre, in the same room—533—as I had when I came here to speak.

Mursharanov is certainly a wonderful doctor, perhaps even a genius. Of course like any other outstanding personality he is endlessly attacked. He is the kindest and most selfless of people.

Larissa is still unwell, but better than she was. Fazil Mursharanov says that had she left it another two months he would not have taken her on.

We must try and arrange it so that Larissa can stay on here as long as possible. He has taught me how to cure my teeth by massaging particular points.

Larissa is asking me to stay here with her, but I don't know how long I can be away because of Moscow and Italy.

We telephoned home, and for the moment nothing awful has happened in our absence.

18 March

I was induced to appear at the All Unions meeting of film-makers. It was terrible. This is what happens when one is not speaking out of a real inner necessity, but for 'a good cause'. I vow never again to make just any speech on the request of the authorities.

At the end of my crazy appearance I quoted Engels, saying 'The more an author conceals his views, the better for the creation of an artistic work.'

The voices in the hall grew louder. I was told later that these words had incited the public—I myself didn't notice anything. However, the reaction of Zimyanin, who was present at the meeting, was conspicuous. He has obviously never read Engels in his life and therefore thought that I was being provocative.

I went home with the feeling of having caused a total catastrophe. I still suspect that my appearance has done me (or could still do me) a lot of harm.

Today Sizov tried to get in touch with me. But I am down with 'flu, or a cold. Yesterday evening I was running a temperature.

Jas Gavronsky has asked me to drop by his place as soon as I am back on my feet. It seems there are some new developments regarding Italy; well, there is a God.

I hope to fly to Rome soon, in order to work out a draft contract between me, Sovinfilm and RAI, which will favour everyone (except me, of course!). It would be fantastic—in case I do not return to Moscow again—if one of the functionaries of the film department could be persuaded to come to Rome and sign the contract there. From Rome it would be easier for me to put pressure on Goskino and Yermash. In any case, I must pack up everything now—but what should I take along? The problem is—should I pack things for a long period? Or should I in any case take my heavy and cumbersome archive with me? I just don't know what to do.

28 March

I have discovered where that Engels quotation is from: K. Marx and F. Engels, *Works*, 2nd edition, vol. 37, p. 36, Letter to Margaret Harkness, London, April 1888.

Lora telephoned again. She told me about the Visconti prize. It is a prize that was established after Visconti's death, and is awarded annually to foreign directors. Up till now it has been given to Bresson (which is very good) and Wajda (rather less good). The prize will be given me at a special ceremony in September. Apparently it is very prestigious.

I have written a screenplay for Arayk, in two parts, for a short film.

I've made a note of Sophia's telephone in Stockholm. She has a letter from Bergman for me. As soon as I arrive in Rome I have to ring her before 12 (Moscow time): she is always at home.

I must start negotiations with the producer the moment I get to Rome.

Perhaps I should ask to be given a flat somewhere straightaway.

30 March, Moscow

List of some of the prizes awarded my films:
The Steamroller and the Violin (1960)
   1. 1st Prize, New York Student Film Festival   1961

Ivan's Childhood (1962)
2. Venice, Golden Lion Grand Prize   1962
3. San Francisco, Golden Gate Prize for best
   director   1962
4. Acapulco, Nalence's Head   1962
5. Warsaw, Polish Film Critics Club Prize for best
   film of 1963   1963
6. Lublin, Czarcia-Zapa Prize for best foreign film   1963
7. New York, D. Selznick, Silver Laurel
   (American Critics' prize)   1963
8. Delhi, National Exhibition Prize, etc.   1963

Andrey Rublyov (1966)
9. Filtre Prize for best foreign film   1973
10. Helsinki, prize for best film of year   1973
11. Diploma, Stratford International Film
    Festival   1973
12. Cannes, FIPRESCI Prize   1969
13. Azolo (Italy) Grand Prize, International
    Film Festival   1973
14. Belgrade, Festival of Festivals, 1st Prize for
    best film of Festival   1973
15. Belgrade, Prize for best film (Filmworkers'
    Union)   1973
16. Belgrade, 2nd Prize of Audience Jury   1973
17. Paris, Crystal Star of French Academy for best
    female role   1972
18. Paris, Film Critics' Association Prize   1968

Solaris (1972)
19. London, Film Festival, Prize for best film of
    year   1972
20. Cannes, Grand Jury Prize (2nd Prize)   1972
21. Cannes, Prize of Evangelical Centre   1972
22. Stratford International Festival, Diploma of
    Honour   1973

Mirror (1973)
23. Italnoleggio, State Distributors' Prize in
    St. Vicente   1 Apr.   1979
24. Italy, David-Donatello Prize/Lucchino
    Visconti   1980

Stalker (1979)
25. Cannes, French Critics' Prize   1980
26. Cannes, Prize of International Christian
    Association   1980

31 March, Moscow

Night. I went to Sovinfilm today and talked to Boris Mikhailovich Pavlov. We discussed a number of problems, and then rang Sizov and went over to see him at Mosfilm. It was decided that I must go to Rome immediately to sign an interim contract, in order to start preparatory work on the film; and that the contract proper, specifying the sums for services in the USSR for RAI, could be signed later.

Evidently I shall be flying on Monday, or—better—on Tuesday. It will depend on the plane timetable.

Lora and Tonino telephoned today. If it were not for Easter I should be flying out on Sunday.

Tomorrow I am flying to Kazan to Lara for two days.

3 April

ON DIFFERENT MERIDIANS—*Trud** (27.3.80)

The celebrated Italian Lucchino Visconti Director's Prize for 1980 has been awarded to Soviet filmmaker Andrey Tarkovsky.

The jury declared Andrey Tarkovsky's work to be outstanding in originality, poetry and range.

Arrived back from Kazan today after twenty-four hours there with Lara. She telephoned today. She had a dream about Maria Ivanovna, who was asking Lara to be consistent and 'put everything in order.' I feel so miserable without Larochka!

11 April, Rome. Leonardo da Vinci

Back in Rome, and back in the same hotel; not only that, I am in the same old room—511! I feel that is somehow significant. I went to the Television Studios. Endless problems with the contract because in TV there is no such thing as an 'interim' contract, nor could there be. I shall have to get in touch with Sizov immediately and consult him, particularly as this 'interim' contract was his idea.

I explained at the TV how 'we' have to be talked to.

*'Labour'.

12/13 April, Rome

Night. Tonino and Lora and I went to see Antonioni today. He is going to America to arrange about working on a film with Coppola. Enrica has changed too.

I tried to telephone Sophia today, but couldn't get through. Tomorrow she is going to ring.

Took Mama's gold watch to be mended.

Morning.

Sophia telephoned from Stockholm. I didn't quite understand what is happening about Bergman, but in any case I don't think there is any letter from him. He simply intends to invite me to Sweden.

Still have not seen either Samokhvalov or Narymov, and I must.

13 April, Rome

Sophia rang this morning from Stockholm. She is going to Riga. She gave me Bergman's address just in case.

13/14 April

Night. Spent today with a retired general who uses a metal detector to hunt for treasures in Etruscan graves, and steals them.

Tonino suggests that we cut *Stalker* for the Italian market rather than letting the distributors do it. That seems sensible. First and foremost the sequence on the meadow (without the Stalker).

15 April

Rang Narymov this morning and said that Larissa's salary would be 300,000 a week. Must find out as soon as possible how Larissa is to pay money into the Embassy, and how much.

Editing *Tempo di Viaggio* from first thing this morning. Cut six minutes from the first half.

Had supper with Acalla (an actor who went to Moscow with the Piccolo Theatre of Milan) and his wife, Julia Dobrovolskaya, together with Tonino and Lora.

16/17 April

Editing. Cut it to 1 hour 3 minutes. It is much better, but we have to rerecord, and Franco T. says there is no money. We'll have to find a way round it.

This evening Tonino and Lora and I went to see Rosi. Carlos was there again, and a lot of squits with big names, and a few Spaniards.

Tonino has talked to the distributor who bought *Stalker*. He suggested that it would be worth asking Goskino to send the film to Cannes. He may be going to buy some footage of the making of *Stalker*. We shall see.

17 April

Morning. I don't know why I didn't write this yesterday: Sartre died the day before yesterday. (So did Rodari.)

Very sadly, in a last interview he repudiated many of the principles which he had upheld and preached to the young. But we were aware long before that of where he was heading towards the time of his death. It wasn't that he aged as death approached, but his perceptions became so superficial.

For instance he admitted that he had not divulged his impression of the USSR (when he was there in 1954) because he was afraid to 'think ill' of us.

Well, well.

I must read him.

He wrote an awful lot!

17/18 April

Edited *Tempo*. Unfortunately there will be no rerecording on Monday. We couldn't make it.

Supper with Samokhvalov and Narymov, and distributor of *Stalker* (with his suite) who asked our people to help Gino Agostini to get *Stalker* over to Cannes. Samokhvalov promised to help. We shall see. Tonino and Franco T. had seen him the day before.

There seems to be no progress with the contract: they (i.e. ours) want the Italian TV people to go over to Moscow to sign.

21 April

Went to see Narymov this morning and telephoned Yermash. He wants the Italians to fly to Moscow to sign the contract.

Went on editing. I'd like to finish by tomorrow.

Went to TV, met Fichera, Renzo, Canepari and some others. I told them of my conversation with Yermash. We discussed all the details of the contract.

I bought some medicines: something for my teeth, and ointment for eczema. And some fructose. Here it only costs 3800 l. a pound!!!

22 April

Editing is finished (on the *Journey*). I hour 3 minutes.

I met Jas Gavronsky at Tonino's. He is the RAI representative in Moscow and is going there to pay off Volchich. I asked him to take some Adelfan for Anna Semyonovna. Telephoned Moscow. Olga is not working.

Arayk has gone to Kazan and will go back with Larissa.

I have a sore throat; must take some medicine. (Medicinal tooth-paste costs 2500, and Adelfan 1160.)

If only the contract could be settled!

Here it has been decided that Columbino will go to Moscow with the draft. They'll thrash it out with him, then he will go back to Rome for Grassi's signature, and back again to Moscow to sign the contract.

I must ask them (the RAI people) to convince Goskino that it is not possible for me to go to Moscow. (At any rate until the contract has been signed.)

24 April

Felt ill yesterday from first ·thing in the morning: sore throat, and obviously a temperature. We worked: Tonino and I started work on the script.

I felt gradually worse and in the end had to leave and come back to the hotel. It's cold in the hotel, they've turned the heating off in Rome but the weather is foul. There have been two thunder-storms and it's very cold.

This morning I woke up ill. For the time being I shall stay in bed.

25 April

Morning. In bed. Feeling ill. 'Flu.

Must ring Samokhvalov today and find out if Pavlov is coming with an 'interpreter' on Monday to deal with the contract. And what about our arrangement with Yermash? Do the Italians have to go to Moscow?

I asked Franco T. yesterday to find me a Russian translation of Spengler's *Decline of the West*.

I should really like to have Jill Claybergh in the principal role!

Two interviews with me have come out: *Ronda* and *Cosivecha*.

I feel there is an enormous amount of work still to be done on the script of *Nostalgia*. Is it right that Gorchakov is killed by chance in the street? Maybe he should die of a heart attack? He does have a weak heart.

For the moment Tonino and I have decided to leave unchanged:

1. The madman on the horse.
2. The *Madonna del Parto*.
3. Bagno-Vignoni. With the illness, the dream, the man with the bicycle.
4. The beginning in the Palm Hotel.

Spoke by telephone to Samokhvalov about whether Pavlov and Yerovshin would be coming from Sovinfilm. He said that despite the new information they would be coming because it had been 'planned'. Wonderful reasoning . . . !!

Oh well, let them come! I must impress on the TV people how important it is to get the final contracts out of them.

Samokhvalov and the Ambassador are going to Capri for two days.

I have been invited to a celebration at the Embassy on 1 May.

I must clearly start a special notebook for ideas related to work. It is not at all practical to have to rummage my way through diaries in search of crucial notes. I could buy a really beautiful notebook here.

I have been in bed all this time. Gutman rang, he wants to take a parcel to Moscow.

Eugenio Rondini, the sound mixer, telephoned. He sympathized and invited me to go out to his house in the country in a few days' time.

Whatever happens I must meet up with Gutman tomorrow.

I have a filthy cold, coughing, streaming nose and streaming eyes, a really nasty 'flu.

Must telephone Moscow tomorrow, perhaps Larissa has arrived.

28 April

For some reason Pavlov and Yerovshin have been delayed. It seems to me that Narymov is being rather cautious in his dealings with me. It may be because Rostotsky is here and has let it be known what he thinks of me, or because Narymov himself has been ticked off by Moscow for putting me in this set-up. I could be wrong, but it seems to me that something is going on.

Fono-Roma are on strike so we have not been able to rerecord the 'Special'. The strike will be on tomorrow as well.

Tonino and I did some work. We have thought of a brilliant second half, marrying *La Candela* and *Nostalgia*.

29 April

Tonino and I worked pretty unsatisfactorily. The new version is not going well. Tonino says it's because 'we want so much.' Of course we do.

At Fono-Roma, where I was retaping the music from the 'Special' recordings, I met Rostotsky, who rushed to hug and kiss me.

I can imagine what he was trying to cover up. God, what a bastard he is!

I telephoned home and talked to Tyapus.

Better not to think about it . . .

30 April

I have arranged the music for recording the 'Special'.

It has been pouring all day—the weather is quite frightful.

Tomorrow I am going to the Embassy with Samokhvalov:
1 May

1 May

An appalling day! Samokhvalov invited me to the Embassy, and in fact I was glad to go, particularly as I met Valentin Iv., who turned out to be a charming, friendly man. He promised to help over the release of the film. We're going to try and meet on Monday.

But as for that *truthite*, the *Pravda** correspondent in Rome—I found him infuriating. Vulgar, stupid creep. I could hardly bear to sit at the same table with him (at Leontiy A's).

In a word, a mass of negative emotions.

I am pinning my hopes on the Ambassador.

I could describe today's events in detail, but it's too distasteful. What unspeakable people!

2/3 May

Night. Tonino and I did some pretty good work—the screenplay (his outline) is coming on well.

In the evening we were invited to Renzo Rosso. He is a writer and works on Channel 2 of RAI. He has a nice wife, a dubbing actress. We talked a lot, and of course argued a lot. He is a subtle, good-hearted and intelligent man.

*Pravda means truth.

3 May, Porto Nuovo, Boschetto, on the way to Loreto

The first episode, in the mist. *Madonna del Parto*. The pregnant women come crowding here like witches, to ask the Madonna to ensure them a safe delivery, and so on. The mist lies in layers around the church.

An amazing thing happened to me today. We were in Loreto, where Franco Terilli was praying to his patron, one of the popes. In Loreto there is a famous cathedral (rather like Lourdes) in the middle of which stands the house in which Jesus was born, transported here from Nazareth. While we were in the cathedral, I felt it was wrong that I can't pray in a Catholic cathedral; not that I cannot, but that I don't want to. It is, after all, alien to me. Then later, quite by chance, we went into a little seaside town called Porto Nuovo, and into its small, tenth century cathedral. And what should I see on the altar but the Vladimir Mother of God.

Apparently some Russian painter had, at some time, given the church this copy of the Mother of God of Vladimir, evidently painted by him.

I couldn't believe it: suddenly to see an Orthodox ikon in a Catholic country, when I had just been thinking about not being able to pray at Loreto.

It was wonderful.

We had supper in Franco Terilli's house. Dino was there as well (Tonino's brother) and Maria, and a wealthy couple who deal in water. The supper was delicious.

4 May, Rome

We spent the night in Franco and Julia's villa in Boschetto. I had a terrifying dream, and when I woke up I remembered it very clearly, and had a strong feeling that it should be interpreted in the best sense imaginable. Then I went back to sleep. And when I woke up again I could not remember it. I can remember that it was something to do with the Mother of God of Vladimir. And it was something very good.

9 May

Two meetings with our people in RAI. They started by naming some unheard-of sum, but it was pointed out that RAI is a state organization, and that if it were to accept the Soviet terms, it would not be able to put on anything apart from *Nostalgia* for the rest of the year, because that would have absorbed the entire annual budget.

I had to draw up phoney charts of phoney scenes because RAI had to have precise costings for the filming to be done in the USSR.

Tonino and I have not yet finished the script.

They are evidently going to draw up an interim contract in order to start shooting. So I shall be able to stay in Rome and work, and the main contract will be signed without me. And it will be easier for Larissa to make arrangements for coming here with Andriushka.

I have had enough of negotiations, and of the bungling. Lora's Italian is not good enough.

10 May

Tonino and I have been working quite satisfactorily. I have decided to change the 'Moon' to a misty cloud, either at dusk or at dawn.

We went to an exhibition by a ghastly artist friend of Tonino's called Sugi. He paints corpse-like figures—hideous and repulsive; and he doesn't even have a style of his own.

All unspeakably dreary and depressing.

In the evening we had supper with de Chirico's widow in her flat in Piazza di Spagna. Unfortunately none of his works are in Rome except for some lithographs. Isa Lvovna has taken them all to Paris. There is going to be an exhibition there, and afterwards in London and Munich.

11 May

Tonino and I went to look at a ruined church with a tree growing inside it. Beautiful. There is a peasant's house beside it.

On the way back Tonino showed me a villa, on the outskirts of Rome, which has been abandoned because of ghosts. It looks amazing.

12/13 May

Went to the television studios. RAI and Sovinfilm are beginning to talk the same language.

'Our' people are going to sign an interim agreement now, guaranteeing that the work will be carried out, and then they are leaving. Then in June RAI will sign a contract in Moscow.

For the moment I shall presumably stay in Rome to work on the costing of the film with RAI.

Renzo Rosso interviewed me before he went to Cannes.

Stalker is apparently going to be shown by a French distributor.

There was a fairly provocative piece by a woman journalist in *La Republica*.

Tonino and I worked quite well.

13 May

At the television studios all morning: the interim agreement was signed, which means I am at least entitled to embark on some preparatory work.

This afternoon Tonino and I worked. Next Thursday (22nd) the script has to be delivered for Cristaldi to read.

Fichera said evasively that he would rather have an Italian actress for the interpreter.

Spoke to Sophia in Stockholm last night. I asked her to pass on to Bergman the idea of a collaboration between the three of us: Bergman, Antonioni and myself. If he refuses, it would be worth thinking about someone else. Kurosawa? Bunuel? I don't think he wants to make any more films.

Oh, yes—some important news: today, 13 May, *Stalker* was shown by a French producer (distributor) who has bought it for 500,000 dollars. (!)

So far I only know the reaction of one critic—the one that liked the 'Special' so much. Kozevich (?). There will obviously be something in the papers tomorrow.

The film was evidently shown as a 'surprise', as Wajda's *Man of Marble* was last year.

This evening at supper I gathered from what Narymov said that Goskino intend to give us visas again for three months, so that we shall not have the right to take Andriushka with us. I don't think that legally or in fact this will stop us making a row and demanding that our son accompany us. But I am frightened. This is an unforeseen and alarming development.

14/15 May

Staggering notices in all the papers on *Stalker* at Cannes. A resounding success. Rondi calls it a work of genius, a great film. In fact it would be embarrassing to repeat all that he says. Altogether—a furore.

Tonino and I have been working: we still can't get the script right.

Spent the evening with Enrica and Michelangelo. Did some good meditation.

Talked to Olga in Moscow. Larissa is not coming for another two days. Tyapus was already asleep. (Darling boy.)

It's a pity that the picture (*Stalker*) cannot now go to Venice.

Not that it really matters now after press notices like that. I don't remember any director ever having things like that said by the critics.

15 May

Tonino and I finished the outline of the new script today. Toni said, 'That's a film I'd like to see.' It really has worked out quite well.

Rondi telephoned from Cannes. He said that *Stalker* was a sensation. No one can talk about anything else. Kurosawa's *The Double*—a film about the Samurai—is very good, but not nearly as good as *Stalker*. I thanked Rondi for his reviews. He immediately called me a genius. Well, I suppose it's better to be a genius than a nonentity, all else being equal.

I had a telephone call from Cristaldi, who is on his way to Cannes. He has agreed to produce *Nostalgia*. Tonino suggested to him that it would be no bad thing if he were to pay us for the screenplay as such. The excitement over *Stalker* is just what is needed to get our project off the ground.

16/17 May

Worked all day.

Sophia telephoned yesterday from Stockholm. Bergman was very interested in our idea of working together on a film, only unfortunately he is completely booked up until 1983. He very much wants to meet me. Sophia says he has seen *Rublyov* ten times.

Martine Offroy rang from Cannes, and talked about the tremendous success of *Stalker*; on the insistence of the audience, the jury and the critics it is going to be shown a second time.

Gaumont are showing an interest in the production of *Nostalgia*.

17 May

The script will be finished and ready tomorrow. Tonino was dictating it to his typist all day.

I telephoned Moscow—Larissa is back! How I have been longing for her. But it doesn't look as if her stay in Kazan has done very much for her health. In two weeks' time she is going to Kazan again for two days. The two days that I spent with her there were far too short, I hardly had time to say anything. I have eczema on my face again. The ointment Lora got me doesn't help at all.

Read Tynyanov's *Kukhlya*, and a volume of short stories by Leonid Andreyev. Tynyanov is a writer of great talent, but with a terribly Stalinist orientation. I liked Andreyev far more this time, because of the psychological precision of his characterization.

18 May

Today I relaxed while Tonino finished dictating his script. I went to St. Peter's Square. I saw and heard the Pope's appearance in front of the people—the crowd filled the entire square with flags, banners and placards. It's odd that although I was surrounded simply by large numbers of curious people, such as foreigners and tourists, there was a unity about them which impressed me deeply. There was something natural, organic in it all. It was obvious that all these people had come here of their own free will. The atmosphere reigning in the Square made that perfectly clear.

I also felt it was wonderful that as I was wandering round the streets, before going by chance into St. Peter's Square, I had been thinking that today was Sunday and what fun it would be when I got back to Moscow to be able to say that I had been present at a Papal audience at the Vatican. Samokhvalov once saw a papal audience too, he told me.

19 May

The script is finished. Now it has to be translated. Lora will do a literal and I shall make the finished version. It is going to be read by Tovoli, the artist, and above all by Cristaldi.

Alberto Moravia came to see Tonino today. He wanted to meet me. He limps, and looks old and ill. He is seventy. He struck me as a man who does not deserve his literary fame, and pays for it in loneliness, since those around him are aware of this. I somehow felt sorry for him; he reminded me of the Moscow painter and illustrator

Tauberg, although I must say Moravia is brisker and more elegant than he.

20 May

Medicines which I really need:
1. Locorten B with neomicin
2. AZ 15 Liquid for gums
3. AZ 15 toothpaste
These help me a lot.

Went to RAI and signed a paper so that I can be paid (by the day).

Saw the American film *An Unmarried Woman* with Jill Claybergh. She's a very good actress, no one could be better for *Nostalgia*.

Franco Terilli says the unions (TV) will be against having an American actress in the film. I shall have to talk to Cristaldi about it.

There are two problems, or even three: 1. Claybergh. 2. Studio shots. 3. Quantity of film.

21 May

Met Luciano Tovoli. We are going to meet again tomorrow at his house and discuss everything. He is a bit concerned about having committed himself to working for Antonioni. But in any case Michelangelo will not be ready to start filming before January 1981.

I telephoned home, and talked to Lara and Tyapus. It really looks as if Lara is still not well. She is longing to see me; and I her. How is this all going to end? This endless waiting, never being able to live together.

The première of *Stalker* took place in the Peace Cinema in Moscow, and was a tremendous success. It also had a great success in Tallinn.

I told Larissa about Cannes. She is going to complain to Uzbekfilm about the fact that up till now we have not received a single penny for the screenplay, even though the film has already reached the cinemas.

22 May

Today I fell; I bought two pairs of shoes; I spent 130,000 lire. Quite mad. What for?

I must translate the script into Russian as quickly as possible, so that I can sit down with Tovoli and Franco and decide on locations.

The RAI are apparently worried about the future distribution. The most crucial first step now is the selection committee, which has the final say on whether a project is accepted or rejected. It will all hang on whether the RAI officials give it good chances of distribution.

I talked to Tyapa and Larissa over the telephone. She rang Yerovshin and asked him if he was actually aware that she could not go without her son. He said that he was very well aware.

I don't know what line I ought to be taking, because from outside it looks as if everything is as it should be.

I now have to concentrate on what is known as the initial estimate, but only in general terms and without committing myself, in order to explain to the Italians what it is all going to cost.

We had supper with the Tovolis. Everyone assured me that his wife, Laetitia, was stingy, but I liked the meal—it was moderate, no need to over-eat.

Tonino is worried about our project.

Are Tyapa and Larissa really going to come here? I cannot believe it . . .

23 May

'Our' young men at the Embassy tried to talk me into taking on some little *puttanella* (tart) of an actress. She allegedly has connections which they consider terribly important. I immediately shook her off. I trust they won't dare to come to me with any more of their idiotic suggestions.

I met the representative of the Donatello Prize committee today, and she invited me to Sicily to receive the Visconti Prize. She is an elderly Russian, who can't talk Russian properly any more.

I told her that despite my work I would take the trouble to come, but probably with my wife. Or maybe just with my son. Of course I did not say any of that to her, only to myself.

Tried twice to telephone Larissa but she wasn't there. The second time I talked to Arayk. He told me about a film which is being made about the shooting of *Stalker*.

26 May

Today we discussed the question of the translator.

I talked to Larissa. She is not feeling well at all. Did Mursharanov really not help her? Anna Semyonovna has apparently had very high blood pressure and is in bed. My poor Larochka! She is planning to go to the country with Tyapa. I don't quite understand how, if Anna Semyonovna is ill in Moscow. I shall ring her again tomorrow.

My beloved one . . .

27 May

Today we discussed business. Tonino has spoken to Cristaldi, and that is all fine, except that we have to change one scene (for the moment) in order to make it clear to the producers that we do not need to dub the Russian or use subtitles.

They managed to find Norman, who has aged a lot but still holds himself well; I want to ask him to be interpreter and assistant. It was he who interpreted for our delegation, when Natasha Bondarchuk and Banionis and I went to the première of *Solaris*.

I telephoned Larissa, Anna Semyonovna is much better, she has been up for the first time since her illness. Larissa has done all the things I asked.

She talked to Sidelnikov, and all the material on the serf composer is here. His name was Maxim Sasontovich Beriozovsky, and he was born on 16 October 1745 in Glukhov. In 1765 he was sent to the Musical Academy of Bologna, where he studied under Padre Tartini the Elder, who was a pupil of Mozart. He became an honorary member of the Bologna Academy, as well as being a member of other musical academies. He wrote the opera *Demophones*, based on texts by Metastasio, for the Livorno Opera. He composed a great deal of superb music and became very well known in Italy.

In 1774 he returned to Russia at the wish of Potyomkin, who proposed that he found a musical academy in Kremenschug. He fell in love with a serf actress belonging to Count Razoumovsky. When the Count heard of it he raped the girl and dispatched her to Siberia. Beriozovsky went to St. Petersburg where he started to drink heavily and in 1777 took his own life.

In Bologna there lives someone called Napoleone Fonti, aged seventy, who knows a lot about Beriozovsky and what happened to him. His scores are in Bologna and Livorno.

Larissa has even found a possible translator, called Gioffi Setifabio, who graduated from the All-Union State Cinema Institute in 1973. She tells me that Sasha Mishurin is coming to Rome on 3 June. I must see him. Of course I shall ask him to take a parcel for Larissa. And one or two letters—for Kochevrin, Sizov and Nekhoroshev.

28 May

Yesterday we worked in Vides, Cristaldi's studio—Franco T., Norman and I. We have worked out a provisional costing for the film—up to half-way.

I always feel ill on Wednesdays, because that is my regular day for fasting.

I talked to Lara on the telephone. I might be able to use Dakus for one of the Moscow scenes and then bring him back here.

29 May

Norman and I have drawn up a detailed description of all the work, now it's up to Franco to produce his estimates, and then we can arrive at an exact sum.

I don't much like the way Antonioni is behaving. He telephoned Tonino and mentioned, quite by the way, that he will be starting work on his film in October, and would need both Tovoli and Schiaccianoci—the art director. Tonino asked, 'What about Andrey?' and Antonioni said that the art director and the cameraman could be somehow shared between us.

I'm afraid he wants to 'sacrifice' the art director and have Tovoli for himself. But Tovoli and I arranged things last summer. I'd do better to give up the art director, whom I'm meeting for the first time tomorrow; Antonioni can't insist on Tovoli as well. So much for Antonioni!

This evening Tonino and Lora and I went to a cocktail party to celebrate the launch of Renzo Rosso's book, *The Sign of the Beast*. Deadly boring! But there were two interesting people there; one a psychiatrist with whom I had a very interesting conversation, and we arranged to meet; and the other a professor of Romagna University, who taught Tonino—very intelligent, and apparently a superb translator of Rabelais.

Heart pains in the evening.

30 May

Spent the morning with Schiaccianoci, the set designer, working out the cost of the sets—around 70–80 million.

I liked him a lot, but I shan't be working with him because of Antonioni. The same goes for Tovoli, who wanted me to wait until

Monday, when Antonioni will finally let him know whether his film is going ahead or not. If it is not, then Tovoli would be my cameraman for *Nostalgia*; if it is, he won't be. In other words, it was up to me to wait.

I dismissed Tovoli.

I have already spoken over the telephone to Rotuno, cameraman to Robert Altman and Fellini. He is arriving here tomorrow from Malta, and will come and discuss our working together on *Nostalgia*.

As for the designer, I still don't know. But if Antonioni is not going to make his film, Schiaccianoci would be ready to work for me.

31 May

This morning I met Grilli, the special effects man. He made a note of all our financial requirements.

By this evening Franco was in a state of total panic, because he is afraid that the whole thing is going to come to 1,200,000,000 lire. Tonino and I then killed ourselves trying to cut the estimate by the vital 300,000,000.

Morning is wiser than evening.

Just watched Marco Bellocchio's *Leap in the Dark*. Cold and sober. Dictated by reason. The cameraman is not bad—Pepe Lanci. I shall have to choose between Rotuno and Lanci.

Tomorrow Tonino is going to Sant' Arcangelo for the elections.

Franco Terilli and Norman and I had supper at Fiumicino, on the coast. Franco showed me 'Shanghai'. In fact we might be able to film 'the madman's house' there.

If art, and artistic creation, are in the end merely a metaphor, then everything poetic is no more than a pseudo metaphor.

1 June

Tovoli rang me yesterday. He is terribly worried and insists that he wants to see me. I find the whole situation embarrassing.

Franco has finished his calculations: it comes to 1,500,000,000 lire. I don't know what we are going to do. The two of us will talk about it tomorrow.

Sasha Mishurin has come here from Moscow with a tourist group; Vika Tokareva is with him. The four of us had supper together. Sasha is very nice; and, of course, overwhelmed by Italy.

Lara telephoned today; poor thing, she feels very unwell. Tyapa spoke as well, and it was obvious how much the boy is missing me.

2 June

Tonino is in Sant' Arcangelo.

Rondi interviewed me, calling me a genius and comparing me to Dante. I don't believe he is joking, only it looks as if he must be because otherwise he would seriously mean it.

Tonino telephones constantly from Sant' Arcangelo; today he spoke to the RAI people, and afterwards told me that everything is going to be fine.

Yesterday I went to RAI, and saw a documentary about the first poetry festival in Ostia, the place where Pasolini was born. It could have been a very interesting film, but it didn't come together. An accumulation of material and nothing else.

I talked with Larissa. Sizov has arrived and she is going to see him.

After the film I had supper with Antonioni, Lora, Enrica, Carlo di Carlo and a journalist and his wife; he is the Paris correspondent and wants to interview me.

Incidentally, the journalist told us that after the film, or rather, after it had been shown at Cannes, everyone was wildly enthusiastic and said that it was the best film of the festival (which was what *Le Monde* said).

6 June

Today I read a wonderful essay by Lorca—passionate, profound, truly poetic ideas.

Lara told me that when she asked Sizov if he knew how *Stalker* had gone at Cannes, he said, 'It was a complete flop. The audience walked out in droves.' It would be interesting to know who gave him that information. Larissa interrupted him and told him about the press notices and the two prizes. Then Sizov said, 'So why didn't they enter it?' Larissa was amazed, and said that was exactly what she would like to know.

Lora and I went to the school of meditation in Piazza di Spagna, at Enrica's. We meditated together.

Tonino telephoned from Sant' Arcangelo.

Rondi wants to see outlines of all my screenplays. (I must find out where they all are, and also have some idea about royalties.) I talked to Larochka and Tyapus. Lara said that Arayk had 'managed to get hold' of some strawberries, and that they (Tyapus and his friends) simply couldn't get over them. Oh, God!

Lara said that my permit is for three months, not two, so I don't have to worry.

In the evening I watched Cocteau's *The Return of Orpheus* (on television).

Where have all the great ones gone?

Where are Rossellini, Cocteau, Renoir, Vigo? The great—who are poor in spirit? Where has poetry gone? Money, money, money and fear . . . Fellini is afraid, Antonioni is afraid . . . The only one who is afraid of nothing is Bresson.

At the Cannes Festival the papers said that Fellini's last film was a total disaster, and that he himself had ceased to exist. It's terrible, but it is true, his film is worthless.

Good night, Larochka!

7 *June*

Nothing happening. The good weather has started, but the forecast is for a summer of terrific heat.

8 *June*

Tonino is back. What a wonderful, gentle, generous man he is. And as naive as a child!

He has a problem with his daughter, who married a cretin and now does not want to live with him. He bullies her, and has no intention of leaving her house (i.e. Tonino's).

9 *June*

Tempo di Viaggio was shown at the RAI, in its final version. They liked it a lot. I still don't understand what the RAI people are up to. We are having a meeting tomorrow to clarify things.

I talked to Lara. On Thursday she is taking Tyapa and Anna Semyonovna to the country. Before the contract is signed, it is not going to be possible for us to get visas valid for the whole time we have to be in Italy.

For the moment I am writing all sorts of rubbish in this diary; the worthwhile ideas that occasionally occur to me—I forget.

If we could completely ignore all the rules and generally accepted ways of making films, writing books, and so on, what wonderful things we should be able to create. We have forgotten how to *observe*. Instead of observing, we do things according to patterns.

It's not surprising that I so often remember Castaneda and his *Don Juan*.

Last night I dreamt that I was in Moscow, I think in the Polyanka, which was full of cars and people. Suddenly, in the midst of the noise and rush of the city, I saw a cow, a most beautiful cow, the colour of dark chocolate, with a head like Isis and horns like a lyre, and deep, human eyes.

She came up to me, I stroked her, and she crossed the street and went off down the pavement. I still remember the smell she left on the palm of my hand: the penetrating, tender, homely smell of life and happiness.

10 June

An awful day: there was a meeting at the television offices where my friends and I were told that if the picture is going to cost more than 900 million, RAI will have nothing to do with it.

Tonino accused one of the officials, Fichera, of incompetence. He was responsible for finding a market abroad, which he had either not had time to do or else was unable to do, which made the situation for today's talks much worse. But it is all bad anyhow. We are going to meet again on Friday, to make concessions to each other. There's very little we can do, and very little RAI will want to do. I suggested to Fichera that he back out of his services to the USSR.

What did they imagine? They knew that screenplay could not be filmed for less than 1800 million. Or are they simply incompetent? It is all far worse than I thought.

Sophia has arrived from Stockholm but I haven't seen her yet.

I talked to Lara on the telephone. Sizov wants me to send the *Stalker* press notices to Yermash, to put him in his place.

Last night I dreamt that I had woken up in some place I did not know, lying on the ground, where I was sleeping next to Mama. A country landscape, half familiar. I walked over to a stream, and washed my face. I could not understand at all how it was that I came to be there. Mama said I had drunk too much the day before, and that was why I did not remember coming there. It was a terrible dream . . .

Could it mean I am going to die?

Lord, help me!

11 June

The film is hanging by a thread.

We reduced it today by 270 million.

1. Half the horse scene.
2. All the studio scenes.
3. Only 10 days out of Rome.

4. 12 days of shooting (?!)

But it's no good, because we still need 1600 million.

Producers don't want to make anything worth making, all they want is money. Rosi is out of work, Antonioni is out of work.

Only a miracle can save us.

12 June

Narymov rang this morning. We arranged to meet on Saturday, but we have to telephone on Friday evening. He said that they are very interested in our project in Moscow, and advised me to be tougher with RAI and not let them push me around.

Meeting Narymov tomorrow—at his place—at 2.30.

Rondi telephoned, very upset that *Stalker* is going to be shown at Pesaro before it is shown in Taormina.

We decided today to offer RAI a short, cheap (1200 million) version of the film.

All the same a producer has appeared (*Pocho mafioso*, says Tonino) who promises to find a billion in four days' time. And Martine Offroy rang, she is interested. So there is hope! God willing!

Had dinner with Sophia and her grandson, they are in Rome on holiday. He (Christian) is a handsome sixteen-year-old, very nice.

We came to an agreement about an invitation to Sweden, if need be.

13 June

Franco and Norman and I worked on the figures.

Went to see Narymov. My film will be shown at Pesaro, at the Soviet Film Festival. It will be the final event. In some ways that's a good thing.

Had supper with my Stockholm friends.

Fichera is postponing the date for signing the contract by a month, because of the money. Tonino and I will try and raise the money ourselves. And the sooner the better, so that Larissa can come to Taormina with me—because they won't let her out until the contract is signed.

I couldn't talk to Lara today.

Sophia telephoned.

14 June

Yesterday I forgot to write that Martine Offroy had telephoned from Paris to say that Gaumont had not only bought up *Stalker* from the French distributors, who bought it originally for 500,000, but that they were also buying the distribution rights for *all* my films. They bought *Mirror* some time ago. (So why have people been saying that Gaumont are in a bad way?) They also want to show *Nostalgia*. Thank God!

Sophia gave me the name of a Finnish director and actor, Lasse Röjsli. He has just been made director of all the Swedish theatres. Sophia says he is among my longstanding admirers, and can send me an invitation. He, rather than Bergman, who is on thoroughly bad terms with the Swedish authorities.

I tried to ring Larissa but didn't get her, unfortunately. She has taken Tyapus to the country.

We had dinner with Rondi. It was the first time he had invited people to his house since his mother's death. He fusses around like a widower, everything is pedantically correct. He gave me his book, with a touching dedication: 'To the unique genius of cinema, Andrey, from his friend Gianluigi, Rome 14.6.80.'

He treated us to a superb dinner with wonderful wines. He wants to ask Bergman to come to Taormina, in order to say a few words about me there, or at least to write them. He would like the Italian President to present me with the prize. I don't know what any of that will come to, but anyhow I thanked him for his thoughts.

Whatever happens, it looks as if it will all take place at the highest level.

I feel so homesick for Moscow and my dear ones.

21 June

So—having killed ourselves to reduce the cost, and done all that was humanly possible, we are still short of 250 million. And we can't make the film without money. It's all over. The whole thing is collapsing.

We went out to Antonioni's bit of land in the suburbs, where they have a swimming-pool. We sunbathed, and I've burnt my shoulders.

I talked to A.S. on the telephone. Everything is all right over there so far. Lara hasn't rung. I shall have to ring her on Monday: Masha Chugunova telephoned, she needs to be in touch with me about something.

I am missing them all so much, let alone Lara and Tyapus and Dakus.

It really is not possible for a Russian to live here, not with our Russian nostalgia.

Parting will devour them both,
Sadness gnaw their very bones . . .

The one thing capable of resisting the universal destruction is love
. . . and beauty. I believe that only love can save the world. Without
it, all will be lost. It is already happening.

Gianni (Antonioni's friend) was telling us horrifying things today
about England, which he found hardly recognizable after an interval
of two years. Spiritual degeneration. Money and make-believe
replacing the life of the spirit.

Today is Alexander Kaydanovsky's birthday. He has separated
from his wife. Lucky man!

'There is no odor so bad as that which arises from goodness
tainted. It is human, it is divine, carrion. If I knew for a certainty
that a man was coming to my house with the conscious design of
doing me good, I should run for my life, as from that dry and
parching wind of the African deserts called the *simoom*, which
fills the mouth and nose and ears and eyes with dust till you are
suffocated, for fear that I should get some of his good done to
me—some of its virus mingled with my blood. No, in this case I
would rather suffer evil the natural way . . .

Philanthropy is not love for one's fellowman in the broadest
sense.'

(Henry Thoreau, *Walden.*)

'I do not value chiefly a man's uprightness and benevolence,
which are, as it were, his stem and leaves . . .

His goodness must not be a partial and transitory act, but a
constant superfluity, which costs him nothing and of which he is
unconscious. This is a charity that hides a multitude of sins . . .

I never knew, and never shall know, a worse man than myself.'
(ibid.)

22 June

How strangely people live. They seem to be in command of the
situation—and they do not understand that they have been given
the chance of living and actually using the opportunity to be free.
Everything in this life is terrible, apart from the freedom of will that
we possess. Once we are united with God we shall no longer be able
to exercise it, it will have been taken away from us.

I can understand why Anna Akhmatova behaved so strangely

then. She was being racked by nostalgia for this life, which (when you pause to think about it) is terrible, carnal, spiritual and free. This morning I went out to the country to Fr. Victor's church. I don't think he recognized me. I lit candles for the souls of the departed, V. N. and M., and prayed for all of ours. It was lovely.

Saw Cassavetes' *The Killing of a Chinese Bookie*. One can see it was his handiwork, but I feel so sorry for him I could weep.

I feel sorry for all of the best of them: Antonioni and Fellini and Rosi—of course, they are not at all what they seem from a distance.

Sophia telephoned about Bergman's coming to Taormina, to meet me and congratulate me. He is hardly likely to want to, evidently.

6 July

Norman's flat. Today I slept until 11 a.m. My teeth are aching and I feel utterly shattered. I'm terribly worried about Lara, A.S. and Senka—he is sitting his first Phystech exam. today. For the second time in four days I rang home and nobody answered. Very odd. Nor was there anyone at home at Senka's. I do wonder how it went today. I don't understand Irina—wherever she has gone, I'm sure she should not have left him alone so long just at the time of his exams.

Lora and I had dinner with Norman. Lessi was ill, and could not move at all for two days. She is better now.

I am staying in the very centre of Rome, next to Piazza Navona. This is close to everything. Why did I not move here sooner? I'd have saved money.

7 July

I am convinced, and this is something that has often struck me, that an artist needs both knowledge and the power of observation only so that he can tell from what he is abstaining, and to be sure that his abstention will not appear artificial or false. For in the end it is important to confine yourself within a framework that will deepen your world, not impoverish it, help you to create it, excluding all pretentiousness and efforts to be original. As far as possible all links with life have to be excluded, with no loss of truthfulness, discarding only the superfluous trash that appears (or may appear to some people) to be a sign of authenticity, of convincing argument. For such arguments lie outside the parameters of image–thought, in an area where quantity can never be transmuted into quality.

Out of sheer curiosity I have been reading Yefremov—*The Razor Blade*. My God! Did no one ever tell the man he suffered from graphomania? Did he actually die not knowing he was a hack?

Tonino and I talked over the telephone about the screenplay he is writing with Frederico F. I gave them one or two ideas (actually rather good ones); the fact that they've completely lost sight of the reason for the voyage in that liner. And what sort of person the character is, whom Gielgud is going to play—he simply cannot remember why he is there or where they are sailing. (They are on their way to bury an urn with the ashes of a famous singer.)*

I have lanced my gum. Of course it feels better now. We'll see what happens tomorrow.

8 July

We did a bit of work at Vides. Received an invitation to an American festival (the 7th Telewide Film Festival); it's no doubt thoroughly second-rate, but in a most beautiful place—the Rocky Mountains where Ford made his Westerns. The Festival is in September, so it's no good; but all the same I must show the letter to Yermash.

Franco and I decided today that if all goes well—and we are able to go ahead with the film—we shall drive to Taormina for me to receive the prize; if Franco is unable to go, then I shall go alone by plane.

12/13 July

Was in town in the morning. Then I helped Norman edit his documentary about the Greek director, Angelopoulos. We have to go on with it tomorrow. Supper this evening with Donatella and Armando. We sat there till 2.30 in the morning talking nonsense about the meaning of life; truth; expediency, and so on. Very stupid. Have to be up early tomorrow.

13 July

Spent the whole day editing Norman's film, and we shall be at it again tomorrow. I am worried about August. It's impossible to prepare for shooting that month—everyone goes off on holiday and you can't get hold of anybody, and in September we shall have to start shooting.

It's late—I must sleep.

*The film being discussed is Frederico Fellini's *The Ship Sails On*.

14 [?] *July*

There is still some hope that something may happen while I'm in Taormina— the money may still be found.

Tomorrow Tonino is going to Sant' Arcangelo, and I am going to Taormina to receive the Visconti David Donatello Prize.

I showed the film to the cameraman and the others (Tonino). The projection was appalling. Norman translated.

This evening Norman and Pepe Lanci and I had supper with Marina—an actors' agent. A beautiful flat with a terrace overlooking the Tiber. I'm tired. Empty conversations and one interesting lady—an actress.

19 July, Taormina. Hotel San Domenico

In Sicily for the first time. I don't yet have any understanding of it. Catania is a gloomy town, with heavy, dirty buildings which have their own kind of air and their own visage.

The Hotel San Domenico in Taormina is in what was once a monastery. Huge corridors; sumptuous staircases; the rooms used to be cells. There's a garden and a view over the sea. The sea here is very clean.

I've seen Rondi, but haven't yet talked to him about the things I intend to discuss with him. Maybe tomorrow.

Marina, the interpreter, is improving. There is something new about her. I am tired, going to bed. Here until the 27th, when I fly to Rome in the morning.

22 July, Taormina

Sunbathed. Had lunch with Rondi and his wife (I've already lunched with them twice by the swimming-pool). Walked around the town, went to look at a delightful little town on a rock (next door to Taormina).

Taormina is a wonderful place too. The sun is not at all the same here as in Rome. It's hot! I'm not feeling particularly well.

Tilda brought my things over from Rome today and left a note saying she would ring.

Missing Lara and Tyapus and Dakus dreadfully. How do they keep going without me, the darlings!

Rondi said he would telephone Fichera again, in order to find out definitely what RAI intend to do about *Nostalgia*.

23 July, Taormina

Lay in the sun. Was interviewed by two journalists. Tilda has arrived from Rome but still hasn't telephoned me. Early to bed.

24 July, Taormina

Narymov has arrived with a very pretty daughter. Surikov wired to tell me to come a day earlier. To hell with them. I shan't have time to do anything in Rome.

There was a big, fairly boring press conference, and after it Rondi congratulated me on my success.

Incidentally, in the evening, at supper, Rondi almost had a fight (!?) with the waiter because he wouldn't bring him coffee from the bar. There was quite a little scene.

I rang Franco in Rome.

And Brigitte Fossey's agent rang to say that Fossey is prepared to drop everything to come and film with me. (Discuss it with Norman, urgently. Tomorrow I'll ask Rondi to talk it over with Fichera, he is arriving here tomorrow; Columbino is already here.)

Larochka! Tyapus! Dakus! How I miss you all! Please God we shall see each other soon. Tomorrow morning I'll try and ring Moscow.

25 July, Taormina

This morning I talked to Anna Semyonovna. Lara will be there today. Tyapus must be staying on in the country.

I've been thinking about *The Idiot*, and it seems to me that it would be possible to disrupt the sequence of the plot, and the episodes, because structure is not at all the same in literature as it is in film.

This evening there was a rehearsal for the prize-giving ritual. Bought three Indian dresses. I've bought almost everything. Only one or two oddments left to do tomorrow.

Donatella was very helpful.

We're dog-tired.

30/31 July, Rome. Via di Monte Brianza

Yesterday, after that sleepless night, I was physically incapable of writing a word.

Norman and Donatella and I collected the suitcases.

Saw Rosselini today, the Gaumont representative; he is not in favour of the idea of making *Nostalgia* as a joint project. Tomorrow we shall have a meeting—Norman, Franco, Fichera, Rosselini. I think it's hopeless. Tonino says (from Sant' Arcangelo) that nothing is lost yet. I'm sick of the whole thing.

I must spend my money sensibly. I'm not likely to be here again soon.

10 November, Myasnoye

Night.

'Even in Goethe we come across heavy lines, even in him we can be confronted by lack of clarity or banality of thought. It is not a question of thought, or of colour, or of faithfulness to literary rules; it is something else, living but incomprehensible, something that will always elude any definition of artistic genius . . .

. . . the clearest images of the great artists and their words are never clear to the end, rather as the limpid sky over our heads, when we gaze into it, turns out to be not pale blue at all, but a darker shade, deeper, fathomless. And so the works of a great genius, for all their crystalline clarity, will sometimes make us gaze apprehensively into their depths, and define the clarity as the clarity of the deep . . . and that is all; what lies at the bottom of those depths eludes us.'

(Andrey Bely, *The Tragedy of Art*, 'Dostoievsky and Tolstoy'.)

'Our world is the purgatory of heavenly spirits bedimmed by sinful thought' (words of Dostoievsky).

'(Art) is a religious necessity for the spirit, where vision is of ultimate truth and craft the ultimate activity: the transfiguration of oneself and others.' (Andrey Bely, 'Dostoievsky and Tolstoy'.)

7 December, Myasnoye

On the 25th (I think) Sergey Vassilevich Kalinkin died. Cancer of the stomach. There was a funeral meal.

I have an appalling impression of the country people.

Must leave as soon as possible.

1981

Truth does not exist in itself; it lies in the method. It is—the way.

1981

20 January, Moscow

I am inclined to write a letter to the Praesidium of the Congress taking place at the beginning of March. No, I don't mean March, I mean February. Mustn't forget: exhibition; lack of reviews; festivals; prestige; foreign currency; letters and invitations through Goskino; award—!?

That I cannot support my family as a result of the way Goskino distributes my films.

Am I needed? If not, then why was I honoured with an award?

21 January

Release: western films—*Who's Who*, *Concord*; cf. listings for Jan.

'Men of wisdom maintain that what is useful for people of every rank and calling is philosophy—for the acquiring of knowledge, and virtue—for activity.' (Montaigne, *Essays*.)

Have started to give a course of lectures at the College of Theatre and Directing.

22 January, Moscow

Sasha Sakurov told me that at a Party meeting at the Film Institute Anatoly Golovnya (a former cameraman) announced that *Stalker* is a pernicious film. The Babushkino district council took note of the old Communist's opinion, and gave orders for the film to be considered as such from now on, and not shown to the students lest it cause their moral collapse.

'They (the Romans) drank wine in smaller sips than we do, and diluted it with water.

> . . . quis puer ocyus
> Restinguet ardentid Falerni
> Pocula praetereunte lympha?

(What deft page, swift to serve, will cool, with fast flowing water, the ardour of the Falernian wine?—Horace, *Odes*, II, 11, 18)'—Montaigne, *Essays*. Book I, Chapter XLIX, 'On ancient customs'.

Arkady and I have been working. I dismantled his plan; we have worked out another.

The Pilgrim, who refuses to kill Abalkin. (Everything back to front.)

Wherever the Pilgrim seems to destroy himself, he is affirmed.

Faith is against knowledge (*The Death of Ivan Ilyich*).

Fisher of Angels—not good.

A person fulfils his duty to society in the name of an idea, always doing violence to someone or something. Dependence. Links with others. Society. In the face of death the links are cut: freedom. Thoughts of the soul. Independence from society. The surrender of what has been acquired through violence. Wrongness and its acknowledgement. Personal rightness lies in moral purity. The devastating vulnerability of the hero. Frailty and helplessness. (Yet he spent his whole life 'ploughing' in the name of an ideal!)

3 February, London

'They say that the philosopher Stilpon, weighed down by old age, deliberately hastened his end by drinking pure wine. Such, too, was the cause, albeit not by his own design, of the philosopher Argesilaus' demise: his life-force, already impaired by age, was snuffed out.' (Montaigne. Book II, Chapter II, 'On drunkenness'.)

Tatiana Storchak and I flew in late yesterday. I'm ill: 'flu (?). The doctor came. Runny nose, headache, cough. I feel ghastly. No impressions so far—only the left-hand traffic and the fact that the city immediately reminds one of a stuffy old Moscow sitting-room.

Evidently sense of style is the most important thing for the English; although at an unconscious level it may not matter to them at all.

Why did I have to go and get ill! Yesterday I wrote a letter to the Praesidium of the Congress about the monstrous way the exhibition and distribution of my films is being handled.

4 February, London

Still no better. Tatiana Storchak and I went to the Embassy.

There was a mini press conference in the bar of the Academy.

This evening John (Roberts) and I went to the Shakespeare Company's production of Erdmann's *Suicide*. Roger Rees is a remarkable actor.

28 February, Moscow

There were so many things in England—Edinburgh, and Glasgow, and El Greco in Edinburgh, and then London again and the Basil Hotel, and Roya, who for some reason wanted to give me a Persian carpet, and the National Film School, and lots of other things. I even had proposals put to me:

1. The Shakespeare Company invited me to direct *Hamlet*.
2. The National Film School want me to lecture, or else to be in charge of a course in directing.
3. Oxford wanted me to lecture on cinematography.
4. Someone called André Engel, from Hamburg, suggested collaborating as co-producer or producer on any film I embark upon. He is already in touch with RAI (though Tonino) and will give his answer in a week's time as to whether or not he will become involved in my project.

The French are going to bring out *Stalker* in the autumn. However, I think they have already sent letters about my going to Paris to prepare a shortened version of the film. Pyotr Kuszmich Kostikov said that Goskino have no objection.

Sophia telephoned and said that I would soon have an invitation to Stockholm with my family, to the première of *Stalker*. The film school would like some lectures, and are offering ('we should deem it an honour') money for making a film.

7 March, Moscow

On Wednesday there was a reception at Jas Gavronsky's. I was beaten into the ground by a Yugoslav couple—Dushan and Xenia. (He is a journalist on *Borba* and she is a film critic.) After Jas's party they invited Larissa and me to have 'a little glass', and that little glass turned out to be fatal. I was ill for the whole of the following day. However, at least it makes it clear that drinking is not for me.

I had a dream last night about some wonderful, fairy-tale, exotic fields, and sunshine, and peace and happiness. And Larissa and I seemed to be looking at them out of a window. Could such happiness really come to us?

The same dream again: happy and full of light.

17 March, Moscow

Sophia rang twice from Stockholm. The first time, to find out whether I had received the invitation (to go to Sweden with Tyapa and Larissa) to the *Stalker* première. Needless to say I have not received any invitation addressed to me via the Soviet Embassy in Sweden and Goskino.

The second time she telephoned, very upset (in her capacity as go-between and interpreter), because they had received a reply saying that I was in Italy! I advised sending a telegram personally to Shauro and Yermash. Not that it's likely to help. Actually, I never for a moment imagined that anything could come of that invitation.

Yermash is ever watchful. I went to see him a few days ago. He is frightfully 'worried' about the fact that I am still not working, that I have to wait for the Italians and their film, when what I ought to be doing is starting straightaway on *The Idiot*. He had summoned me to 'put a tick' beside my letter to the Praesidium of the Congress. I told him that in the two hours that we had been talking, we had achieved absolutely nothing. I called Matveyev a lackey . . . I said I was willing to do my job, but not to be a lackey.

We had an argument.

Tonino telephoned—on his birthday. How could I have forgotten it?

Proposals:

Course of lectures in Film School (London).

Make a film with Angelo.

Make a film on money from the Swedish Film Institute.

Direct *Hamlet*.

(Maybe Ostrovsky, *Late Love*).

Sizov also told me that the Studio has drawn up documents to have Tolya Solonitsyn awarded the title of Honoured Artist of the RSFSR. The bastards! He had to be desperately ill, perhaps even dying, before they would give him the title.

25 March, Moscow

Yesterday three out of the twelve students turned up at the course in directing. I decided not to lecture any more. In the evening I went to the Taganka Theatre, and saw *The Master and Margarita*. Awful; not a single actor.

I was talking to Shkalikov from 2 o'clock till 6.

I explained to him that I am not a camel. He—or rather, they—would like me to go to Sweden with Storchak, and not with my family as the invitation specified. We had a furious row.

It's all going to be decided now. But they are putting on such heavy pressure. They don't want to set a precedent by letting me out with my family. And they quite simply mistrust me. Bugger the lot of them. They're going to finish me off, there'll be nothing left of me.

And there has been a second telex from RAI to say that the advisory council has passed the plans for *Nostalgia*.

'. . . For in much wisdom is much grief; and he that increaseth knowledge increaseth sorrow.' (Ecclesiastes.)

27 March, Moscow

Sophia telephoned again. The Swedes applied to our Ministry of Foreign Affairs (since Yermash refused), but so far nothing is clear.

Anyhow, after talking to Shkalikov I let the Swedes know that I would not go alone without Larissa.

Today is my second-last lecture of the course. I don't think much of these students, I must say. They're a dim lot.

28 March, Moscow

Feeling very ill. Cramp in my heart, and a terrible ache at the back of the head. Zemfira Vassilevna came today. On Tuesday morning Tyapa and I are going to her clinic. I think Tyapus has something wrong with his heart and that Z.V. is hiding it from me.

This evening I went to see Yura Bezelyansky. He is very nice.

29 March, Moscow

Tonino telephoned yesterday from Italy. (He spoke to Olga.) Larissa says he sounded very cheerful and said we should soon be seeing each other. I don't know, I don't know . . .

What should I do if the Italians come here to discuss the contract? Obviously Larissa and I will have first to sign the contract and then demand that Tyapa come with us. But what if that makes them cancel the whole thing, the journey, the project? I just don't know what to do.

'And in truth, philosophy is but sophisticated poetry: from whence do these ancient authors have their authority, if not from the poets? Indeed the first of them were themselves poets, and wrote of it in their own art. Plato is but an unravelled poet.' (Montaigne, II, Chapter xii.) 'And that perhaps was why Timon, by way of insult, called him the great miracle forger.' (II, xvi.)

31 March, Moscow

Yuri Trifonov died on Saturday, at the age of 55. Cancer.

Very odd: some woman telephoned today from the Swedish Embassy, calling herself the cultural attaché, and asked if I knew whether or not I was going to Sweden. I said I had already replied, and that if there was any news on that front the Swedes would know about it before I did, and that I hoped that if that happened she would telephone and let me know. Then she suddenly announced: 'They promised to give us a decision on the question of whether you were going or not—today, 31st of March.' I was rather taken aback. It means that for the entire week following my talk with Shkalikov they still haven't known whether we were going. Or else they have known, but are in no hurry to announce their refusal. It doesn't make sense.

Sophia keeps on telephoning from Stockholm in desperation, and tells me endlessly that everyone has put off their holidays, and all the papers are writing that I am definitely coming, and of course we are not going anywhere. Goskino told the Swedes in the Moscow Embassy that we are not going because I don't want to. Larissa rang Storchak and asked why they were saying that. Storchak said it must be because they were flustered.

Flustered. I see.

The electricity board people have just come and cut off our supply because we haven't paid the bill.

Lara thinks I should go to Sweden alone so that I can talk about our business. I'm sure she's right, but I hate the idea of going by myself.

My God, does this happen in any other country? The *authorities* forbidding a husband and wife to travel out of the country on an invitation? It's not as if she were not an employee of the Mosfilm Studios just as I am; she is my assistant on every film I make, she deals with all the business side of my work—they know that perfectly well. They are frightened, the bastards! They know what they've been up to! We have had enough of it. How long can one go on!

I rang Kostikov and said that if my refusal was going to make things difficult for Goskino, I would be prepared to go alone. There has been too much talk in Stockholm. My reasons for changing my decision:

1. I don't want it to be thought that I am safeguarding my own interests at the expense of Goskino.

2. I may be able to find out something about future developments.
3. As far as possible the way must be kept open for the contract with the Italians, although I have lost faith in them.

5 April, Moscow

Completely absorbed by a fascinating book (translated from English)—Uspensky's *In Search of the Miraculous*, about the teachings of Gurdjiev. *A New Model of the Universe* is by him, Gurdjiev, as well.

9 April, Moscow

On the 11th I am going to Stockholm for five—only—days. A sea of troubles.

Met Sasha Pancratov. We talked about religion; and about faith and knowledge. I've lost my strength. I have to decide on a course of action. That is something new and frightening.

'Sin is what is not essential'—Gurdjiev's words, quoted in Uspensky's book (*In Search of the Miraculous*).

Perhaps my last lecture, on Friday, should be based on a discussion of the nature of the short film as a genre.

11 April

Sitting in the plane, before take-off. I was seen off by Masha, Arayk, and of course Larochka and Tyapa. My heart is jumping a lot, and the back of my head aching badly. I hope I don't have an attack. Lara told her mother everything, and Tosia and all her relations. That may not be a good thing.

Two weeks ago, or rather, one week, or a few days, I suddenly remembered that my number is 13. And from habit, I started looking for it on cars. I couldn't find it. I was expecting 13–13. For some reason I had a feeling that if I did, it would be a good sign. In Sheremetevo, as I was coming into the airport, I noticed a black Volga next to the entrance. The number was 13–13. I still can hardly believe it.

Evening. The hotel room is pretty average. Sophia is very nice. I telephoned Tonino. Couldn't quite understand what he meant. I think he was saying things were moving. Had supper with Bibi (Anderson). I don't think anything is going to work out: I'm only here for five days, and the Embassy will have to be asked for an extension. I've arranged with Titkin (the cultural attaché) to go and see him on Monday morning. I'll have to change it to Tuesday. It would be better for Almark to be here first. Something going on in the state of Denmark.

13 April, Stockholm. Grand Hotel

Saw Jure Lina. *Had a talk with Bibi A.* Met Sven Nykvist. Went to the Maharishi centre in Sophia's house. There was a gathering of students and audience at the Film Institute. The all-important thing is to extend my stay in Stockholm.

The idea of a royal summons. Sasha Titkin is an idiot.

Sophia's story of the four planets for Oven.

Phone-call from Bibi about a peace film, which can only be made with a Russian director.

I rang Lora (in the morning). Nothing new, apparently. But Martine has already spoken to Rosselini. Going to telephone her again on Tuesday.

14 April, Stockholm

A lot of work—interviews etc. Going to see the Ambassador tomorrow to talk about extending my stay. I'm terribly afraid nothing will come of it.

Wonderful dinner, fantastic people. Sven Nykvist. Pår Almark has already been with the Minister of Culture, to ask the Ambassador for an extension for me. What was the upshot of his meeting with the Ambassador?

15 April, Stockholm

Saw a bad, 'mathematical' film made by a very good man. I talked with him. I'm afraid it is not going to be easy for him: he is frightened, and has no faith in himself.

I've been paid 2000 kroner ($200) for the TV.

Went to see the Ambassador, who promised to let me know if it would be possible to stay on here. I was thrilled, until I heard that Almark had asked for permission 'at least until Sunday'. My whole stomach turned over.

Evening. I told Pår Almark, the director, Boris, and Bu—the producer—all about it. There is a producer, there is somewhere to live, and there are . . . As Lara and I decided. But I am afraid. Must ring Lara.

16 April, Stockholm

Oh, what misery this is. I talked to Tyapus and Lara. She gave me to understand that she is insisting. But I am frightened. What if something happens to them? I never imagined it possible that I might find myself in such a position! Lord, help me!

Jure telephoned just now. He wants to come round. Laura Mikasian rang too. She is worried and wants to get some sort of help to Seryozha Paradzhanov.

Jure rang and came. He almost convinced me that I ought to go ahead with my idea. He for one is convinced it will work. He gave me new heart. Jure said that Maxim Shostakovich stayed abroad with his son while he was giving concerts in West Germany.

17 April, Stockholm

It's all becoming confused. Sophia rang Jure Lina.
Heard the *St. Matthew Passion* at the Cathedral. Marvellous.

19 April, Goteborg

I was meant to go for a walk with Titkin, and didn't go. I left. P.A. helped me. Now all I can do is trust in God! Lara, Tyapochka, pray for me!

23 April, Moscow

At home in Moscow. 'I have been in hell.' I flew back on Tuesday. Yesterday I went to see Sizov in hospital. He told me what a panic the unfortunate bosses had been in.

I've brought back vast quantities of books by and about Gurdjiev.

Incidentally, here is the text of the note I left for Titkin in the hotel in Stockholm:

Dear Sasha! I'm sorry I let you down, but I am so tired, that when my Swedish friends invited me yesterday to spend a few days in the country, I could not refuse. Don't worry, and don't raise a hullabaloo, which could only make things worse. I am alive and well. By the way, on Monday Filip Timofeevich Yermash will be able to answer any questions that the Embassy may raise with you about all this.

Again, I apologize.

A. Tarkovsky.

PS. In any case a great deal will depend now on what answer I am given by Goskino.

24 April, Moscow

Ill; 'flu. We are all ill. Someone called Casati is coming to Moscow (he works for Gaumont on the financial side) together with Norman. Tonino says they are 'waiting for visas'.

26 April, Moscow

Christ's Resurrection. Ill. Pascal: 'Man is a thinking reed.'

4 May, Moscow

What an extraordinary degree of pride and blindness is contained in those Principles of ours! In our views—on things about which we really have no idea; on knowledge, of which we have no inkling of even a hundredth part, on faith, on love, on hope . . . We talk about it so much, as we imagine, when in fact each of us has something quite different in mind. We have no firm footing in the wider context, in the whole, the system, the general, the One. We grab a word from out of its context or a concept, or a state of mind, and we chatter on about it incessantly. Our so-called thought process is mere psychotherapy . . . which we practise in order not to go mad, to preserve the illusion that we have won the right to mental equilibrium. How worthless we are!

8 May

Went to see Arkady Strugatsky. We decided to abandon *The Witch*. Arkady says he is ill, he is going into some cardiological institute, where of course he 'won't be allowed to work.' I feel sorry for him; but he has been messing me around for the last four months. He's ill, but he drinks, and he goes on hoping that he'll be able to do proper work. And of course he can't.

I was feeling ill. That same 'stream' again, as if I was looking at everything through a stream of water. And the headache. A sort of spasm? It has happened several times now.

I shall write *The Witch* myself.

NB: *The Witch*: Kalyagin must be poor, in rags, unshaven, pathetic and happy (no one can understand why).

Marina has given me two of grandmother's little ikons, to be worn around the neck; God . . . What a grandmother I have!

9/10 May, Moscow

Reread, and realized I should have written 'had' in the last sentence; then it occurred to me that it wasn't an error at all.

Sophia has been in Moscow. I saw her today. She's a strange person. All the same we talked about the possibility of my being invited together with my family. I explained to her that if the invitation comes from Bergman, they won't let me out with Larissa and Andriushka. There was a rumour going around Stockholm that I wanted to stay in Sweden, and that she—Sophia—had somehow prevented me from doing so.

Jas Gavronsky has arrived in Moscow, we are going to meet tomorrow. It's odd: I can't really believe that the collaboration with RAI will come off. Yet I love Italy. I feel relaxed there. I felt less good in England and Sweden; despite my Stockholm friends.

16 May

Yesterday Kolya Dvigubsky and I came to an agreement (in principle) about his collaboration on *Nostalgia*. He is going to do some repairs quite cheaply. He promised to fix me up with his workers. He can refurbish a four-room flat for 2000 roubles.

Lora telephoned. Tonino has brought out a new book—*Moongazers*.

I must finish the translation of *Nostalgia*.

Going to give a talk tomorrow at Dubna, for which I shall be paid 200 roubles.

Met Yura Klimenko, who is planning to work with Ghia Danelia.

Ghia is in a bad way. His son has been arrested for drugs. (Apart from being an addict, he's also a homosexual.) Ghia was in hospital, and overdosed on sleeping pills. They brought him round, but he is a wreck. Poor Ghia!

19 May, Moscow

Today I attended the opening of the VIth Congress of Cinematographers, and listened to a speech by Kulidzhanov, who called me an elitist director, and expressed regret that—in effect—I, endowed with talent as I am, do not make films like Matveyev.

In other words—a denunciation.

Should I perhaps speak myself, and tell them some home truths?

I am upset. My heart is painful.

21 May, Moscow

I was not given the opportunity to speak at the Congress, though none of the ones who were had actually been queuing for it.

22 May, Moscow

Tolya Solonitsyn came today. He doesn't look too bad, only his breathing is heavy. And his hands are thin.

They didn't dismiss me from the Board. Titkin telephoned from Stockholm—he really has got a cheek—to enquire whether I needed anything.

I told him of the scurrilous rumours that greeted me in Moscow. He said he couldn't imagine who was responsible or what it was all about.

24 May, Moscow

'. . . The secrets of philosophy have much in common with the fantastic inventions of poetry . . .' (Montaigne, *Essays.*)

'. . . Our waking is blinder than our sleeping. Our wisdom less wise than our madness. Our fantasies are worth more than our judgements . . .' (ibid.)

28 May, Moscow

Lora telephoned today; Tonino wanted to let me know that there's a clash between the interests of RAI and of Gaumont. (Allegedly something to do with RAI putting on Tarkovsky and not Italians. All very odd.)

Tomorrow, Friday, there will be a meeting (yet another) and it will finally be decided (yet again). Tonino is going to telephone. Unfortunately my solicitous friend Lora is going off with Inna Konovalova, who has been invited somewhere, and won't be able to telephone.

1 June, Moscow

Tonino was supposed to telephone on Friday and tell me what happened at the meeting, but no call came through. Either the meeting didn't take place, or else the whole thing has fallen through and Tonino doesn't dare tell me.

This is what Kulidzhanov said about me at the Congress, despite *Stalker* having been acknowledged by *Komsomolskaya Pravda* as a box office picture.

Extract from Kulidzhanov's speech to the Cinematographers' Congress:

'There is another film which could almost be called science fiction. I refer to *Stalker*. It is a work which is full of allegory and elaborate symbolism, and it is not easy to understand; it does nonetheless illustrate the accomplishments of its author—Andrey Tarkovsky. He is a talented director, and I have to say frankly that it is regrettable that he should aim at what is called an elite audience. What a joy it would be for us all to see Tarkovsky make a new film, dealing with the important problems of our times, or of historical times, a film which could move millions of people and which they could understand.' (?!)

Tonino telephoned. He said that things are bloody difficult in the Cinema, but that everything is under control. Before that someone from RAI rang Jas to say that Norman is coming on 9 June.

Ksiusha says that there were invitations for me—and my wife— to all the festivals in Belgrade. And I was not even told about them.

3 June, Moscow

'. . . Our feelings are deceived and lie when they take that which seems to be for that which is, for they do not know what is. But in that case, what does, in reality, exist? That which is eternal, that is to say that which had no beginning and will never have an end, that which is not subject to any alteration in time. For time is something moving . . .' (Montaigne, *Essays*.) 'To save a man against his will is tantamount to committing murder.' (Horace.)

4 June, Moscow

'An instantaneous death is the highest happiness in human life.' (Pliny.)

'. . . something which is not in itself discreditable will inevitably become so when it is acclaimed by the crowd.' (Cicero.)

Maybe I am obsessed with freedom. I suffer physically when I do not have freedom. Freedom is being able to respect a sense of dignity in yourself and in others.

5 June, Moscow

Today again I had a kind of spasm in my head, and something quivering in my eyes (in my right eye); and my head is aching again.

Freedom, freedom!

I have a feeling that it was no accident that Arkady Strugatsky broke off our working relationship. He evidently felt that contact with me could be somehow risky for him. I shall never forget how he came dashing over to see me in order to put his—our—finances in order, when he heard that I had had a heart attack.

6 June, Moscow

Father rang. He is in Moscow, and Tyapa and I are going to see him tomorrow. Just like me (or rather, the other way round) he has those spasms in the head which stop him seeing properly. Does that mean it is hereditary?

23 June, Moscow

This morning Casati and Norman had a meeting with Sizov; Sizov seems to be persuaded of RAI's serious intentions, if they are capable of serious intentions; he was given full details of what they plan.

The schedule is 12½ months.

Among other points raised was du Plantier's visit to Moscow, in order to talk to me; about *Boris Godunov*. That suggestion threw them all into a trance. 'But why not Bondarchuk?' was their reaction; the answer to which was: 'Because the director has to be a religious man and a poet.'

'The Lord gives each person a cross to bear according to his strength.' (Montaigne, *Essays*, III, Ch. vi.)

'We do not move in one direction, rather do we wander back and forth, turning now this way and now that. We go back on our own tracks . . .' (ibid.)

That thought of Montaigne's reminds me about something I thought of in connection with flying saucers, humanoids, and the remains of unbelievably advanced technology found in some ancient ruins. They write about aliens; but I think that in these phenomena we are in fact confronting ourselves; that is, our future, our descendants who are travelling in time.

25 June, Moscow

Norman, Franco, Casati and I went to see Surikov at Sovinfilm. He gave us his figures:

Me—80m.

Lara—40m.

Tolya—40m.

Mosfilm services—$230,000 (i.e. Sovinfilm's requirements have increased almost threefold). !? They clearly don't want to make the film.

My God, it's infuriating; the one person whom I respected, and who—I thought—respected me, made a point when he met Casati of telling him that I am a frightful man with an impossible character, who 'will suck your blood', as he put it, making out he was joking. But he wasn't joking at all, he was carrying out orders from Yermash. How low can you get. Any revenge on someone like that would be justified.

I am not living. For many months now I have been waiting, waiting, waiting . . . God, help me!

26/27 June, Moscow

Went to see Kolya Shishlin in Old Square. He advised me to write a letter to Yermash, and then to Chernenko, and perhaps to Andropov. But I don't want to ask Kolya to pass on the letters.

Perhaps I should try some other way? Through Zimyanin? But he wouldn't take anything on. Or Dushan? Or Uwe? Contact Mitterand? How? Something has to be done fast, because it's clear that Yermash wants to sabotage the project. I've got to do something.

8 July, Moscow

'Ut olim flagiliis, sic nunc legibus laboramus—just as once we suffered from crime, so now we suffer from laws.' (Tacitus, *Annals*, III, 25, quoted in Montaigne's *Essays*, III, Ch. XIII.)

How can you live, what can you aim at, what can you wish for, if you are surrounded by hatred, stupidity, selfishness and destruction? If your house is in ruins, where can you escape to, where can you save yourself, where can you look for peace?

'I am so fond of freedom, that were I to be forbidden access to some corner of the Indies, I should in some way live less at ease because of it. And so long as I can find land or the open air elsewhere, I would never lurk in any place where I had to hide myself. My God, how hard it would be for me to endure the conditions in which I see so many people, mailed down in one district of this Kingdom, barred from entering the principal cities, or the courts, or from using the public roads, as a result of falling foul of our laws. If those whom I serve were to threaten so much as the tip of my finger, I should take myself off in chagrin to seek out others, wherever they might be. All my small wisdom, during these civil wars in which we live, is used to ensure that they do not impinge upon my freedom to come and go as I please.' (Montaigne, *Essays*, III, Ch. xiii.)

10 July, Moscow

Another miracle. Despite everything, strange and wonderful miracles do sometimes happen to me.

I went to the cemetery today, to Mama's grave. A cramped little enclosure, a small bench, a simple grave with a wooden cross. The wild strawberries are putting out shoots. I prayed to God, wept, complained to Mama, and asked her to pray for me, to intercede . . .

Because really, life has become completely unbearable. If it weren't for Andriushka, death would seem the only tenable idea.

As I was leaving Mama I picked a wild strawberry leaf from her grave. It drooped on the way home, so I put it into warm water and the leaf revived. And I felt calmer and purer in my soul.

And suddenly there was a phone-call from Rome. It was Norman, to say that the Italians are coming here on the 20th. Of course it was Mama. I don't doubt it for a second. My dear, good Mama . . . my darling . . . thank you. And how guilty I feel towards you.

15 July, Moscow

'I have always been regretting that I was not as wise as the day I was born.' (Thoreau, *Walden*.)

Surely our feelings and perceptions cannot all be identical. I suspect they may be quite different. The world is accessible to an original mind, it is hermetic only in a relative sense. It contains far more holes and far more absolutes than are immediately apparent. Only we can't see them, we don't recognize them.

Perhaps I am an agnostic, in the sense that I reject everything that humanity presents as new knowledge about the world, on the grounds that the methods used were inappropriate. The formula $E = mc^2$ cannot be right, because there can be no such thing as positive knowledge.

Our knowledge is like sweat, or fumes, it's a function of the organism inseparable from existence, and has nothing whatever to do with Truth.

The only function of consciousness is to produce fabrications. True knowledge is achieved in the heart and in the soul.

20 July, Moscow

Xenia says that at a symposium at the Union of Cinematographers during the Festival some Swede said that Tarkovsky was the best director in the world, and an Englishman announced that *Stalker* was the best film in the world.

I went to see Xenia and Dushan, where I met someone very important; a director, head of the Film Institute in Belgrade, member of the government. He promised an invitation for all three of us, and as we were saying goodbye, assured me that all would be well.

'I believe that every man who has ever been earnest to preserve his higher or poetic faculties in the best condition has been particularly inclined to abstain from animal food, and from much food of any kind.' (Thoreau, *Walden*.)

'He who has true faith in the All-present Higher Being may include anything in his diet.' (Only in a year of famine.) (The Veda, quoted in Thoreau, *Walden*.)

'When the soul has lost control of itself, we look and do not see, we listen and do not hear, we eat and do not taste our food.' (Tse Tsi, quoted in *Walden*.)

'The difference between man and beast is not great; ordinary people lose it soon enough, noble people carefully preserve it.' (ibid.)

23 July, Moscow

A lot has been happening. Shkalikov was very unpleasant to Larissa over the telephone (she rang him).

Sizov is very aggressive, as if afraid of being accused of being well disposed towards me.

This morning Surikov told Larissa that the Italians are crooks. (That was his answer to Larissa's question about the two telexes from RAI, in which the Italians wanted to know about visas and dates for their visit here to sign the contract.) Surikov stated bluntly that there hadn't been any telexes. When Tonino telephoned, Surikov said the telexes had come (so presumably the Italians are not crooks after all).

I talked to Kostikov and told him that our son is not going with us, and we want it to be laid down in the contract that we have the right to come to Moscow from time to time to see our family.

And everything seems to be changing for the better. Time will tell.

Arayk talked to Galya Br. She wanted to talk to her father as well about Andriushka, but it turned out that he will be in Moscow in the middle of September. I think that once the contract has been signed (please God!) the question of Andriushka will be seen in a different light, if those are Yermash's orders.

The Yugoslav 'minister' has already talked to Yermash about inviting me to Yugoslavia, and apparently Yermash had 'no objection'.

Today Casati rang (I was out) and Lara and I were rather scared. But all he wanted to know was which hotel they would be staying in. The Ukraine.

26 July, Moscow

' "They pretend", as I hear, "that the verses of Kabir have four different senses; illusion, spirit, intellect, and the exoteric doctrine of the Vedas."

'If a man does not keep pace with his companions, perhaps it is because he hears a different drummer.'

'However mean your life is, meet it and live it; do not shun it and call it hard names. It is not so bad as you are. It looks poorest when you are richest.' (Henry Thoreau, *Walden.*)

27 July, Moscow

De Berti, Canepari and Cásati arrived yesterday. They are willing to do anything, even to agree to Goskino's last demand (x 2.5).

We all met, including Tonino, and decided:

1. To say how important the production is, culturally and ideologically, for all future contracts between RAI and the USSR.

2. It might be possible not to build a set in the country, but to find an existing house. (So that we don't have to bother about it afterwards.)

3. Cut the (overall) time from 13 months to 12—though this is not crucial; we shall have to think about it.

4. Start in October. (Better to have a break at some point in the course of the work.)

28 July, Moscow

The question of the contract is complicated by the fact that de Berti is not entitled to put his signature before that of the consultative board. It might be left unsigned.

I've reduced the estimate for the country set that I am going to shoot in Italy.

'Even if we travel from end to end of every land, nowhere in the world shall we find a country that is alien to us; from everywhere it will be equally possible to raise our eyes to the sky.' (Seneca.)

De Berti telephoned the vice-president in Rome. He can:

1. Leave a letter explaining the position and undertaking to sign the contract finally after the consultative board has met.

2. Hand over 25,000,000 lire to Sovinfilm as a guarantee, which Sovinfilm will keep if RAI back out of making the film.

They are treating the Italians abominably. No cars, no allowance, no interpreter, no reception. I can just imagine how things would be if it were Bondarchuk instead of me—they'd all be crawling on their bellies in front of the Italians.

This evening we had supper (revolting meal) in Archangelskoye, with the Italians and Tonino and Lora.

The impression produced was ghastly; the streets were full of drunks, and the heat unbearable. They're forecasting 35° for tomorrow.

29 July, Moscow

The talks went well today. I began to have the impression that our people intend to let me make the film (they are stipulating in the contract that one person has to go to Rome to look at my material).

30 July, Moscow

We saw the Italians off. There was a dinner in the Aragva. Everyone is pleased. The contract will be signed soon. I can hardly believe it. In fact I shan't believe it until I find myself actually in Rome.

31 July, Moscow

Tonino would like me to tape the account of my journey in Siberia.

'The first thing promised by philosophy is the ability to live amongst people; benevolence and sociability.' (Seneca.)

1 August, Moscow

'For me one person is like a whole nation, and a whole nation is like a single person.'—words quoted by Seneca in his VIIth letter to Lucilius.

'The idea is the eternal image of all that is produced by nature.'— Plato.

'We enter, and do not enter twice, the same stream.'—Heraclitus.

4 August, Moscow

'It is shameful to feel one thing and say another, but how much more shameful to feel one thing and write another!' (Seneca, *Letters to Lucilius*, II, xxiv.)

Today at last I finished the translation of *Nostalgia*. Now I must get the second half retyped, in time for Lara to take a copy to the country on the 7th. I shall evidently be going tomorrow with an engineer from Shilovo.

The script has turned out really well.

6 August, Myasnoye

Arrived in Shilovo early this morning, after very nearly over-sleeping. Volodya Ivanov met me. Tyapus is sunburnt and looking much better. He can swim. Tomorrow he and Dakus share a birth-day. Lara and Olga are coming tomorrow; and perhaps Sasha Medvedev and Arayk.

The engine isn't working. Everything has to be put in order.

I feel utterly exhausted.

Darling Tyapus! He was missing me so much! He's so looking forward to his birthday. Larissa said she would try and come to-morrow morning.

Of course the script ought to be retyped in the course of today. But that's not difficult, if it's all clear.

7 August, Myasnoye

Tyapus was given his presents and was very pleased with them. Particularly his little tape recorder and cassettes. He was waiting for his mum and Olga all day long, poor little boy. Arayk brought him a water-melon from Yerevan. Olga is waiting for some money, so she couldn't come. She is coming soon, according to Larissa.

11 August, Myasnoye

Made a fence with posts and barbed wire. Sasha made a lot of gloomy jokes on the subject. Today he went off to Moscow. I want to paint the inside of the cistern—for cold water for the bath-house.

There's a smell of smoke—I think the peat bogs are on fire. Any-how there's a smell of burning peat. We still haven't insured the house, or the bath-house. Brilliant—in this heat.

It's impossible to live here. This beautiful country has been totally fouled up. They've made it menial, destitute, and lawless . . .

13 August, Myasnoye

I've started to dream. It must be some step forward in my meditation. But what? My life is filled with my Italian problems. What if it falls through, if they don't allow it? What an appalling thought. I cannot bring myself to ask Galya Brezhneva for help. So many frightful things are said about her. Lara and I are going to have to talk it all over thoroughly. We *cannot* make a mistake.

Today after weeks of heat it has been raining since early morning. That's good.

Despite everything, a balanced, independent, lonely way of life can give the peace that is vital. I must look for peace. I must start to do meditation seriously—there I go, thinking again in Italian terms —and Buddhism.

How wonderful it would be to live somewhere in Italy or Switzerland and be able to go off on holiday to Ceylon, just to have a look.

I don't remember, incidentally, whether I've already written something about Gurdjiev's theory? I was not convinced by it, because, as an agnostic, I found myself faced with a 'universal' conception of the construction of the universe and of man's role in it.

I don't believe know-alls. I can accept faith, but not knowledge. And Gurdjiev proposes an actual 'method' of existence, based on a construction that is *clear to the author from beginning to end*—which is meaningless within the terms of our causal and infinite world.

That's all on the subject for the moment. Even if there are no arguments, thought still ought to be clear.

I feel shivery; perhaps I've poisoned myself with something.

For some reason I keep thinking about Antonioni. When all is said and done, he is the best Italian director today. Fellini has an open, expansive temperament. That is his very essence.

If only things work out with the Italians! Opening the Gospels at random:

'Verily, verily I say unto you, he that entereth not by the door into the sheep-fold, but climbeth up some other way, the same is a thief and a robber.

But he that entereth in by the door is the shepherd of the sheep.

To him the porter openeth, and the sheep hear his voice: and he calleth his own sheep by name, and leadeth them out.' (John, Ch. 10).

Could that be about my plans? Oh, dear Lord . . .

I wonder—can I remember the outline of *Nostalgia*? I'll have a go:

1. *Madonna del Parto*

2. Foyer of the Hotel du Palme. Reminiscences and 'translation.'
3. The windowless room. Eugenia. The well. Conversations. The dream.

14 August, Myasnoye

Why are plots in which people win by far the most common, in literature, theatre and film? Of course, that sort of development corresponds with how people live through the hero's experience, but they would still live it if the hero were to be a total loser. Stories of failure could well be a fruitful new departure in art.

Truth does not exist in itself; it lies in the method. It is—the way. *The way.*

18 August, Moscow

At home. I'm tired. I can't sleep properly anywhere except in my own bed. And alone.

19 August, Moscow

I am not living; for many months now I have been waiting, waiting, waiting . . .

God, help me!

20 August, Moscow

Faith and sincerity in the 'conversation' with the future audience —that is the one and only criterion. There are no others, nor could there be.

22 August, Moscow

Terribly worried about Larissa. We are penniless. And I'm really worried too about Andriushka, he's got to go to school very soon. There are things to be prepared—his room, trousers. Of course I'm sure Lara will deal with it all. If only she is well; she is so tired, poor thing.

I've heard rumours that things are not going too well with Solonitsyn. His doctor says that in the year following the operation you can expect anything—either good or bad. And that this is only the beginning of the illness.

How wretched I feel . . .

23 August, Moscow

Why do I feel so bad? So wretched? I used at least to dream, and in some of my dreams I could find some sort of hope. But now I don't even dream. Frightening—life is so frightening! Oh, Lara, if it weren't for her . . .

Nostalgia.
After Beriozovsky's letter, it needs something else before the scene in the House at the End of the World:
The bulb explodes in the bonfire (poem)?

God, what misery! Never have I felt so alone!

'. . . an acute and prolonged feeling of sinfulness leads to a sense of oppression, whereas the function of a religious life is to *overcome* oppression.' (Nikolay Berdyaev, *Self-knowledge.*)
'I have a real revulsion for nationalism, it is not merely immoral, but always stupid and ridiculous.' (Berdyaev.)
'. . . I love Russia with an ardent, but nonetheless strange love, and I believe in the universal mission of the Russian people. I am not a nationalist but a Russian patriot.' (Berdyaev.)
'Without Christ, the Slav sense of being destined to perform some cosmic feat of heroism is turned into a racist aspiration.' (Vyacheslav Ivanov.)

3 September, Myasnoye
Yesterday, quite unexpectedly, Sasha and Yuri Kochevrin turned up (in a car belonging to a friend of Sasha's). They left again this morning. Sasha came in order to talk over various problems to do with the scriptwriting course: Kokoreva is convinced that I am going to be in charge of both the directing and scriptwriting courses. They needed names of readers for candidates' work (Klimov, Nekhoroshev), and I'm supposed to be producing a list of two or three directors and scriptwriters—so far only Sasha Medvedev and V. Sedov.
Yuri really enjoyed being with us. He even wanted to know if it was possible to buy a house here.
Tyapa went off to school very happily (September 1st).
Lara has been stung twice by a wasp (or a bee).
Today I finished the cess-pit, and the piles of rubbish—I got rid of three of them. Terribly tired. Tomorrow I want to start on the raspberries. Of course it's heavenly here. We've got such a lovely house. And bath-house!

Seneca, *Letters to Lucilius*. Letter xxx could be the basis on which to build the character of the Philosopher at the beginning of the screenplay, *The Witch*. (The title is not right.)

'The best way is to avoid people who are not like you and who are preoccupied with other desires.' (Seneca, Letter xxxII.)

'Nothing that vanishes from our sight is destroyed—it is all hidden in nature, whence it came and where it reappears. There is an interval, but no destruction. And death, which we repudiate in terror, interrupts life, but does not put an end to it. The day will come when we appear again in the world, even though many would refuse to return had they not forgotten all about it.' (Seneca, Letter xxxVI).

Again 'the eternal return!'

'. . . Neither infants, nor children, nor those whose reason is impaired fear death—shame upon those to whom reason fails to grant the serenity accorded by foolishness . . .' (ibid.) (for *The Witch*).

'I give myself to be burned, bound, or beaten to death with iron.' —Gladiators' oath (Seneca.)

1982

There is nothing more difficult to achieve than a passionate, sincere, quiet faith.

1982

January, Tbilisi

Bazhanov is wonderful; great charm, clever, subtle, tactful—it's a joy to be with him. Larissa and Tyapa are enchanted by him. He is living in appalling conditions, and not one from among his string of visitors, nor any of the people who happily accept presents from him, is willing to bestir themselves to help him find a flat. He has no water, gas or bath, and he is ill. He is a wonderful, kindly man.

We saw Simon and Lany, and went to Kakheti and Tikhan with Seryozha. Silnach was particularly beautiful. I met Gayaneh Khatchaturian, and Dato Eristavo, a remarkable character, and a healer.

We went to see the Agababobys, and Eldar Shengelay. I still have a few visits to make; etiquette is taken seriously. Andriushka loves it here, so does Lara, but I must say I feel it is Asia.

Through the cinema club I have given five talks. My gums were inflamed, but settled down again quite quickly, perhaps thanks to Dato.

Surikov is not yet back at work. On the 3rd—by the end of the week—I must ring Sizov again before I leave. I have so many good impressions of Tbilisi. Incidentally. Svetlana Dzegutova is a wonderful, kind, sensitive person—but a fantasist.

Morning! Ceylon, Ceylon. Dato Eristavo was telling us yesterday how he had found his teacher, or rather, how the latter had found his pupil. His teacher is a thirty-year-old Kazakh, related to the secretary of the district committee. Once when he was ill and in hospital, some ordinary shepherds came in and sat around his bed; in the end, he got up and walked, and walked out of the hospital. Then in 1980 he appeared in Tbilisi and found Dato, who was leading a very dissipated life at the time. There are only two of them in the Soviet Union connected with Ceylon and that particular esoteric school. He—Dato—and the grandson of Samuel Marshak.

Today Larissa reminded me of how Tatiana Alekseyevna had upset her when Lara, entirely out of the goodness of her heart, had dashed off to help Father move flat and various other things. She terribly wanted to bring Father and me together, because we love him deeply. Tatiana Aleksandrovna announced over the telephone to Anna Semyonovna that Alyosha was going to inherit everything. For God's sake! As if anyone was thinking about legacies. It hadn't entered any of our heads. That idiotic woman is not actually capable of understanding genuine feeling. Father really is being punished by God, having to put up with her year after year. And now Alyosha is dead, and I think that Tatiana Alekseyevna will die before Father; it is all meant.

7 January, Tbilisi

Night. Today Seryozha did a deal with Yuri Barabadze—he got a fantastic Khersur dress out of him and gave it to Larissa. It is amazingly beautiful, and really suits Lara.

We went to see Dato Eristavo who treated Larissa. She had a very strong negative reaction. Tomorrow Lara has to have her teeth done. Inna Agababova promised to arrange it.

Things don't look too good for the tickets—decent sleepers are only available on the 12th. Dato Eristavo gave me a photocopy of Rozenberg's book, *Questions of Buddhist Philosophy*. I've started reading it.

About *Stalker*—the only film he's seen—Dato said, 'It's not a film, it's a teaching.' He also talked about 'the field of investigation', and said I was a 'newcomer'—meaning that in the past I had been there, outside. I must find out exactly what he means by that.

8 January, Tbilisi

Had a depressing conversation with Zhurbinadze about Sergey Paradzhanov, about his life and what lies ahead for him. Gayaneh Khatchaturian is a remarkable artist.

The world of my hallucinations belongs in effect to spiritual naturalism. Staggered by Pirosmanashvili in the museum. Georgiy Shengelay made a bad film about Pirosmane. Pirosmane lived as he wanted, he was a happy man, as it were, organically whole, with nothing about him of the social martyr.

Andriushka went to the Rustavelli theatre with Lara and Sergey to see *Richard*.*

*Robert Sturua's much acclaimed production of *Richard III*.

I gave a talk at the Institute of Physics. I'm tired. I don't want any of it. This evening we all went to the theatre to see Robert Sturua's *Chalk Circle*. Razmas was wonderful! Lado and I talked about Seryozha. I intend to go to the Central Committee, to the Public Opinion Committee—or whatever that unique body is called—to talk about Sergey. I cannot bear to watch it all going on.

9 January, Tbilisi

For many millennia, man has been striving after happiness; but he is not happy. Why not? Because he cannot achieve it, because he does not know the way—both those reasons. Above all, however, because in our earthly lives there must not be ultimate happiness, but only the aspiration towards it, in the future; there has to be suffering, because it's through suffering, in the struggle between good and evil, that the spirit is forged.

10 January

Today, 10 January, 1982, we celebrated Seryozha's birthday, at his place in Zarisi. (His birthday is on 9 January, according to his passport, as he says, but he always celebrates it on his son's birthday, I think in December.) It was a wonderful evening; a group of very different people, but all united in our love for Seryozha.

13 January

On the Tbilisi–Moscow train. We very nearly missed the train, with all our boxes, crates, bundles, bags, which all accumulated at the last minute, with vast quantities of gifts; Seryozha was late. We were seen off by Gayaneh, Seryozha and his friends, the propaganda office; Eko and Lyalya Agababov brought along some food . . .

16 January, Moscow

We're drinking delicious Georgian wine and remembering our friends in Tbilisi. How lovely it was there! What a wonderful man Seryozha is! How kind, and generous. I am glad to be alive at the same time as he. Lara thinks he is marvellous, so does Andriushka. It makes us sad to think about him. He is not only a genius in terms of his work, he is a genius in everything, he is unique!

17 January, Moscow

Volodya Shinkarenko came. He has had the idea of filming Tolya

Solonitsyn, whilst he is still alive. As the poet* said, 'Come, we're not in Chicago, my dear?'

Volodya Shinkarenko and I went to see Tolya. He is very sick. He has seen Djuna three times; he has growths in the rib cage, right and left, and they must be in his liver as well. Please God he will not be in agony!

19 January, Moscow

Spoke with Djuna about Tolya Solonitsyn. She said—'It's too late.'

Our Alyosha Naydenov is helping, very effectively, to organize filming an interview with Tolya. I am thinking very seriously about Alyosha, I like his work, he could develop into a very fine cameraman; he must be given some help.

There is a saying, originating in one of the Gospels, to the effect that there is no need to distort your own persona in order to recognize God. There is a particular look, just and serious, which quietly manifests itself at the moment when you decide to embark upon spiritual practice.

21 January

Went to see Djuna yesterday. She wants to tell me something not for the microphone. Must talk to Lara about it, and invite her to come and see us. Again, she said it was too late for Tolya.

I saw Sizov, he said that everything was in order for Italy; I am to go to Rome on 15 February, to sign the contract, either with Yermash or with Sizov.

Saw Sasha Kaydanovsky about *Nostalgia*. Read him the screenplay, offered him the part; he agreed. Oh, Tolya, Tolya!

29 January, Moscow

Suslov died yesterday. He had everyone on a short rein for a very long time. I wonder what will happen now.

29/30 January, Leningrad. Astoria

I have one appearance in Leningrad, tomorrow, for 300 roubles; there couldn't be any more, for various complicated, unexpected reasons.

Of course I've seen Sasha, Yura, Kostya. They showed me the

*S. Mikhalkov, *Mister Twister*.

Leningrad antique shops, which are marvellous. I want to buy some china for Lara's birthday, even if it's not the right moment. What a fine man Sasha Sakurov is, and how hard it is for him, being in Leningrad with so much talent; not that it would be much better in Moscow. They showed me an amazingly beautiful tiled stove. Wouldn't it be lovely to have it in our house in the country!

1 February, Moscow

Back from Leningrad. Lara's birthday. We celebrated at home, with only the family. Lara was very pleased with my presents, I'm so glad!

But we've been met by every kind of calamity, the main one being that people from 38 Petrovka Street* came round to tell me that a criminal case is being brought against me; I am convinced that Goskino don't want to let me go to Italy. Larissa has already had a word with Svetlana. Larissa promised to find out through Alexander Alexandrovich; she can also make use of knowing Yakovlev, Shelokov's replacement. She'll go to his office tomorrow. They're out to get me by whatever means they can.

3 February

Thanks be to God! Lara has put everything right, the whole thing has been dropped. They said it was some kind of misunderstanding. There's only one misunderstanding, and it's the one I suspected.

Abbado telephoned from London yesterday, he wants to put on *Godunov*; and today John Roberts rang also from London, wanting to know what news there might be of my plans. And what plans are Goskino sitting on?

Read a rather noxious little book by Yeremey Yudovlevich Karpov, a fantasy about a journey through Asia and India; about the god, Lotos. He is so clever, and so infallible in his judgements on every topic, it's nauseating. From a literary point of view it's not up to much; racy, illiterate, brash—in a word, an example of Soviet naturalism.

I had a terrifying dream last night, about a vast fair or exhibition of electronic amusements, things like encounters between machines and beings from other planets. A terrifying, ironic mystery; and then, on top of that, I dreamt that I had become a member of the Politburo and was on my way to a session, where I was going to meet the other members.

*Ministry of the Interior.

There was a phone-call from the correspondent of *Unita* about the much-discussed preface to the volume *Russian Fantasy*.

12 February, Moscow

Svetlana Dzegutova telephoned today from Tbilisi, and this evening—Garik. Seryozha Paradzhanov has been arrested. No one knows any details yet. His flat hasn't been searched. It is sealed.

13 February, Moscow

'Mine is not a pleasant story, it does not possess the gentle harmony of invented tales; like the lives of all men who have given up trying to deceive themselves, it is a mixture of nonsense and chaos, madness and dreams.' The words which are used as an epigraph to Hesse's *Demian*, and which could equally be an epitaph to *Mirror* (as could the lines which follow them).

All that I wanted was to tempt into life things that wanted to come out of me. Why was it so hard? That is precisely the explanation of the scene with the stammerer, which is essentially the epigraph to the film.

Nostalgia—perhaps if Gorchakov is Kaydanovsky, the night scene in the hotel should be based on Kaydanovsky's likeness to Van Gogh rather than on the beauty of the hero's hands.

Gorchakov deliberately winds his scarf around his ear, and he knows that Eugenia is following him.

'I consider that reality is the last thing we need worry about, because, tediously enough, it will always be there, whereas more beautiful and more necessary things require our attention and care. Reality should not in any circumstances satisfy us, it is not in any circumstances to be worshipped or respected, for it is accidental, it is the refuse of life. And the only way to change this vapid reality, forever disappointing and joyless, is by denying it, and thereby proving that we are stronger than it is.' (Hesse, *A Life Story Briefly Told.*)

Rereading Hesse. He and I have so much in common. He would be quite at home, for instance, with those ideas about St. Anthony.

'Gold must become a flower, the spirit must become body and psyche, in order to live.' (Hesse, *A Guest at the Spa.*)

'There are two paths to salvation. The path of righteousness, for the righteous, and the path of grace, for sinners; and I am a sinner. I have again made the mistake of trying to achieve salvation through righteousness.' (ibid.)

—*1982*—

r February, Moscow

Anna Semyonovna was 79 today. The two of us are close in so
.any ways. I have never in my life met anyone more spiritual than
.e; with her wisdom, her kindness, her deep understanding. And at
.e same time she has a meekness and a tolerance that clutch your
.eart to the point where it hurts. When I look at her I often feel
.hamed of myself. All is vanity of vanities and weariness of spirit.

3/24 February, Moscow

Sasha Sakurov and Yura Reverov are having a really bad time.
They are not being given anything to do. Pavlyonok and Bogomolov yell at them and put them down in every way they can. It's
the result of a denunciation from Heifits, who is trying to shove his
two sons into the production. And the bosses know how the lads
feel about me, and they are taking it out on them instead of on me.
They accuse them of being under my—of course deleterious—influence.

It is really becoming impossible to breathe. These days everyone
involved in the press, or cinema, or television, finds himself obliged
to hear or read quantities of words which contain very little meaning;
and as a result anyone of any depth experiences actual hunger. By
contrast, for those that have ears to hear, the spirit can reveal itself
in examples and in simple words which do not stifle it in any
way.

'Faith without works is dead'—James. 'Be master of your tongue
and do not multiply words, lest you multiply your sins. The Lord will
guard your soul as long as you guard your tongue. All sins are hateful in the sight of the Lord. But most hateful of all is pride of heart.'
—St. Anthony, in *Lives of the Fathers*.

'Penury is nothing other than abstinence and contentment with
your lot.'—ibid.

'Do not suggest or teach to anyone else anything that you have
not already done yourself.'—ibid.

27 February, Moscow

'Whenever we are faced with a battle against temptation in the
place in which we have been called to dwell, we move somewhere
else, imagining that there exists some place that does not have the
devil in it.'—St. Anthony.

'Anthony led Amon out of his cell and said to him, "Offend that
stone, strike it a blow." Amon did so. Then Anthony asked Amon,

"Did the stone give you any answer, did it show you any resistance?" "No", replied Amon. "You too", Anthony told him, "will attain that level of detachment"; and this was indeed the case.'—Abba Amon, in *Lives of the Fathers*.

28 February, Moscow

'I have never wished to be worshipped, I should be ashamed to find myself in the role of an idol; I have always longed to be necessary.

'Whomsoever you go to see, do not speak to him before he asks you to.'—Abba Evagrius.

'Worldly curiosity is empty and vainglorious.'—Commentary on *Lives of the Fathers*.

'If a woman came to talk to a monk, or if a monk found it necessary to talk with a woman, they would sit at some distance from each other, on opposite banks of a stream, and their conversation would take place in that way.'—*Lives of the Fathers*.

3 March, Moscow

'Before you start to speak, consider what it is that you are going to say. Say only what is necessary and proper. Do not boast of your reason, and do not think that you know more than others. The essence of the monastic life is self-reproach and the conviction that you are the most unworthy of all.'—Abba Isaac.

'Stand at prayer in the fear of God, do not lean against the wall or shift your weight from one foot to the other as the ignorant do.' (From the teachings of Abba Isaac.)

5 March, Moscow

'The holy hermit fathers uttered prophecies about the last days. They posed the question, "What have we done?" One of them, Abba Iskerion, a man of exemplary life, declared, "We have observed God's commandments." The fathers asked, "And those who come immediately after us, what will they do?" He answered, "They will do half the deeds that we have done." The fathers asked again, "And those who come after them?" "They", replied the Abba, "will not lead the monastic life at all; but disasters will overcome them, and they, the victims of disaster and temptation, will turn out to be greater than us and greater than our fathers." ' (*Lives of the Fathers*)

'One day an elder, a native of Fivanda by the name of Pavva, took a withered tree, thrust it into the ground on the mountain, and told John Kologa to water the withered tree daily, until the tree bore fruit. There was no water nearby. It was necessary to set out in the morning in order to fetch it and bring it back by evening. By the end of the third year the tree sprouted and brought forth fruit. The elder took the fruit and brought it into the church to the community and said to them, "Come, taste the fruit of obedience."' (ibid.)

'At some distance from their cell was a graveyard, and a ferocious hyena lived there, which slaughtered people and cattle. The elder said to John in the graveyard, "I have seen the hyena's droppings, go and fetch it and bring it here to me." John answered, "And what am I to do if the hyena attacks me?" The elder smiled and said, "If the hyena attacks you, bind it up and bring it to me." That evening John went to the graveyard. The hyena attacked him, but he, as the elder had ordered him, threw himself at it to capture it. But it ran away from him, and John ran after it, shouting, "Stop, my father told me to bind you." It stopped. John bound it. In the mean time the elder was sitting and waiting for his pupil. And so John came back leading the hyena. The elder was astonished when he saw him. Wishing to teach his pupil humility and save him from arrogance, he took an iron rod and began to beat him, saying, "You fool, have you brought me back a dog?" The elder untied the hyena and let it go.' (ibid.)

8 March, Rome

Rome. I flew here yesterday. Sizov and Bondarchuk were in the same plane. Their Florence première of *Red Bells* has fallen through. At Sheremetevo there was an awful incident with the customs. The official told me to open my suitcase, and he took one of my diaries out of it, and gave it to his assistant to examine. Apparently you have to have special permission to take out manuscripts, and I didn't have it. Then he went off somewhere, and at that moment his assistant found a photograph of Solzhenitsyn and his daughters in my diary. I had no idea it was there. He demanded an explanation, and I said that the photograph was there entirely by accident. He put it back and closed the diary. Then the senior official came back. The assistant said nothing, he was silent. The other, the senior one, asked me something about ikons. I said I had nothing like that at all, although he obviously could see my cross in his machine. But he didn't pursue the conversation either. I was lucky.

Today I saw Canepari, de Berti, Rosselini and the others at the studio. And Picera.

I telephoned home and talked to Larochka. Dear Lord, look after them.

10 March, Rome

I still can't believe what I feel. I seem to be in a dream. Any moment now I shall have to wake up. I talked to Lara. She's not well. She's on edge because of my going away. Oh, God. I talked to Andriushka.

13 March, Rome

Yesterday I forgot to write that I had met Andilopolous and his wife. No particular impression.

Spoke to Larissa, she is better. I think she's going to supper at the Italian Embassy on Tuesday, if she's well enough. Talked with Andriushka, he said he had had three fives,* in Russian language and literature.

Saw Enrica and Antonioni in the evening at Ugo Attati's—new friends to whom Tonino introduced me.

15 March

Had a talk with Zemfira Vassilevna about Lara. She's in a state of total nervous exhaustion. Her friend is coming. On Wednesday, I think, Larissa has a meeting with an important official. Talked to Tyapus. He was boasting about his fours and fives.

I was interviewed by Rondi. He said that in the summer I was going to be given some government prize.

My darling Larochka and Tyapus, how are they, in Moscow.

'I gazed around me, and my soul was wounded by the sufferings of mankind.'—Radishchev, *Journey from Petersburg to Moscow*.

18 March

It has been pouring since morning. It's damp. Reading Bunin. I don't want to launch straight into a screenplay. It's too soon. On Monday I want to go and look at outdoor locations with Pepe. But first and foremost I must go to Porto Nuovo, to my Vladimir

*Top marks.

Mother of God. Incidentally, I want to use the interior of that wonderful church.

Reading Bunin. Any false element in the poetic weave of a work will destroy its vital force—surely, directly and rightly. Look at Rasputin: half legitimate, half topical questions, half love, half truth. But Bunin is whole, monolithic, and his prose is tender and powerful.

'In Moscow Street I wandered into a coachman's tea-room. I sat there among the voices and the crowd, in the steamy heat, and looked at the fleshy, scarlet faces, the red beards, the rusty, flaking tray on which two white tea pots stood in front of me, with wet string tied to their lids and handles. Observing the mores of the people? No, you are mistaken: merely that tray and those wet pieces of string.'— Bunin, *Lika*.

Amazing stuff, almost like Tse. Bunin writes about Oryol in *Lika*, about the shops, the restaurants serving beautiful meals on the terrace, the starched table-cloths, the footmen in tailcoats, and so on. And that was all at the back of beyond, before the Revolution, my God! And what is Oryol like now? I dare not even think. All falling down, the ruins lost in mud, poverty, darkness. 'A footman, the tails of his coat swinging.' My God, the very concept seems crazy; in Oryol, in the station.

'How beautiful some unhappy people can be; their faces, their eyes with their very souls gazing through them.'—Bunin, *Lika*.

'I went into the church. From loneliness and sadness churches have become a habit.'—ibid.

I feel I have a brother in Bunin: his nostalgia, his hope, the rigour of his demands, which undiscerning people put down to resentment.

Telephone conversation with Larissa. I gathered she had spoken to some official about her trip, and had been told that her passport wasn't ready, that it hadn't yet been processed. Lara was alarmed. I don't think there's any need to be alarmed yet, he was only a minor official, he really doesn't figure, and he's afraid of everything. Surikov promised to explain the situation. We'll see. Lara has an important meeting on Monday. He also said that the question had already been considered at a high level, or is going to be.

Talked to Tyapus. He is working hard at school, my darling boy. I sent word with Olya that there was a parcel on its way to them. Larissa hinted that things are bad financially. She started to ask about audience letters. I interrupted her, and told her not to, because I would be back in Moscow. One way and another the call left me feeling anxious, but somehow in my heart I feel it will be all right. It can't not be. The Lord will not allow anything bad to happen.

19 March

RAI have sent a telex asking Larissa to come as soon as possible.

20 March

My God, what a compelling power of love and compassion for the defenceless and the despairing Bunin achieves sometimes in his stories. Yet people say he is cold. Towards whom? Or what? Andriushka must read Bunin, I must remember to mention it to Lara.

An odd idea has occurred to me for a screenplay in order to earn money. About someone landing on another planet, where he can't understand anything of the atmosphere of this other civilization. Something of my dream, a little of Lem's *Return from the Stars*. But that's not what is important. The activities of other beings, what they look like, the objects, the phenomena—everything. What an absurd notion! The embodiment of the absurd! Very frightening at the same time. The point is to create a new real world in a kind of agnostic sense. Perhaps I should do it as a kind of hypercommercial gesture.

I should love us to live in a good, comfortable flat, for Larissa's sake. I should love her to be able to rest, and be entertained, and as far as it's possible, to have treatment. It's not easy for her to live with me, taking on the impossible burden of our lives, and by doing so giving me the confidence to believe that I chose the right path. And of course I am not all sweetness and light as a character. Not everyone could take it. The one thing of which I am certain is that I couldn't live without Lara.

This evening we celebrated Lora's birthday at Tonino's house. Dino and Maria came from Sant' Arcangelo, so of course the food was phenomenal. I told Tonino my idea for a documentary film. He agreed. We shall have to work on it a bit. I do so like Dino and Maria. He has terrible business problems, but he doesn't talk to anyone about them. Tonino wants to help him in a roundabout way. He's a very noble character, that Cretan, Dino.

21 March

Spent the evening at the Embassy club. I had to speak in front of our people, and of course deal with some idiotic questions.

Rondi rang and said that he was with Fellini and that they were about to celebrate my fiftieth birthday. Incidentally, Rondi said earlier that the Italians are planning to give me some sort of national award.

22 March

Went to Terilli today with Franco, and to Porto Nuovo with Pepe to pray to my Vladimir Mother of God. It made me feel so much easier.

Talked to Lara. They've postponed her meeting till Wednesday. They also told her it would take two months to process the documents. I think that if that meeting really takes place, she will be able to sort out both problems at once. We shall see. Blessed Virgin, pray for us. Today I prayed and prayed.

I heard today that this year at Cannes they are going to award some sort of highly prestigious prizes to the world's best directors, and apparently that includes me.

Lara has no news. Naturally Shkalikov said that he couldn't discuss the details over the telephone, but that he would try to have her documents dealt with as soon as possible. He is mystifying, of course.

24 March

Yesterday the television people agreed to send a telex asking Larissa to come to Rome as soon as possible.

All day long I've been having depressing thoughts about Lara and Andriushka. The present doesn't exist. There are only the past and the future, which, practically speaking, are a cypher in terms of temporal state, and only connect with a person through the assertion of his will, through his action, which allows the future to filter through it, leaving the past.

What is expressed in mathematics is not so much objective laws of the world as laws of the human psyche, laws of logic, of the human mind. It's really a kind of mental game, and yet the exact sciences, as they are called, command extraordinary respect—physics, astronomy, and so on. It's very odd, in fact I would say an amazing, paradoxical misconception.

I saw Tonino and Jacob, the director of the Cannes Festival. He said first, that at the 35th Cannes Festival twelve, and not five, best directors in the world were going to be given awards, or diplomas, or something; and that I was one of them, and could I go to Cannes for the ceremonial presentation. I told him I could, but asked them as far as possible to keep quiet about the award. Second, they asked me to sit on the jury. I told them it was unlikely, as I had already promised to sit on the Venice jury, all the members of which this year are going to be holders of the Golden Lion. Third, they want to have *Nostalgia* at the Festival; Tonino and I said yes.

What I asked them was whether this year, taking advantage of being in Cannes, it might be possible to meet someone in the French government, with a view to letting Anna Semyonovna, Olya and Tyapa come over on holiday after the film. But that'll have to be later, because it has to be thought about very seriously. What if I have another heart attack because of all this, a second one, and how could I explain to them why, and ought I to explain? They promised to arrange the meeting. What is happening at home? Lord, bless and preserve them!

Talked to Larochka and Tyapus. He received the parcel, and he was so delighted, the little boy. Lara was in good heart too. She is insisting that Shkalikov let her go to Rome, and wants to reprocess the documents. He apparently insists, despite everything, that she hasn't been commissioned by Mosfilm.

The crucial meeting has been put off to Saturday, but Lara doesn't think it will happen before next week. She says everything is fine at home. Yura Reverov, Kostya Lapushansky and Volodya Mashin are all helping her. Endless phone-calls, everyone's worried. In the mean time Sizov is in hospital, I think with a heart attack. Tomorrow I must send him a telegram, to the studios. There are rumours at the studios that he is having problems with Lotyanu and Bondarchuk, or rather, with their films.

The most important thing and the hardest is to have faith. Because if you do have faith, then everything comes true. Only it's impossibly hard to believe sincerely. There is nothing more difficult to achieve than a passionate, sincere, quiet faith.

28 March

Tonino and Lora and I went to visit Antonioni at Speclo. The house is staggering, it cost him something like 750,000 dollars. There's a beautiful olive orchard. But inside the house everything is much too clearly defined, like in an architectural plan.

29 March

Not only are space and time and cause all forms of the thought process, not only does the essence of life lie outside these forms, but our very lives consist of gradually submitting to these forms, and then, eventually, freeing ourselves of them once more.

Yet again—St. Anthony and his temptations. The same thing all over again. And indeed the compass of human freedom is bounded on the one side by evil and on the other by good. But I have never heard of anyone struggling to rise and at the same time slipping back, falling. To rise is necessarily to struggle.

30 March

Telephoned Moscow. Andriushka is ill, his temperature in the morning was 39°. Poor little boy. Larissa hopes that the interview will be tomorrow at 7.0. Maybe. As for her leaving, none of the top people are there, and Surikov assures her that her documents were ready at the same time as mine. So the picture is clear. They are up to something—they don't want Lara to come and join me. I am so worried about Larissa and miss her so much. Lord, grant that we shall be together.

31 March

The future Lady Hamilton used to pose naked in *tableaux vivants*.

The famous Lobachevsky was Chancellor of Kazan University when Lev Nikolaevich Tolstoy first went there as a student (1844–5).

Last night I had a dream about Seryozha Paradzhanov in prison, but it was some sort of strange prison, not a real one.

We had supper with Michelangelo. We had a really nice conversation. He is a remarkable man; very reserved, but subtle, with an extraordinarily tender soul. I consider him to be the best Italian director. We watched Ozu's *Autumn* on television. I don't remember precisely what autumn. Dreadfully boring; rather like a Mendeleyev table.

'. . . the principal evils besetting people and the disorder of their lives stem from government action. One striking illustration of this premise is the fact that the government not only condones, but actually encourages the production and distribution of wine, that lethal poison, just because its sale brings in a third of the budget.' (From a letter from Lev Tolstoy to Kuzminsky, 1896.)

1 April, Rome. Via di Monte Brianza

Yesterday, from Narymov's, I spoke to Larissa and Tyapus. Tyapus is ill, poor darling, with a high temperature and a head-

ache . . . poor little boy. He talked to me for a bit, poor little thing
. . . Larissa said that Kulakov, allegedly 'on his own initiative',
wants to let Larissa go to Rome on the 4th, but she thinks it's some
sort of ruse. I think the same, but nonetheless it is an indication that
only Goskino are to blame for all the hold-ups. They still haven't had
that meeting, and Larissa says it might be tomorrow, Friday.
Tyapus worries me. Larissa is anxious about the lack of money. I
told her she had time (before Lora leaves for Moscow on the 20th)
to think about what to bring, or rather, what to send her.

I spent the evening with Narymov and Khamreyev. Ali is a
terrible, quite prodigious, bletherer. He went on about everything
under the sun—Afghanistan, corruption in high places . . . I found
it alarming to have to listen to all his ravings. But he made a superb
plov.

2 April, Rome. Via di Monte Brianza

Talked to Lara. It now seems more certain that the interview will
be on Tuesday, the 6th. Lara is really downhearted about not being
able to be with me on the 4th. And Tyapus was in tears after talking
to me yesterday. My God, what barbarians they are!

Kulakov told her that he couldn't let her go by the 4th (why not?).
Anyhow, she convinced him that she has every reason to believe her
documents are now ready.

And Larissa said that Tolya is improving. Incredible! Actually, I
keep thinking about that screenplay, *The Witch*. I am sure that despite everything, Tolya will recover.

Norman and Laura and I went to a concert of early church music
in one of the old churches. It was nice. Of course everything sounds
quite different in a church.

On Sunday, my birthday, I shall go to church.

Why is it that people's perception of reality, received through the
sensory organs, is identical? What is X? Does X = the senses or
reality? The thing is that our senses are given us—with all their
limitations—for us to 'create' or fashion for ourselves our own material world. Objectively speaking (for want of a better word), the
world is utterly, endlessly dense—it's like the nucleus of the heaviest
of the planets. But because we are possessed of—limited—sensory
organs, and consciousness, we have created our own world out of
our *partial* perception of material reality; the world in which we live.

Our reason cannot reach the other parameters or other dimensions which exist, and so it fantasizes about them in the form of mathematics and physics. Science involves the discovery not so much of objective laws of nature, as of the laws which govern the functioning of our consciousness. A kind of music; image; symbol; sign. A mathematical symbol of truth, corresponding to our capacity for knowing it with our brains.

3 April, Rome

Yesterday a greetings telegram arrived for me at RAI from Surikov; today one from Yermash, (through Narymov), also signed by Kulidzhanov. And that was the total celebration; much as was to be expected, I suppose.

My darlings! I have no one else—only Larissa and Tyapus, Anna Semyonovna and Olya! My dearest Tyapus! And Danechka!

Norman and I saw a Truffaut film this afternoon with a wonderful actress, Fanny Ardant. The film is not up to much, but the acting is good. And Ardant is quite lovely.

In fact, if I could use Trintignant and Ardant, it would be pretty good . . .

Tomorrow, or rather, today, in two hours' time, I shall be 50. God, my life has gone by so quickly . . .

4 April, Rome

Tonino rang early this morning from Madrid, to wish me a happy birthday. He was on his way to the Prado, and after that to a *corrida*. Jure Lina rang, not knowing it was my birthday.

Then I went back to sleep, and dreamt I was in Madrid, with Tonino, on a very high terrace. He went so close to the edge that I was frightened and asked him to move away, which he did.

Telegrams have arrived from Sasha Sakurov, Ira and Anna Reverov, Kokoreva and Verochka Semyonovna, and Marina . . . from the Ivanov young men, those same ones. And of course the best of all and the most important to me—from home, from Larochka, Tyapa, A.S., Masha and Volodya Sedov.

This evening Rondi laid on dinner for me in a smart restaurant called Cesarina.

Lizzani and his wife, Fellini and Giulietta Masina, Rondi, Lora and I. It was somehow very nice. I tried to telephone Moscow from there, but it was no good. The operator said the receiver was not in place in Moscow. Now I am back here: Lora booked a call for me, and I am waiting for them to ring. Maybe I shall be able to talk to Larissa after all.

5 April, Rome

I wasn't able to talk to Larissa in the end. No line.

Narymov rang and said I must telephone Yermash, urgently. I had no time today. What does he want now?

Lora and I went to see Ugo and Beatrice this evening; later on Michelangelo Antonioni joined us.

6 April, Rome

I've spoken to Yermash. He wants me to go back to Moscow before Larissa leaves. I asked why Larissa still hadn't left. He told me that everything was fine, only we have to talk things over, for one thing, and for another, Larissa Pavlovna, don't you know, has business to see to. I said I'd go back on the 20th.

Then I talked to Lara, and told her of my conversation with Yermash. She says that there are rumours circulating about our going to Italy, all quite detailed, rather like what happened over Sweden. I told her I probably wouldn't be able to come because of work. She is anxious about money, so I reassured her that Lora would be coming. Lara had a party on my birthday, and did some baking, several people came. There were lots of letters and telegrams. I've been given a 'Badge of Honour'.

Yes—Larissa's interview is tomorrow at 8.0 in the evening. This time it really seems to be happening. With God's help!

'Great art is often topical. Sophocles was tried and fined for reducing to tears and despair the thousands of people who saw his tragedy, by showing them the state of the country.' (Victor Shklovsky, *Lev Tolstoy*.)

'The proof of the immortality of the soul is the fact of its existence. Everybody dies, you will say. No: everything changes, and we call these changes death, but nothing disappears. The essence of every being—the material—remains. Let us draw a parallel with the soul. The essence of the soul is consciousness of self. The soul may change with death, but consciousness of self, that is to say, the soul, does not die.' (L. Tolstoy, quoted in Shklovsky's book.)

Unfortunately this is sophistry, for the material of the soul may live, and the soul disappear. Consciousness of self is not necessarily immortal.

It is possible to lack spirituality, to be in an animal state, to have anaemia of the soul. These would still be states of the soul. By animal state I mean being devoid of any tendency to rise. It's not convincing; and anyhow, consciousness of self is not material. It may be the result of its activity, but it is still not material. Of course, if thought is material, then ... but in that case there is nothing more to say, it has all been said ...

7 April, Rome

Today I am fasting, and finding it extremely hard. Before Lora went off to Sant' Arcangelo she said I could come at any time while she was away. I went to her place, and the porter wouldn't let me have the key. So much for that!

8 April, Rome

Went to the Questura to have my passport stamped. Actually, they didn't stamp it. I must talk to Casati. Feeling really low ... Missing Lara and Tyapus.
Talked to Lara, Tyapa and Anna Semyonovna on the telephone. Lara had been for a walk with Tyapa and Dakus—Andriushka is feeling better and is going to school on Monday. Lara said she had preliminary talks with someone else, and that it was going to be difficult; because of bad reports on me and because of *his* being ill (?).
But they've promised to let Larissa know on Monday when he will see her. She says she'll do all she can.

Had supper with a friend of Norman—a dubbing editor. He is a superb cook, but I didn't eat much. However, it wasn't boring.

Last night I had an awful dream (in Italian—for the first time); I seemed to be in Italy(?) and found myself listening in to a telephone conversation between my wife (Larissa) and a man (I could hear all of it, perhaps I was even eavesdropping), who was asking her for an assignation, and she agreed, and specified a time and place.
I was crying terribly in my dream, and could see myself in the mirror in tears. A really awful dream ...
The conversation was in Italian and I could understand it.

Tolstoy writes of France (in 1857) that there was not one person 'who is unaffected by the feeling of social freedom which is the great delight of life in this country, and of which no one can have any idea unless they have experienced it themselves.' (V. Shklovsky, *Lev Tolstoy*.)

Tolstoy wrote to Botkin from Lucerne on the 27th (9th) July about the 'pain of solitary enjoyment' (cf. *Nostalgia*).

9 April, Rome

'Before he died Lev Nikolaevich came round, and said quietly: "Whatever is that?"' (V. Shklovsky, *Lev Tolstoy*.)

'He (Tolstoy) remembered Herzen's words: "If only instead of wanting to save the world people wanted to save themselves, if only instead of wanting to free the world they wanted to free themselves —what a lot they could do for the salvation of the world and the liberation of humanity."' (ibid.)

How can man live without God? Only by becoming God, which is not possible . . .

I must find Friedrich through Khamreyev; and write to Jure, the Grossens and Pår Almark.

Last night I had a dream: it was spring; rain and puddles; I was taking Dakus for a walk. Some boozer fell into a puddle, terrified, and started fending Dakus off with his feet. Dakus of course had no intention of biting anybody . . .

'Tolstoy . . . said of Turgenev that he reminded him of a fountain of imported, foreign water: he was constantly afraid that he might run dry.' (V. Shklovsky, *Lev Tolstoy*.)

12 April, Rome

A beautiful, radiant day! Angela had a tremendous—and entirely positive—effect on me. She completely took away my depression, and made me believe in myself. And another reason it's a good day is that I'm convinced that something important and good has happened in Moscow: perhaps Larissa has been given an appointment.

'Altogether, memoirs and diaries have to be used with great caution if you are going to discover the truth, and not merely become involved in quarrels which were long ago settled by death.' (V. Shklovsky, *Lev Tolstoy*.)

'We tend to over-estimate the cultural level of the Russian nobility in its day-to-day life. The nobility settled down on their estates when, under Catherine II, they were released from military service, and they started to abandon their estates in the 1860's. One must not judge the ambience of the country house by our museums, which have preserved the most artistic and valuable objects from the wealthy estates.' (ibid.)

Angela also said—I quite forgot—that I am going to mean something more to my son than a father, something even more important!

13 April, Rome

On the 10th and the 11th the weather was beautiful, but now the mornings are overcast, and towards evening it starts to drizzle. It's damp. I went to Lora's hoping to telephone Moscow, but couldn't; maybe tomorrow.

14 April, Rome

Something appalling has happened: my interview has been published with two really bad comments, one by the woman journalist, and one by Antonioni, who says that the making of this film will give me a chance of escaping from the trap into which I have fallen in the USSR.

The journalist woman has put in some nonsense about my background, and my being at odds with the ideology of the USSR. Frightful. Tonino has arrived.

I couldn't telephone home. Tomorrow.

15 April, Rome

Rondi telephoned yesterday to say that on 10 June I am to be presented with a very important government award—some sort of gold medal (worth about two million, according to Tonino). Pertini is going to make the presentation.

What does it all signify?

Talked to Lara from my new study. No change. The man who was meant to help Larissa is ill. She is trying to do something through Svetlana Barilova (presumably through A.A., who is a friend of hers). I don't feel that is going to be enough.

Spoke to Tyapus; he's still not well, still coughing, poor little boy.

And I spoke to A.S.—she asked me to bring, or rather send, some aspirin with vitamin C, some plain aspirin, Adelfan, and something for her eyes (must find out exactly what when we next talk).

The world exists for us and is assessed by us, by our consciousness.

Is it possible to go beyond human consciousness and make a new, non-subjective assessment of reality? It is not considered to be possible, but I somehow feel it may be (Castaneda and his Don Juan).

Tonino telephoned and said it would be worth writing a letter to the *Eropeo* repudiating the picture drawn of me by that wretched journalist woman—or rather, it's I who am wretched—and Michelangelo. Tonino and I will talk about it tomorrow.

'Vera Zasulich killed General Trepov, who had ordered the revolutionary Bogolyubov (Arkhip Emelyanov) to be flogged. *The jury acquitted her.*' (V. Shklovsky, *Lev Tolstoy.*)

'Andrey, do not be afraid of anything! You are strong and can do *everything*.'

16 April, Rome

Norman took me to Angela. She gave me various pieces of advice and started to 'treat' me. I talked to her a lot about my problems.

She said she could work on U,* to make him recover and want to help. (Must find a journal with his picture.)

'. . . our exterior life is always entirely repulsive, just as the act of childbirth is repulsive unless our passion casts its own light over it, all our material life is horrible and repulsive, from food and defecation to demanding other people's labour for oneself.' (Tolstoy, letter to V. A. Alekseyev, Dec. 1884.)

Sometimes I am filled with a sense of absolutely breathtaking happiness, which shakes my very soul, and in those moments of harmony the world around me begins to look as it really is—balanced and purposeful; and my inner, mental structure or system corresponds with the outer structure of the milieu, the universe—and vice versa.

At those moments I believe myself to be all-powerful: that my love is capable of any physical feat of heroism, that all obstacles can be overcome, that grief and yearning will be ended, and suffering be transformed into the fulfilment of dreams and hopes.

This is one of those moments.

I believe that Larissa will succeed in bringing Andriushka here,

*Marshall Ustinov.

and that we shall drink orange juice and eat ice-creams in the Colo di Rienzo, in the café Leroy. I don't just believe it, *I know* that's how it will be.

Nikolay Fyodorovich Fyodorov; librarian. (His teaching posited the physical resurrection of the dead.)

Almost all social and individual problems are based on people's dislike of themselves, personally, on their lack of respect for themselves. People are far more ready to believe in the authority of others. It all starts with love of yourself, first of all. Without that it is not possible to understand anyone else, not possible to love.
'Love your neighbour as yourself . . .'
That is point zero, the lowest reading—i.e. nil—'I', the persona.

17 April, Rome
Talked to Lara this morning.
I must go and see Tonino. His daughter was with him yesterday, and he cannot get over the state she is in. Poor girl!
Today I met the head of the Théatre National de Chaillot in Paris, the director, Antoine Vitez.
He heard I was in Rome and wanted to meet me. He was very complimentary, especially about *Hamlet* ('the mousetrap was a touch of genius!') and *Stalker* (the film which made him think for the first time in his life about the end of the world and the end of Socialism.) He is one of the three best theatre directors in France. He asked me to think about the possibility of directing something for him at the Chaillot in the '83–4 season. He is a friend of Wajda, who is going to put something on for him, and is in France at present working on a film about Danton.
I told him about Paradzhanov and asked him to do anything he could to help. He is very nice . . . but French. He spent some time in Moscow, worked with Pluchek, knew Lilya Brik and Katanyanov and so on . . . all of what is known as the high society of Moscow. Goodness!
He knows my father's poems.
He arranged to meet me, and when he arrived he couldn't recognize me. I knew him straightaway, even though we had never met.
Bumped into Gideon Bakhman who now lives in Rome. We met in Venice in 1962; twenty years ago . . .

18 April, Rome

'She (Sophia Andreyevna) is wrong, because she wants to justify herself, but in order to grasp, and say, the truth, you have to be penitent...' (Lev Tolstoy, *Diaries.*)

'... If only he (Herzen) had been incorporated into the spirit of the younger generation of the '50s, become part of their flesh and blood, we should not have had any revolutionary nihilists. To demonstrate the weakness of revolutionary theories you only have to read what Herzen says about how violence is invariably hoist with its own petard, by the very cause which gave rise to it.' (Tolstoy, letter to Chertkov, 9 Feb. 1888.)

Tonino is desperately anxious about his daughter. I was there this evening. I treated him; we shall see how he sleeps tonight—I hope really soundly.

Yesterday I tried unsuccessfully to telephone Lara. It's so hard to get through to Moscow, they still can't have mended the phone. Though actually it's far more likely to be for other reasons— [K.]G.B.

19 April, Rome

Talked to Larissa. Tyapa is still not well, poor little chap.

U. is going to be off, ill, for the next ten days. Larissa said she was expecting a call today from another quarter.

20 April, Rome

Spoke to Larissa. It doesn't look too good in Moscow: some sort of rumour about what I allegedly intend to do has been made into the official version of what is going on. And so they don't want to let her go. I asked to have a telex sent to Surikov saying that Larissa is needed in Rome immediately. U. is ill. She spent the whole of today waiting for a telephone call from someone else who might be able to help in the present situation. I rang around 7.30 Moscow time. Larissa is thoroughly depressed, naturally enough, but not giving up hope. I must chivy RAI over the telex. I told her to inform the authorities, when they are next in contact, that I can't be there at the end of April because I have to meet the actors.

I also asked if the man who may be helping us is an influential figure; she says—very.

Things are so bad in Moscow. It immediately made me feel

wretched; and the back of my head is aching. Just as one would expect in the circumstances.

Tolya Solonitsyn can't walk. The disease has gone right into his spine.

21 April, Rome

'Goodness means service of God, accompanied by the sacrifice, the constant loss of one's animal life, just as light is accompanied by a constant loss of fuel.' (Tolstoy's Diary, 8 June 1891.)

There is a legend about St. Peter's Square, here in Rome: somewhere in the square is an invisible gate, through which a person can disappear from this world, as many people already have. Only it's very difficult to find the invisible passage: in order to go through, you either have to stand directly facing it, or else you have to be in some special spot in relation to it—I forget exactly; but the legend exists.

Norman tells me he has based the outline of a screenplay on it; only some member of the Catholic hierarchy, or somebody who is well in with them, said the film would never be made, that the theme is taboo.

'. . . Summaries (that is, detailed advanced plans—A.T.) are something I find unthinkable . . . because if the first part has been published, the second part cannot be regarded as finished until it is finally in print, I can still change it, and I want to have the option of changing it. My objection to summaries and having things read in advance is not pride, but a certain awareness of my calling as a writer, which precludes the subordination of the spiritual activity of writing to any practical considerations whatsoever. There is something monstrous about such a concept, which fills my soul with disgust.' (Tolstoy's reply to the request of an American publisher to provide a pre-publication 'summary' of *Resurrection*.)

I had a meeting with the Ambassador. He's quite civil. A bit stupid . . . He has been around: he was Ambassador in Norway and England, and he was in charge of the cultural division of the Ministry of Foreign Affairs. Nikolay Mitrofanovich. It was all rather odd, and a bore. A bit ridiculous. One cinema here is showing all my films in succession. The conversation turned to cinema, and audiences; Italians and Americans; and I felt ashamed as I thought about people coming to the cinema to see my films. Ashamed, because nothing that I have done is actually cinema, and my films should not be seen. They have to be lived through together with me, and who can possibly do that? As it is, they make me ashamed.

The will in which Tolstoy renounced his right to the ownership of his books was written and signed by him in the woods, near Yasnaya Polyana.

'The poet and artist in his true works is always national. Whatever he may do, whatever aim or idea he may have in his work, he expresses, whether he will or no, some elements of the national character . . .' (Herzen, *My Past and Thoughts*.)

23/24 April, Rome

Norman and I have been to Milan, by plane. We saw J. L. Trintignant, who is working on a film there. Tomorrow is the last day of shooting. What a delightful man he is! He would really like to work for me: both because he wants to work for Tarkovsky and because he likes the part (I told him a bit about it).

He told me, incidentally, that one must not rely too much on actors' agents; it's better to be in touch with the actors direct, because agents' deals are not always in the best interests of the actors. (We talked about Fanny Ardant.)

Milan is very beautiful—a solid, cosy, bourgeois city with some wonderful buildings and inner courtyards. (I found the courtyard of the hotel where Gorchakov stayed.)

Saw Leonardo's *Last Supper*. In fact it's not very easy to see, it's being restored, there's scaffolding everywhere.

Trintignant made a powerful impression on me.

27 April, Rome

Saw Casati. The Gaumont contract has still not been signed, but Franco reassured me about money for taxis from April on, and everything else as laid down in the prior agreement. There's a problem about the Italian nationality of the film, because of the actors. But I have definitely decided to use Trintignant.

Telephoned home. Tyapus wants a remote control motor launch.

Dakus has 'learned some new songs', as Larissa put it. I spoke quite openly over the telephone about the rumours about my staying in Italy. Let them know that I am not scared of them.

I had a letter from Stockholm, from Jure L.

Last time we talked Larissa said that Sophia had rung, and that Boris Fogelman and Pår were waiting for me to telephone Stockholm.

Covent Garden has cropped up again. They're going to telephone.

'The greatest thing in life is to know God from your own experience.'—Dr. Ralph L. Byron, oncologist (USA).

'Look how your body is made. We have 30 trillion cells. Each of
them has 10,000 constantly active chemical reactions. Far greater
faith is required to believe that this body happened by chance than
to believe that it was made by a reasonable God.'—same.

Larissa said that the meeting will almost certainly be tomorrow
at 8.0. They specified the time. I'm afraid it may be the result of
Kolya S's help.

True poetry goes with a sense of religion. An unbeliever cannot
be a poet.

'The fact that a scientist is a Christian does not make him any
better or worse a scientist. If the study of science destroys religious
faith, one can be certain that there is a correction to be made: what
it destroys is false faith, or to be exact—false religion.' (Van Mersel,
professor of experimental zoology, University of Leiden, Holland.)

'Whatever mystery science solves, it will be faced with a much
greater mystery.

'All the proofs that can be summoned by science go to prove that
the creation of the universe occurred at a specific time.' (Lincoln
Barnett, American scientist.)

'The more discoveries science makes in the physical world, the
more we are faced with conclusions that can only be solved by faith.'
—Einstein.

I remember how thoughtful the late Landau became after he had
given a negative answer to my question as to whether he believed in
God. It was in the Crimea, I think on the beach—some time before
his tragic accident in Koktebl. He was silent for quite some time,
and then said—yes, perhaps he did believe.

I was young and full of hope, the sun was shining, there was the
sound of the sea, the cries of seagulls . . . It was a long time ago. I
don't even remember who was with me in the south, or exactly
when or where it was.

'We are like children playing on the shores of the infinite ocean
of truth.'—Newton.

'In the course of the last century science has become more modest.
There was a time when it was assumed that science would discover
everything infinite or unknown. Modern science has taken to look-

ing at things more humbly, for it found that man cannot give final answers or reach wholly satisfactory conclusions. *Man himself* is limited in his pursuit of knowledge. The scientist has far more reason to believe in God now than he had fifty years ago, because now science has recognized its own limitations.'—Autrum, Munich (natural scientist).

'One of the most fundamental laws of nature, confirmed by science, is that in the physical world nothing is without cause. It is simply not possible to imagine creation without a Creator.'—Von Braun, USA.

'Science has left the question of God completely open. Science is not entitled to judge in this area.'—Max Born (physicist, Nobel Prize winner).

It's one o'clock in the morning. I heard a racket going on under my windows, and looked out through the shutters: the police were arresting three youths. They laid them down on the cobbles and gave them a bit of a beating (there were three policemen). Then two police vans drove up, followed by another two; and the men were taken away.

It was curious to watch. Like being in the cinema, only true. It left a nasty taste: fear, mixed with revulsion and hatred . . .

'There always comes a point beyond which science cannot go. If we go back from simple forms to still simpler ones, we eventually come up against the question: where did the atom of hydrogen come from? And to that question science has no answer.'—Wilde (physiologist, USA, Nobel Prize winner).

'We are just as far away today from solving the questions of philosophy as we ever were.'—Guterud (physicist, Norway).

Philosophy is poetry, the play of fantasy, a series of intellectual constructions which distinguish the personality—affirmation of the individual existence of the 'I'.

'Can human reason, which I assume to have emerged from lower animals, inspire confidence, when that reason draws us into such strong feelings?'—Charles Darwin (in the last years of his life).

'One of the biggest mistakes is to imagine, as most people do, that scientific method is a reliable path to the Truth.'—Wood (scientist, USA).

28/29 April, Rome

In an old notebook that I was throwing away I came upon this: 'Sitting in the café Leroy in the Colo di Rienzo, not far from the hotel (Leonardo da Vinci), at the table where one day we shall all be together: I, Lara and Tyapus. 11.19, 28 April, 1980.

My God, I've just noticed that today is the 28th of April as well— that's more than mere coincidence!

29 April, Rome

Last night I dreamed about Brezhnev, he was talking to me very amiably. Dio Mio!

Spoke with Lara. She had an interview with somebody. She was advised to write a letter with all the arguments and complaints, and they promised an answer by May 3rd.

I have a feeling it may be Chernenko, thanks to Kolya S's contacts. How grim . . .

30 April, Rome

Tina telephoned this morning from Berlin. She is going to be here around the 8th, and will bring the agreement; she promised to help (I think), because at the end of May she is going to be in Moscow. (Larissa is sitting there penniless, poor thing. Not that that is anything new.) How can one live like this?

Tina wants to film me for a short television documentary.

1 May, Rome

'Wine stuns a person, allows him to forget himself, artificially cheers him, irritates him; the less developed a person is, the more narrow and empty his life, the more he enjoys being stunned or irritated in this way.'—Herzen, *My Past and Thoughts*.

Tonino and I went to see Rosi's *Tre Fratelli*. It was awful. Better than *Christ Stopped at Eboli* but still bad. Disjointed, meaningless. The acting is good. One episode—the teacher's dream—is actually monstrous. Tonino wrote the screenplay. It's his own fault. It's like handing over to someone else the telling of an anecdote instead of telling it oneself. He is the only one who laughs, because no one else has any idea what it is about. You cannot hand poetry over to someone who has no ear. As cinema it is appalling.

2 May, Rome

I went to a service in the church. (Father Victor is apparently 87.) It was lovely.

Saw an unspeakably revolting film called *Possession*. An American mixture of horror film, satanism, violence, thriller and anything else you like to name. Monstrous. Money, money, money . . . Nothing real, nothing true. No beauty, no truth, no sincerity, nothing. All that matters is to make a profit . . . It's impossible to watch . . . Anything is possible, anything is allowed, provided that 'anything' can be sold.

Last night I had nightmares. I was so frightened I woke up.

3 May, Rome

Yesterday Dino—Tonino's brother—remarked (when I said my favourite bit of rabbit is the leg, whereas they consider that the breast, the white meat, is the best) that of course Russians are accustomed to suffering. We all found it ridiculously funny. Maria cooked the rabbits superbly.

4 May, Rome

Spoke with Larissa: she has been twice to Old Square and hopes to have an answer within the next two days.

Sizov was rude to her and demanded that she immediately go to the Regional Party Office for another reference. I told her to wait.

They apparently have given me an award. (Kolya checked.)

1983

A bad day. Terrible thoughts. I'm frightened.
I am lost! I cannot live in Russia, nor can I live here.

1983

22 May, Rome

Just back from Cannes, and not yet sufficiently recovered to put into words what happened there. It was all terrible: the details can be found in the press, they gave the festival very thorough coverage. I have a lot of the articles.

Very tired. *Nostalgia* made a great impression, and was given three prizes. I was congratulated. Oleg Yankovsky was offered a contract, but he had to leave earlier, and of course there was no question of his entering into a contract. I heard all about how Bondarchuk spent the entire time attacking my film, from Yvonne Babi, the daughter of the late Sadoule. He was consistently hostile to my film because he had been sent to Cannes for the purpose of discrediting it, even though all the Soviet film officials who had come to Cannes assured me that he would at least be loyal. They went on about it so much that it was obvious to me that they had sent him to Cannes deliberately in order to prevent my being awarded any prize that would increase my chances of being able to work abroad.

Bondarchuk did a great deal of damage, but so did Bresson, by announcing that he wanted the Golden Palm or nothing. I had to explain all this at a press conference so that we would have equal chances with the jury.

I met Bresson, and Martine Offroy, and arranged to meet Toscan du Plantier in Rome to talk about a film in the future.

I signed a contract with Anna-Lena Wibom for *The Witch*. I now have to face another talk with Yermash—about staying on in the West for more work (Covent Garden and Sweden).

There was a showing at RAI, and the Embassy turned up. One of them (unofficially) congratulated me. The rest moved away from me without a word, or practically without a word. The Ambassador was said to be ill. He obviously doesn't want to meet me. I am going to have to talk to the Consul and Yermash more or less at the same time. I don't want to write.

Must start work. Missing Tyapa terribly.

23 May, Rome

I forgot to write yesterday that *Nostalgia* won three prizes: Best Director Prize, FIPRESCI and Ecumenical.

On the 21st there was an article in *Soviet Culture* about the Cannes Festival, saying that the standard had been very low; that there had been some good Indian (!) and Turkish (about paederasts?) films, that the best film was Japanese—very humane—and that Tarkovsky and Bresson had shared the Special Grand Jury Prize for directing. Anna Semyonovna and all our family and friends in Moscow are very upset, but I told her they shouldn't be: 'The worse, the better.'

I often wonder about how right we are when we maintain that artistic creation is a state of soul. Why? Perhaps because man is trying to imitate the Creator. But should he? Is it not ridiculous to imitate the Creator whom we serve? We make good our guilt before our Creator by using the freedom he has given us to fight against the evil within us, to overcome the obstacles lying on the path that leads to our Lord, to grow spiritually and rise above all that is base in us. Help me Lord, send me a Teacher, I have been waiting so long I am tired.

25 May, Rome

A bad day. Terrible thoughts. I'm frightened.

I am lost! I cannot live in Russia, nor can I live here.

26 May, Rome. *Via di Monserrato*

On the 31st I have to fly to Milan to meet Claudio Abbado. They telephoned from Berlin. Someone wants to make a film of *Hoffmanniana*. I have been given $50,000 in cash. Shouldn't it have been more?

There is a rumour going round Moscow that I had a complete failure at Cannes. My God, that really is the last straw!

Lara and I had tea today with Princess Brancaccio. She is quite amenable to our buying the bit of land with the tower. Franco and his brother Remo are going to be very helpful. We must have a roof over our heads—and soon we shall.

27 May, Rome

The Germans invited me to their festival in Munich. Of course I'm not going.

We received a telegram saying that we have to move house, and we have no idea where to.

Larissa and I telephoned Moscow. Rumours are being spread all over the place about my film being a flop at Cannes. Vindictive slander-mongering.

Spoke to Andriushka and Anna Semyonovna. A.S. seemed to be very anxious about something. She may still be unwell. Lara and I are dreadfully worried. Tyapa had three threes in his last report: algebra, physics and Russian.

Today Franco Terilli took us to the country, where his brother owns a wonderful house; it will only be habitable in three months' time, they have to do major repairs.

I must find a way of working with Dvigubsky. Should I travel to Rome every day? It's not impossible. There's a bus that leaves from the station. And then there's Franco's brother, who lives in the country and works in the Vatican, he drives there and back daily. It would be very easy if I could go with him.

30 May

Franco has telephoned to say that the house in the country is no good. So we're again without a roof over our heads. We can't take the Palestrina house, because there's no telephone and no good connections with Rome. We simply don't know what to do!

2 June, Rome

Returned from Milan today. Utterly exhausted. I met Abbado, Sir John Tooley and Dvigubsky. We had one or two good ideas about *Godunov*. But I am tired, completely exhausted; and we have nowhere to live. We must work, we must come to some sort of decision. We have to do something, and I am not doing anything. I am waiting for something, and I don't know what.

Lara has gone to San Gregorio with Franco. We could rent a place to live there for the moment, until the house is ready. I did some work with Dvigubsky, and after that he went off to Paris, but he's coming back next week. I must start negotiations with Yermash, but first I have to talk to Rostropovich.

5 June, Rome

I am so tired. We went to visit Angela in the country. She completely supports our plan. She would like to draw up a scheme for our future. At present she is surrounded by twelve young men aged between thirteen and twenty—'extrasensories' endowed with supernatural gifts—who came to her for help. Allegedly they are in contact with extra-terrestrial planets and with the mysterious Council of Twenty-four. Obviously the whole thing is pure fantasy, but Angela says she has double-checked everything and that it has all been proved to be true.

Now we have to move (probably to San Gregorio?) and then telephone Yermash, and explain ourselves to the consulate.

6 June, Rome

Went to San Gregorio today and saw the flat. It's cramped and nasty, and the kitchen is minute. But what can we do?

Shilayev—a Sovexportfilm official—telephoned today; he wants to come with me to see the Ambassador. At least, that's what he claimed that he wanted. The question I am going to ask them all is: 'Why did you not invite us to the October Revolution Anniversary celebrations?' At least for the showing of *Nostalgia*. They are showing the film with no translation, clearly so that the audience will understand as little as possible. Had they invited me I should have been able to talk about how the film has to be seen.

11 June, San Gregorio

We moved to San Gregorio on the 8th, in order to be closer to the house we want to buy, so that we can oversee the work. I hope—with the Terilli brothers to help us—that it's not going to slip through our fingers; there are plenty of other people interested in buying this particular house.

12 June, San Gregorio

A new Italian minister has appeared on the scene who wants to help with my letter to Pertini. He said that everything is actually going to be settled very soon. We may find out on Monday what exactly has been settled already, so that when I talk to Yermash I won't sound like an idiot. Incidentally I probably looked like one when I was talking to the Ambassador about the car. He was inquiring about my plans for Dostoievsky. I just told him that I was not too convinced about that project, but I couldn't explain any further. Why not? Merely because the Ambassador didn't have enough time. And a few days ago our Consul asked Lora Yablochkina in passing, whether I was thinking of putting on *Godunov*. It is all very odd . . .

The last few days Lara and I have been terribly tired, and feeling very unwell. We still haven't managed—in three days—to unpack all our cases and boxes. We must finally summon the energy to-morrow.

Pacifico thinks that with a concerted effort, and if all goes well, the tower could be restored and habitable in two months. That means that it all has to be done by 15 July—contract and everything else. Then from 1 August till November—three months of repairs and restoration. God help us and give us strength.

1984

Last night I had a terribly sad dream. I dreamed again of a northern (I think) lake somewhere in Russia; it was dawn, and on the far shore were two Orthodox monasteries, with amazingly beautiful cathedrals and walls.
And I felt such sadness! Such pain!

1984

17 January, San Gregorio

I saw Francesco Rosi, he promised he would talk to Trombadori, and said it was most important to have his advice. He also feels I must be entirely loyal to the USSR, and act very diplomatically.

News from Moscow: Goskino apparently have sent *Rublyov* and *Mirror* to a festival in Japan. If it's true, then it's clear that they want to avoid a scandal. Let's believe that is the explanation.

They are having terrible money problems in Moscow. I must think of some way of helping. What swine those people are! Not allowing me to send money to support my own family! It's tantamount to condemning them to death. They are getting their own back on us by inflicting misery on totally innocent children. Butchers! Monsters! How is it that the earth doesn't swallow them up!

24 January, San Gregorio

Anna-Lena came here on the 21st. We agreed that I would write the screenplay in February, and that shooting would start on 1 August. She was very interested in the idea of the school, but said that her husband had been working on the same idea for some time (!) and that we must meet.

In any case I shall have to go to Stockholm at the beginning of April to start preparations for the film.

The rumour about Palme having talked to Gromyko is not true. (I was wrong, Anna-Lena doesn't actually know whether they have talked together. She'll telephone to tell me.) If they haven't discussed it, Palme is going to write to Gromyko.

I am terribly tired. I have pain in every inch of my body.

26 January, San Gregorio

Yesterday I met Michael Kruger. We talked about the publication of my book and my screenplays. I was thinking of *Hoffmanniana*, *The Bright Day* and *Nostalgia*. *Nostalgia* is coming out in Germany and Monaco; and in New York. Or rather, it is already running, and very successfully. I have thought of a title for the book. The *Mirror* screenplay must be put in order as well, that is going to mean a lot of work, and I have no time at all. I am working on *Sacrifice*. Yesterday Angela introduced me to a professor from Milan who is involved with questions of 'Pranotherapy'—astrology. He promised to take us all to a papal audience in the Vatican.

We must try to extend our *soggiorno* through our new friends in Milan (Sergio).

27 January, San Gregorio

Cornelia Gostenmayer telephoned from Germany to say that they were going to try to find (non-provocative) ways of contacting Moscow. For the moment it's not easy: the best would be to act through commercial representatives, firms, but at present that is not possible in Germany. (She advised me to look for opportunities of that kind in Italy.) Governments change but entrepreneurs remain, and the Soviets know that.

6 February

We went to Amsterdam and Rotterdam, where there was a film festival, and saw Dima Shushkalov. It was boring and dreary. The people in charge had promised to give me a bit of work, and didn't, and even the tickets they had promised—1st class—turned out to be a myth. There was a public lecture, and a 'round table' about Bresson, dreadfully stupid.

In fact I only went because of Larissa, who really wanted to see Dima and Olga. I only hope I can still finish the screenplay in time.

I saw Otar Yoseliani. He said that at one point (before the Venice Festival, and before Sizov's talk with Yermash) he had been told by the Committee that they had already arrived at the decision to deprive us of our citizenship. We saw his documentary about the Basques. Rather depressing and dull.

Otar has finished shooting; editing and synchronizing still have to be done. He is being summoned to Moscow, because his time has run out. He is not afraid to go, he says he has the protection of Shevarnadze. It seems very odd . . . Or maybe it isn't, God knows.

Today yet another letter was sent to Andropov.

11 July

Immediately after the press conference: No energy or inclination to write anything here for some time. But what a lot has been happening!

The Movimento Popolare and the FP organized a press conference for Larissa and me in Milan. The political leader of the Movimento is Roberto Formigoni, who seems to be a nice man, a monk. Slava Rostropovich, Vladimir Maximov and Yuri Lyubimov came to the press conference—they have all given up their Soviet citizenship. The American and European press have been writing about our case for the last two days, and about the press conference.

Lara and I are utterly shattered.

We decided, with Rapetti, on a different publishing house, then we went back to San Gregorio, and on the 18th we went to London. Amongst other things, I gave a talk there, at St. James' Church, on the Apocalypse. It was a great success. We stayed with Ira [Brown], and did a lot of sightseeing.

In London we organized a committee to campaign for our son and our family. Marina Voikhanskaya is taking a very active part. She herself went through a very difficult time fighting for her family. She is a psychiatrist from Leningrad who refused to treat dissident 'patients'.

8 November, Stockholm

On the plane. The Minister of Culture wants to meet me, to help over the family.

Before all my panicky telephone calls I met Olofson (director of the Institute) and had a serious business talk with him, and mentioned the absence of a contract. Incidentally I had the impression that Anna-Lena is not very competent and that she doesn't keep the director properly informed about developments.

David Gothard in London has been very helpful indeed.

We must definitely go to Paris. The Minister of Culture wants to meet me, and this is crucial both for the picture and for the family. So on the 14th—test the children; 16th—pack for Berlin, and fly to Paris, from there to Milan (22nd), where there'll be a press conference on the 23rd, and so Lara and I shan't meet before then.

We're about to return to Rome for the television showing of *Nostalgia*, and then we fly to Berlin, where I should like to talk to the German director Alexander Kluge about a short film on Rudolf

Steiner, and where I also have to finish work on the *Hoffmanniana* screenplay. At the same time I have to start looking for financial backing for *Hamlet*, and write the filmscript. And we must find time for America—whatever happens we have to have visas. Perhaps a film about St. Anthony as well—which means collect material and work on the screenplay, having first signed a contract. Apart from all that, if all goes well with *Sacrifice*, we go back to Stockholm from March to July. Rome again in August, the question of the house has to be settled before that. Then by the end of 1985, editing and finishing the film. In February and March '86, if I want, one month for the *Flying Dutchman* in London. Starting in January 1986—work with the Germans on *Hoffmanniana*.

Last night I had a terribly sad dream. I dreamed again of a northern (I think) lake somewhere in Russia; it was dawn, and on the far shore were two Orthodox monasteries, with amazingly beautiful cathedrals and walls.

And I felt such sadness! Such pain!

Nikolay Ilyin telephoned, and Carlo. They both want to see me.

As for Kluge, it will hardly be possible to do anything for television in the time we have left. Carlo said the television people were interested in *Hoffmanniana*, but I am going to have to decide straight-away whether or not to do the Hoffmann immediately after *Sacrifice*. We shall have to draw up an agreement and organize the money.

Volodya Maximov has introduced us (for the moment only by telephone) to Irina Pabst—a very influential Russian friend of Springers. She has already helped me in the argument with Ullstein, the publishers, over the additions to the book.

We have taken a three-roomed flat in the centre of Berlin. But it has the same entrance as the next-door flat, so we want to change. Tomorrow we are going to look at another flat, nearby.

1985

The one important thing is to find TIME within TIME . . .
It is enormously difficult, but it has to be done!

1985

11 January, Berlin

We have got to know Wieland Schmied, President of the Berlin Academy of Arts and Director of the German Academic Exchange Service. I asked about protection. And I've opened an account in a local bank. Then I telephoned Gambarov, but he wasn't there. I left my telephone number with his secretary, but he hasn't rung back. I keep being given conflicting information; as for the flat, it doesn't seem to be working out with the Academic Exchange people.

1 February, Berlin

Of course the whole thing has fallen through. They wouldn't accept the documents from the family at the Visa and Registration Department: the invitation was not correctly formulated. There has to be a new one:

1. Addressed to the Directorate for Visas and Registration, not the Department.

2. If the application is for permanent residence, then they want certification of my right to live in Italy.

3. It has to be confirmed by the Italian Consul.

27 February, Berlin

Berlin is a ghastly city. We must leave as soon as possible.

At the Festival, De Hadeln was unspeakably rude to me; I might have been in Moscow.

I am leaving for Stockholm first, Lara will fly after the 4th. I've seen Sir John Tooley and we talked about the production of the *Flying Dutchman*. Nothing is clear about any possibilities here with the Germans.

Andriusha Yablonsky has appeared. Things are not going well for him either at home or at work (UNESCO).

Saw Carlo—we did the work for the estimates. (They are going to pay 10,000 German marks.) He says the solicitor asked for a lot of money: $150,000 for the screenplay and $350,000 for directing, plus a daily rate, telephone, flat, heating, etc.

6 March

The Swedes are lazy and slow and only interested in observing rules and regulations. Shooting has to start at 9 a.m. and not a moment later! And that's outside, on location! This must be the only country where they treat the shooting of a film like work in an office. From such and such a time to such and such a time, without a thought for the fact that a film has to be *created*. And where artistic work is concerned, timetable considerations don't enter into it. And the converse is true. They really don't work well, not well at all.

8 March, Stockholm

Back in Stockholm. Suffering from 'severe bronchitis'.

One really important thing happened in Berlin: we went to see Irina Pabst, and there we met her friend, Frau Axel Springers, who sent us a book about her life with a very touching inscription. They want to help us—I think absolutely seriously.

We still don't know when we have to fly to Italy for our documents.

We have been sent an invitation by the President of Iceland, a committee has been formed there as well. And the Paris committee is now on a proper footing—organized by Filippo: papers and finance are already available. Everybody says we have to have passports and citizenship—as soon as we possibly can.

We still haven't got a boy for the film. I am really worried.

8/9 March, Stockholm

Berlin had an appalling effect on me. It's a terrifying city.

We eventually managed to get in touch with Maximilian Schell— he was very ill, like me he had bronchitis. He gave the family (in Moscow) 10,000 roubles. At least they'll be able to pay off the pawn shop and clear the most pressing debts. Maximilian also managed to give them a large parcel of essential clothes, which Larissa bought in Berlin with the money he lent us. He is so selfless in everything he does, and utterly natural. Without giving the question much thought, I realize that all the fine feelings in the world are worth less than one single good deed. And so I don't feel humiliated, because looking at the giver is as great a delight as looking at the gift. For the first time in my life I have experienced real support, and that has given me hope for the future.

Now he wants to carry out his intention of speaking on our behalf to our bosses. If only it helps!

Maximilian is going to be in Berlin on the 26th. So Larissa will have to stay on in Berlin to see him.

9 March, Stockholm

I forgot to write yesterday that Olga Surkova wrote an appalling letter, full of monstrous statements, and claims, and so forth. I ought to answer, but I don't want to be in touch with her even by letter.

'Honest people are never rich, and rich people are never honest.' —Lao-Tzu.

'Never bother another person by asking him to do something you could do yourself.'—Lev Tolstoy.

Yesterday I spoke with Yury Vita; he interviewed me for the evening paper. I explained to him that I would be ready to turn to Palme for help, his political stance so far in newspaper interviews and television appearances has suggested that he would not refuse to support us. Wait a minute! I have just had an idea: a hunger strike of unlimited duration outside the Soviet Embassy in Stockholm. In Sweden of all places, where the Soviets do their best to 'infiltrate' the country with every means available, and are used to relying on the friendly co-operation of the Swedes. Have the hunger strike publicized for several days with television crews from a number of countries present all the time. Make videos of the meetings that take place with leading cultural and political figures. It would be very good if representatives of every country, and someone from 'Solidarnosc' could take part.

The one important thing is to find TIME within TIME. Finish the film and start working on the *Flying Dutchman*. It is enormously difficult, but it has to be done!

10 March, Stockholm

Volodya Maximov told me that Yuri Petrovich Lyubimov has

lost his theatre in Bologna. They apparently said quite openly: 'Now that your position has changed (i.e. he is no longer Soviet), we have no alternative but to turn you down.'

Unbelievable. Even more unbelievable is the fact that Evtushenko has been invited to Hollywood as a director (!?) and actor (!!?) to make a film of *The Three Musketeers* from his own screenplay, and he is going to play D'Artagnan (!!!???). I really can't believe it. It's some sort of crazy farce. Of course Zhenya is a great pusher. Given his eye for the main chance it could be true, in the current political climate. Even if the Americans know the film will be a failure.

Yes, even if it is possible to change one's life—or at least, its appearance—karma remains karma: irrespective of what we want.

I am in touch with the anthroposophists, as well as the Society of Filmmakers, and the various Tarkovsky committees (committees campaigning on my behalf) in London, Italy, Iceland and France; and also with the Italian Movimento Popolare. Make a film about what is happening, and arrange things so that the Soviets know about it, and show the film at every single festival. But it ought to be a 16mm film, not a video. Talk to David [Gothard], T. Committee representative in England; draft leaflets, and a letter to the Swedish government; of course the vital thing is choosing the right moment. Yuri will organize it all for me. Perhaps I shall have to raise money —whatever happens I must telephone Filippo in Paris.

10 June

I talked to Andriushka today in Moscow. He is 1 metre 68 now— exactly the same height as I am! His shoes are size 43, mine are only 42. Lara has felt very ill since we returned here from Florence. The journey was awful, it was stifling on the autostrada. Larissa very nearly fainted, it really frightened me. Lara is flying from Rome to Berlin, via Munich, and I am flying to Stockholm in half an hour's time, via Copenhagen, with our new passports, or rather, travel documents.

June, Italy

Larissa showed me a most beautiful place—Roccalbegna. One can buy a house—or rather, a ruin—here, and build a new house on the site, plus another nine hectares of land, all for 23 million. I think that is what we should do.

July, Sweden

It looks as if the film is going to be all right!

The Mayor of Florence has confirmed that they are going to put a flat at our disposal, 120 square metres, in the centre of the city, with a balcony. Larissa wants to make a studio there for me. For the moment they are allowing us to put up an editing table on a lower floor of the same building, so that we can work there. Larissa is going to buy furniture now, in Berlin, and she wants the Florence flat to be ready by 20 September. That is not going to be easy!

29 September, Stockholm

It's all so difficult. And I'm so tired. I just cannot bear it any longer, being without Andriushka. I don't want to live.

10 November

Tommasi and I did some work on the decor. It isn't clear yet, but we're moving in the right direction.

I must make *St. Anthony*. I could ask for support from the Pope through Formigoni.

No developments as far as Andriushka is concerned. Tomorrow we are going to have a second meeting with Palme.

Larissa and I went to the Ministry of Foreign Affairs in Rome; they want to help us. But how?

We went to see Gino Giugni, a barrister and senator, who has excellent contacts in the government. Andreotti asked him to wait for a week before starting to make representations about the invitations for the family.

Larissa has stayed on in Florence alone to cope with all the problems over the house.

The news from Moscow is bad. What terrible days, what a terrible year. Lord, do not desert me!

Krzysztof Zanussi telephoned. He was very nice and offered us his bachelor flat in Paris if we should need it.

I talked to J. Lina: he has made arrangements for a meeting with the 'Witch'—she wants to meet me.

11 November, Stockholm

Went to see Palme today. He said there were two possibilities: (1) to apply officially through the Ministry for Foreign Affairs for permission for my son to come to Sweden; legally speaking, that is pretty well impossible. (2) He personally will send a letter to the government of the USSR with a request for Tarkovsky's son to be allowed to come to the West (it doesn't matter exactly where to). His letter will be delivered through their Ambassador to the USSR.

Of course (2) is by far the better option.

The doctor has sent the X-rays to the specialist.
Yesterday I was coughing blood. Today as well, but not so much.
I am missing Larissa terribly, particularly when I feel ill.

18 November

I am ill. Bronchitis, and something monstrous at the back of my head and in my muscles, which are pressing onto the nerves and giving me an awful pain in the neck and shoulders. Cold and cough. And the film has to be synchronized. And time is going.

19 November

I went to the physiotherapist. As a result of constant stress, my shoulders and back are in a bad way, and it looks as if I will have to have a minor operation, by the right shoulder blade. He said it would be risky to leave it. I talked to Moscow. Not that I could tell them anything new. With me away, work at the Film Institute is at a standstill.

24 November

I am ill; in fact, seriously so.
Terrible tension between me and the producer about the length of the film—2 hours 10 minutes.
The talks between Gorbachev and Reagan are over. There is some hope for next year.

30 November

Awful arguments over the length of the film. I'm ill. I had to have blood tests and a chest X-ray. Still haven't had the results.

7 December, Stockholm

I feel ghastly.
Slava Rostropovich has arrived. He said he would certainly help, he'll hand my letter on to Reagan. And he'll also come to Florence

in February, in order to see the Mayor (he knows him, in fact they are apparently friends), to talk about the problem of where we are to live. I asked him to find out the name and position of the consultant to whom my X-rays were sent. He is very concerned.

He wants to make an opera film of *Boris Godunov*. I tried to explain to him that I didn't see how it could be done in a film. According to him the suggestion came from Toscan du Plantier, who has apparently bought up the bankrupt Gaumont. There seems to me to be some confusion. They all seem to imagine that if I did a good *Boris* in the theatre, it will be even better as a film.

Of course they are wrong. Theatre is not cinema. And I don't know how to make a film of an opera.

10 December, Stockholm

Yesterday Slava Rostropovich telephoned, he has flown to Helsinki for two days. He asked me to change the date on my letter to Reagan to 15 March 1986.

Lara wants to drop everything and come here to me. I calmed her down by saying that at the moment it's more important to finish organizing the flat before I arrive on the 20th, so that I can rest and start thinking about the *Flying Dutchman*.

The doctor told me that on Friday 13th (a great day to choose) I have to go and see the lung specialist.

I spoke to Ira Brown, asked her to let Covent Garden know about my illness, as it could affect our plans.

Anna-Lena has sent a telegram to Cao, the solicitor, saying that if I don't reduce the film to the agreed length, she is not going to pay me the outstanding $55,000. That seems to be merely a bit of blackmail. Had a very severe letter from the Director of the Film Institute, and sent a very cold reply, saying that I don't understand his position: either he wants a film by Tarkovsky, or else he wants some commercial film an hour-and-a-half long (the generally accepted length). Then I talked to Anna-Lena for about an hour-and-a-half, and after that she apparently talked to the Director, and told him that my letter contained some valid arguments.

Larissa has gone to Roccalbegna, I haven't spoken to her for the last two days.

DEDICATION

'Dedicated to my little son, Andriushka, who is being made to suffer, innocently, as if he were an adult.'

11 December

The older I get the more mysterious I find people become. They seem to slip away from under my gaze. That means that my system of assessment is collapsing, and that I am losing my capacity to judge people. In one way it's good when a system of assessment collapses, but can it be good when all the systems collapse? God protect me from losing everything!

What is the matter with me? Is the TB getting worse again? Pneumonia, or perhaps even cancer? On December 13th I shall be told.

I am ill and in bed. Severe pains at the base of the lung.

Last night I dreamt of Vassya Shukshin, we were playing cards. I asked him, 'Are you writing anything at the moment?' 'Yes, I am,' he answered absent-mindedly, he was completely absorbed in the game. Then everyone got up and someone said it was time to reckon up—meaning the game was over and we had to tot up the scores.

12 December

A few days ago I was lying here in bed, but not asleep. Suddenly I could see my lung from the inside, or rather, one area of my lung, with a gory hole, and blood oozing out. I have never had that sort of vision before.

I'm in a bad way. A severe, hacking cough and a piercing pain in the lungs. Headaches.

13 December

Today really is black Friday. I went to see the doctor at the clinic. They were all extremely nice and attentive, in fact rather too nice. They were doing the tests in their own free time. Slava Rostropovich must have used his influence somehow. There is something in the left lung. The doctor said it might be an inflammation, but that is obviously not true, because the dark patch didn't disappear with the antibiotics I took. Or TB? Or a tumour? He asked me where I would want to be operated, if the worst came to the worst. I wonder if I should have an operation at all. Why go through torment to no purpose. It's a lung, after all, not a woman's breast. They're doing tests on the tissues of the mysterious lump on my head, that appeared a month ago for no obvious reason. They tested me for TB. By 20 December they'll have all the results.

Anyhow, I am prepared for the worst. That time when I blacked out and saw my lung in front of me, it looked more like a gaping hole than a tumour, although I can't be quite certain about that. I don't actually know what a tumour looks like. Only I had the impression that the area around the wound was all clear, there was nothing malignant. I should have taken out life insurance in Italy, now it would probably be very hard to arrange.

15 December

Throughout his life a person knows that sooner or later he is going to die, but he doesn't know when. And to make it easier to live his life, he relegates that moment to some indefinite point in the future. But I do know, and nothing now is going to make it easier for me to live. That is very painful; but worst of all is Larissa—how am I going to tell her? How can I, with my own hands, inflict that appalling blow on her?

16 December

I spent the whole of today in the hospital. They opened the tumour on my head and cut out a little bit for tests. The doctor says the results of the tests are bad, and that nothing can be done about the tumour, unless it turns out to be a particular type, in which case it can be 80% cured. It is clear from all this that I am in a bad way. How am I going to talk to Larissa?

21 December

On the 23rd I am flying to Italy; taking all my stuff with me. I am getting worse by the day. Boris Leonidovich Pasternak was right when he said I would make another four films. I am thinking back to those spiritualist seances at Roerich's. Boris Leonidovich's calculations were not quite right. He knew that I would make seven films altogether, but he included *The Steamroller and the Violin*, which shouldn't really count. But in general terms of course he was right!

1986

Yesterday I went out for a walk, and was suddenly overcome with an inexplicable urge: I took my shoes off and walked barefoot on the cold earth . . .

1986

10 June, Oschelbronn

Since the evening of 10 June I have been in the Anthroposophical clinic in West Germany, not far from Baden-Baden. I have a high temperature, 'flu, a cough, all of it far worse than it was. The doctors say that I am in a state of remission, and that on no account ought I to have any chemotherapy. I feel ghastly.

12 July, Oschelbronn

The staff here are excellent. Particularly Sister Elizabeth; she speaks Italian, and is warm and generous. She emanates peace and goodness.

Yesterday I went out for a walk, and was suddenly overcome with an inexplicable urge: I took my shoes off and walked barefoot on the cold earth—with a temperature, cough and rheumatism. I really am crazy. My head is full of gloomy thoughts.

3 December, Paris

Anna-Lena telephoned today. She said:

(*a*) that a fund was being set up for Andriushka's education, which means that the USA, England and Sweden will meet all the expenses.

(*b*) that the Soviet Union want to buy *Sacrifice*, and that I own the rights. The arrangements for the deal all have to be discussed; on no account must the Soviets be aware that I own the rights.

What incredible news. That Anna-Lena is quite something!

5 December, Paris

Severe pains.

Yesterday (every Wednesday) I was given chemotherapy (for the third time). I feel terrible. I can't even think of getting out of bed, or even of sitting up. Schwarzenberg doesn't know what to do, he doesn't understand why I have these appalling pains.

The film has been shown in England, with great success, and in America. The reviews are unbelievably good.

The Japanese are organizing some sort of relief fund as well, only they find it impossible to understand how such a famous director can be so poor.

6 December, Paris

Must talk to the lawyer about drawing up a document prohibiting the publication of manuscripts or extracts without prior agreement. That will prevent any repetition of the kind of incident we had with the *Figaro* interview. I must find out what is meant by the purchase of film without 'original material'. Whatever happens I mustn't let Carlo Tommasi disappear. He is a decent man, and of course an expert in his field.

I must talk to Andriushka about cinema and literature, find out what he knows.

15 December, Paris

Hamlet . . . In bed all day, didn't get up at all. Pain in the lower stomach and the back. And nerves. I can't move my legs. Schwarzenberg doesn't understand why I have such pain. I think it's the old rheumatism, stirred up by the chemotherapy. My arms are very painful too, it's like a kind of neuralgia. It feels like knots. I'm very weak. Am I going to die? There is one other possibility: hospital, under the doctor who treated me in the Sarcelles clinic.

Hamlet . . .? If it weren't for the pain in my arms and back, there might be some question of the chemotherapy having helped. But now I have no strength left for anything—that is the problem.

[*Andrey Tarkovsky died of cancer in Paris on 29 December 1986, a fortnight after the last entry above, and only weeks after the Soviet authorities had allowed his son out of the country.*

His death coincided with the early days of perestroika. His immensely popular films, banned from Soviet screens from the moment of his enforced exile in 1982, came back into circulation. National and international seminars are now held in the USSR to celebrate and study his work.]

On Cinema, 1966

[This is the text of an interview with Maria Chugunova for *To the Screen*, 12 December 1966.]

What do you consider most important in cinema today?

The truth. When an artist abandons his search for the truth it is going to have a disastrous effect on his work. The artist's aim is truth. Have you read Rossellini's article in *Komsomolskaya Pravda*? It's about the crisis in the cinema. Very alarming. And I entirely agree with him, Rossellini is frightened by the fact that cinema today is orientated totally towards entertainment.

What are your own guiding aesthetic principles?

Above all I try to achieve maximum truthfulness in all that happens on screen, in terms of the photography. For me that means being as close as possible to life. When we started work on the film I felt we were overdoing it, but now it seems to me that we failed to achieve that degree of precision.

Cinema must record life with life's own means, it must operate with the images of actual reality. I never construct a shot, and I always maintain that cinema can only exist by being totally identified with the images of life itself. That is what makes it different from other art forms, that is how it affects the audience. If you start to sketch shots, to compose them intellectually, it will mean adulterating the principles of art.

But in 'Ivan's Childhood' you have constructed shots.

Yes, of course. But *Ivan's Childhood* is a typical VGIK work of the kind that get dreamt up in halls of residence.

How important is editing in your last film? What place does it have generally in contemporary film?

Rublyov is shot in very long takes, to avoid any feeling of artificial, special rhythm, in order that the rhythm should be that of life itself. In fact you can have any kind of editing: short, long, fast, slow. The length of a shot has nothing to do with being modern or not modern. In film, as in any other art form, it is a way of selecting in order to express a particular idea. Basically, editing is the way you organize the rhythm of a film. And the length of a take depends on what has to be shown: it'll be short for a detail and long for a panorama. Eisenstein used editing to create the battle on the frozen Chudskoe lake. He juxtaposes short takes very dynamically, but the rhythm of the editing is at odds with the inner rhythm of the scene as it has been shot. It's rather like pouring out the Niagara Falls by the tumblerful. Instead of Niagara you get a puddle.

What is your view of colour?

For the moment I don't think colour film is anything more than a commercial gimmick. I don't know a single film that uses colour well. In any colour film the graphics impinge on one's perception of the events. In everyday life we seldom pay any special attention to colour. When we watch something going on we don't notice colour. A black-and-white film immediately creates the impression that your attention is concentrated on what is most important. On the screen colour imposes itself on you, whereas in real life that only happens at odd moments, so it's not right for the audience to be constantly aware of colour. Isolated details can be in colour if that is what corresponds to the state of the character on the screen. In real life the line that separates unawareness of colour from the moment when you start to notice it is quite imperceptible. Our unbroken, evenly paced flow of attention will suddenly be concentrated on some specific detail. A similar effect is achieved in a film when coloured shots are inserted into black-and-white.

Colour film as a concept uses the aesthetic principles of painting, or colour photography. As soon as you have a coloured picture in the frame it becomes a moving painting. It's all too beautiful, and unlike life. What you see in cinema is a coloured, painted plane, a composition on a plane. In a black-and-white film there is no feeling of something extraneous going on, the audience can watch the film without being distracted from the action by colour. From the moment it was born, cinema has been developing not according to its vocation but according to purely commercial ideas. That started when they began making endless film versions of classics.

What about Antonioni?

The Red Desert is the worst of his films after *The Cry* [*Il Grido*]. The colour is pretentious, quite unlike Antonioni usually, and the editing is subservient to the idea of colour. It could have been a superb film, tremendously powerful, if only it had been in black-and-white. If *The Red Desert* had been in black-and-white, Antonioni wouldn't have got high on pictorial aesthetics, he wouldn't have been so concerned with the pictorial side of the film, he wouldn't have shot those beautiful landscapes, or Monica Vitti's red hair against the mists. He would have been concentrating on the action instead of making pretty pictures. In my view the colour has killed the feeling of truth. If you compare *The Red Desert* with *The Night* [*La Notte*] or *The Eclipse* [*L'Eclisse*] it's obvious how much less good it is.

What about colour in your film?

We only used it for Rublyov's paintings.

What would you say about the transition from black-and-white to colour?

I think it's well done, it's not too obvious.

Just now you mentioned film versions of the classics. You're very fond of Dostoievsky, and have written about him a lot. Would you like to make a film of any of the novels?

Yes, I should like to make a film of *Crime and Punishment*, and of *The Possessed*. But I wouldn't touch *The Brothers Karamazov*. The novel achieves its effect through a mass of detail, and a confused, cumbersome composition.

What do you think, have there ever been any successful screen versions of Dostoievsky?

No.

What about Kurosawa?

His *Idiot* is a wonderful film. Setting the film at the present time and on his own national soil makes a very interesting film version. It's on quite a different principle, and actually very exciting. Imagine making *Electra* in a modern setting.

If you were to screen Dostoievsky, would you give it a contemporary setting?

No, I would definitely set it in its own period, but I would write a completely new screenplay. I would probably include in the action the things that Dostoievsky puts into his extraordinarily profound descriptions. They are almost the most important thing, they carry the weight of the whole idea of the book.

Could you explain why everyone in this country is so keen on film versions of books?

It's because they have no ideas of their own. And of course it's not easy to make a film with a modern plot. If you stand for the truth, then you have to speak the truth. And if you do that it's not always going to please everyone. So directors turn to adaptations. The ideas are already there in the prose, and the plot has been constructed.

What was the reason for the differences between the screenplay for 'Rublyov' and the shooting-script?

There were various reasons. In the first place the original version was not particularly good, in the second place it was too long, even in the director's version, and therefore it had to be adapted while work was going on. For instance the scene of the swan hunt, which was the first one I cut, was pretentious, it was too 'ancient Russian', it had nothing to do with the central idea.

Your film is said to be too cruel and depressing.

I don't find it so. I should say it was truthful. Anyhow I was trying to make it express what we feel about the age of Rublyov.

Tell me about how you work with your actors.

I don't work with them. I believe Marcel Carné or René Claire was once asked that same question, and he answered, 'I don't work with them, I pay them.' In my view actors should not be told all about their function, or their meta-function, in a particular scene. As a rule what I explain to an actor is the state he has to be in, what he has to be perturbed by, or excited by. It is through a grasp of these basic factors that the actor arrives at a clear understanding of the form and the essence of his actions.

There are some directors who actually show the actors what they have to do, they try to find the exact movements that are going to help them.

What about you?

If an actor doesn't understand what I mean, then of course I might show him. But an actor has to be able to act, the only thing that ought to be explained to him is his own state of mind.

Can an actor improvise?

Yes, indeed, within the framework of the required state of mind. But when an actor can't find that state of mind, you have to be inventive; you sometimes have to think of devices of various kinds to help him. On the other hand, when you are driven to using such ingenuity it can only mean that the actor is not fully competent.

I tremendously enjoyed working with Nikolay Grinko. He's an amazingly gifted and natural actor. He understands everything immediately. There is no need to explain anything.

What do you feel about the training at VGIK?

People have to study, but really if you want to be a director you would do better to be in on the making of one long film. The best course is the advanced course in directing. It's absurd to spend six years studying in the faculty of directing, you might as well spend twenty years there, when you take into account the fact that only twenty per cent of the total time is allowed for your speciality.

You can't teach a person the art of cinematography any more than you can teach him to be a poet. The profession as such can be taught in a couple of months. Piano-playing has to be taught by someone, whereas writing you can only learn yourself, by reading books. And of course you have to be taught how to be an actor, only they are not being taught the right things. They don't know other languages, they can't ride. Nor can they fence, or swim, or dive, or drive a car or a motor-cycle. Doubles have to be used for all those things. The actors can't pronounce their words properly, they are not natural, but on the other hand they pass dozens of exams. What they need to be taught are things like hygiene and diet, and intense physical exercise. But all that has to be done professionally. VGIK ought to enlist the services of leading cineastes who know how to teach. In my view film actors should be taught by good film directors. Sergey Gerasimov is right to teach actors and directors together.

At the moment a lot of people straight off the street are being taken on as actors. And quite rightly. They will have parts in films, and they will become real actors, because they know what they want. There are plenty of VGIK graduates who imagine they are fully-fledged actors or directors, when in fact VGIK is merely a place where you can get a good degree; the whole thing only starts after VGIK, when you leave.

The main trouble with VGIK is that the professional is not interested in it. None of the studios know anything about people at VGIK. It's vital to break down the wall that separates VGIK from film production. I think they ought to have a year's practical, working on an entire production. A year of specialist study and then a year of practical, working on a full-length film. Or maybe the the other way round: the practical year first and then the institute. The point is that VGIK can't go on being divorced from production. When we first came into the studios in our fourth year, we felt as if we were in some dense forest. The rules there were different, we had to do things that we hadn't been taught. On the other hand a studio can't guarantee work for twenty people.

And then—how should candidates be selected? I only realized what I wanted to do when I was in my fifth year; before that I hadn't the slightest idea why I had come to VGIK. Only after working under Marlen Khutsiev did I begin to understand that this was something real, and important, and art. Earlier I had been working on screen adaptations, and working with actors, but without knowing any of the whys or wherefores. I wanted to become a director, and I imagined I knew why, but in fact I only really understood why very recently.

First you have to be bitten by cinema, you have to ask yourself if you are going to be able to do something in cinema, and only then should you go and study. Lots of people who graduate from VGIK have a difficult time. We don't have a satisfactory selection system, and so there is a tremendous amount of wastage. We remain oblivious of all the endless psychological tests that exist to establish what a person is likely to be good at. Surely there must be a way of finding out about somebody's professional potential? Then, of course, nobody actually knows what it takes to be a director. That ought to be established. One is told that it is not possible to develop any system of that kind, but the fact is that nobody is giving it any thought. One way would be for the student to be apprenticed to a master, as they were in the old days. Apart from all that, how can anyone live on twenty-eight roubles a month? The students are quite simply unfit for work; it's hardly surprising that no one will take them on. Engineers are needed all over the place, but directors are pretty well redundant. A director only becomes necessary when he has proved that he can do things better than other people. Then he'll be an artist. All the rest are doomed to eke out an existence on the periphery of art, on the periphery of cinema. Once a person has been studying one thing for a year or two he hasn't the courage to give it up and start doing something else.

There ought to be quite a different form of training. They ought to see more films. The whole 'new wave' was a result of film critics sitting in cinemas and watching quantities of films. It's important to see the work of the great masters, and know it well, in order not to start inventing the bicycle. There aren't so many of them, perhaps five; Dovzhenko, Bunuel, Bergman, Antonioni, Dreyer, and one or two others.

And then there's no time at VGIK to read. All you have time for is getting through the reading for the seminars. You don't read beyond certain works, or even just extracts, on specific themes. That's very bad. A person can only really assimilate what he reads when it has time to become a part of him. If they were to read more at the institute, and watch more films, they wouldn't then start inventing things that have been invented long ago.

What are your plans now?

I have a great many plans. It's hard to say anything definite. I hope to be working again in the spring. I may make a film of *The House with a Tower*, based on Friedrich Gorenstein's short story.

On 'Solaris'

[The following is the text of a discussion Tarkovsky had with Z. Podguzhets in 1973, on *Solaris* and other films.]

Why, in a film which could be categorized as science fiction, are you more concerned with the drama of the hero's conscience than with the dramatic situation in the space station?

When I read Lem's novel, what struck me above all were the moral problems evident in the relationship between Kelvin and his conscience, as manifested in the form of Khari. In fact if I understood, and greatly admired, the second half of the novel—the technology, the atmosphere of the space station, the scientific questions—it was entirely because of that situation, which seems to me to be fundamental to the work. Inner, hidden, human problems, moral problems, always engage me far more than any questions of technology; and in any case technology, and how it develops, invariably relates to moral issues, in the end that is what it rests upon. My prime sources are always the real state of the human soul, and the conflicts that are expressed in spiritual problems. And so I paid more attention to that side of things in my film, even though I did so unconsciously. It was an organic process of selection. I didn't erase the rest, but it somehow became more muted than the things that interested me most.

What is the central idea of your film?

What is central is the inner problem, which preoccupied me and which coloured the whole production in a very specific way: namely the fact that in the course of its development humanity is constantly struggling between spiritual, moral entropy, the dissipation of ethical principles, on the one hand, and on the other—the aspiration towards a moral ideal. The endless inner struggle of man, who wants to be freed from all moral restraint, but at the same time seeks a meaning for his own movement, in the form of an ideal—that is the dichotomy that constantly produces intense inner conflict in the life of the individual and of society. And it seems to me that the conflict, and the fraught, urgent search for a spiritual ideal, will continue until humanity has freed itself sufficiently to concern itself only with the spiritual. As soon as that happens a new stage will begin in the development of the human soul, when man will be directed into his inner being as intensely, deeply, passionately, limitlessly, as he has directed his efforts up till now to his search for inner freedom. And Lem's novel, in my own specific understanding of it, expresses precisely man's inability to concentrate on himself, and points to the conflict between man's spiritual life and the objective acquisition of knowledge. It's a conflict that will never give man any peace until he has achieved complete outward freedom. We might call this freedom social, the freedom of the social individual who is not concerned with bread, food, a roof, or his children's future. Mankind does not move forward synchronously, it stops and starts and goes off in different directions. And only when scientific discoveries occur in the course of technological development is there a corresponding leap in man's moral development. There is an extraordinary cohesion between the two. That was the problem which exercised me all the time I was working on the film. In simple terms, the story of Khari's relationship with Kelvin is the story of the relationship between man and his own conscience. It's about man's concern with his own spirit, when he has no possibility of doing anything about it, when he is constantly drawn into the exploration and development of technology.

And what is the outcome of the conflict between Kelvin and his conscience?

In one way Kelvin is the loser, beause he tries to relive his life without repeating the mistake he made on earth. He attempts to replay the same situation, because he has a conscience, because he feels guilty of a crime, and he tries to change himself in relation to Khari. But it doesn't work. Their relationship ends as it did on earth, the second Khari commits suicide. But if he had been able to live this stage of his life differently, he would not have been guilty the first time, either. And he realizes the reason for his inability to live this second life with Khari. He realizes it is not possible. If it were, then it would be possible to press the button of this microphone that is recording our conversation, replay the tape, wipe off all that has been recorded, and start off afresh. And then concepts like spiritual life, conscience, morality would have no meaning.

Does that mean that the film ends on a note of pessimism?

The film ends with what is most precious for a person, and at the same time the simplest thing of all, and the most available to everybody: ordinary human relationships, which are the starting-point of man's endless journey. After all, that journey began for the sake of preserving intact, and protecting, feelings which every person experiences: love of your own earth, love of those close to you, of those who brought you into the world, love of your past, of what has always been, and still is, dear to you. The fact that the ocean brought forth out of its depths the very thing that was most important to him—his dream of returning to the earth—that is, the idea of contact. Contact in the sense of 'humane', in the sense of 'doing good'. For me the finale is Kelvin's return to the cradle, to his source, which cannot ever be forgotten. And it is all the more important because he had travelled so far along the road of technological progress, in the process of acquiring knowledge.

Do you think Lem is going to be pleased with your film?

I should not want to prepare Lem particularly for the film. He is a person for whose opinion I have a great respect, I admire his talent and his intellect. I am very fond of the film, and extremely grateful to Lem for allowing me to make it. However Lem feels about the film, I don't think he will have any call to be angry or offended by its being badly done, or insincere, or unprofessional. As far as all that goes, I don't feel he is going to be disappointed. I'm sure he will like Khari.

You took your film to Cannes. What did you think about the other films that were shown there?

I was astonished by how low the standard was. I don't understand. On the one hand everything I saw was highly professional, on the other it was all utterly commercial. For example, they would treat a subject that was bound to be of concern to everybody: the problem of the working-class movement, or the relationship between the working-class and other sections of the population. And all of it was done with such an eye to the audience, with such a desire to please. One really had the impression that all the films had been edited by one and the same person. But in film the most important thing of all is to be aware of the inner rhythm. So what can only be individual had become commonplace, hackneyed. It is extraordinary. Even Fellini's film about Rome, the most interesting film of all—it was shown outside the festival proper—is a sort of game of give-away played with the audience, the editorial rhythm is so slick that one feels offended on behalf of Fellini. I remember pictures of his where the shots, the length of the shots, and their rhythm, were tied to the inner state of the character and the author. But this picture has been made with an eye for what is going to please the audience. I find that repugnant. Anyhow, the film tells us nothing new either about Fellini himself or about life.

What did you think of Polanski's 'Macbeth'?

I didn't like it. It's very shallow, very superficial. It completely ignores the moral problem of conscience of the man who is paying for the evil he has committed. I am staggered that anyone can put on Shakespeare and completely bypass the spiritual issues. It is a major failure on Polanski's part. His serious intentions only show in his urge to be naturalistic. The film is so detailed that it ceases to be realistic. The director's aim becomes obvious, and as such, merely a means of achieving an effect. And once the audience can read that so clearly, the aim ceases to be one with the weave of the film and becomes just a patently obvious aim.

What are your plans now?

It's not easy to talk about them, I am always rather frightened of doing so. If you talk too much then nothing happens. But anyhow, I have a screenplay all ready. I want to start filming in the autumn. It will be an autobiographical film, about my childhood. It will look at the same events from two sides: the point of view of the older generation and my own. I think that the use of that parallel could create an interesting way of seeing things, an interesting angle, and the intersection will lend a curious colouring to events that are familiar to everyone in the course of their lives. I am very excited by the screenplay. I am very anxious to make the film, because I am afraid that if any length of time goes by without making it, I shall never go back to the same theme. I thought about the screenplay for so long before I wrote it, and I have given so much thought to the production. And if time passes I am afraid that the idea of the film will live itself out.

On 'Solaris'

What about the film about Dostoievsky that you told me about last year?

I haven't given up the idea of a film on Dostoievsky, I intend to do it. But it will take considerable time. Not so much the making of the film, as the writing of the screenplay. I haven't even touched it yet. I am still collecting material, and reading. I shall start actually working on it later.

On 'Mirror'

[This is the record of a talk by Tarkovsky in the Building Institute, 29 April 1975, on his film *Mirror*.]

I know from experience that on occasions like this there is no point in making long speeches because you always have to repeat yourself when people start asking questions. So let's start with the questions. Please let me have your questions in writing, and while I am waiting for them to reach me I shall try to answer the questions I was asked by the two excellent young men who brought me here by car.

Were any substantial cuts made in *Mirror*, they asked me, before it reached the screen? The answer is, No.

Is there any connection between *Mirror* and Kirsanov's *Mirrors*? No, none.

What, in my view, is *Mirror* about?

It is an autobiographical film. The things that happen are real things that happened to people close to me. That is true of all the episodes in the film. But why do people complain that they cannot understand it? The facts are so simple, they can be taken by everyone as similar to the experience of their own lives. But here we come up against something that is peculiar to cinema: the further a viewer is from the content of a film, the closer he is; what people are looking for in cinema is a continuation of their lives, not a repetition. There are no entertaining moments in the film. In fact I am categorically against entertainment in cinema: it is as degrading for the author as it is for the audience.

The purpose of *Mirror*, its inspiration, is that of a homily: look, learn, use the life shown here as an example. There are so many films now, and they are all so different, that very soon it will be impossible to plan for distribution to cinemas. That will be the beginning of a new phase in the development of film, which is after all the youngest art form, it is only about seventy years old. Films will start to be handed out as cassettes, people will take them home, every viewer will find himself face to face with the film he particularly likes. And what of cinema, the mass medium, you may ask? Mass is not a criterion of quality. The same could be said about the number of people involved in the making of a film. Numbers are not the point. A small team working together is preferable to a large collective.

Another question: What is going to happen to *Mirror*? We don't know yet. For the moment the film is only being shown in three cinemas, and they started with two. They are trying it out first, because the organs responsible for distribution are afraid it might be a failure. When they heard that people sat on and wouldn't leave, one of the highly placed distribution officials observed that *normal* people leave the cinema. The film is going to be on wide screen in September.

About the team that worked on *Mirror*. There is only one major change since *Rublyov*: Rerberg has replaced Yussov as cameraman, but this is how it happened to turn out, there was no question of principle involved.

Will *Mirror* be shown in Cannes? No, it won't.

About the actors in *Mirror*: They are all small parts except for Terekhova, who actually has two roles. In fact audiences keep being confused by that, but it doesn't matter.

[Next come the answers to written questions submitted by the audience.]

Why is the film called 'Mirror', and not 'The Bright, Bright Day' as it was originally called?

The Bright, Bright Day was the name of the screenplay, not the film. There is no basis for giving the film that name.

Can 'Mirror' be considered a surrealist film?

No, it certainly cannot. What is surrealist about it? I was against surrealism even when I understood something about it, and I am even more against it now that I no longer understand it at all. Even the great Salvador Dali has repudiated surrealism. The movement has in fact disintegrated altogether.

On 'Mirror'

How is the first episode of the film, with the stammering boy, to be understood?

I shan't explain that, because I don't want to spoil it for those who have not yet seen the film. In any case that is not my function. I am there to do things, you are there to explain things.

Do you acknowledge the influence of Fellini, in particular of '8¹/₂', on 'Mirror'?

No, I don't, there could not have been any such influence, if only because *Mirror* was made earlier. The hero of *8¹/₂* is constantly on screen, the hero of *Mirror* is off screen. However, I consider *8¹/₂* to be Fellini's best work.

What is the subject of 'Mirror', its idea, moral, plot, development, denouement?

The writer of that question clearly considers that all those things are essential in any work of art. In reality the concept of things that 'have to be' is incompatible with art. A work of art, of whatever art form, is constructed only according to its own principles, and is based on its own, inner, dynamic stereotype. In fact I can answer like a demagogue: in *Mirror* there are subject and denouement, and all the other things listed in the question.

Is there symbolism in 'Mirror'?

No! The images themselves are like symbols, but unlike accepted symbols they cannot be deciphered. The image is like a clot of life, and even the author may not be able to work out what it means, let alone the audience. Pushkin's 'My sadness is radiant' is not a symbol but an image. Tolstoy's dying Ivan Ilych feels as if he is confined inside a narrow intestine pipe, and cannot get out. What he feels is so real and vivid that it obliterates anything else, and even affects what the sick man says. As long ago as the Middle Ages Japanese writers were decrying the interpretation of symbols in art. And quite rightly! The fewer symbols the better! Symbolism is a sign of decadence.

What was the word that the heroine of 'Mirror' whispered to her friend?

It couldn't be repeated in public.

What is the correlation in 'Mirror' between logic and intuition?

I don't know. If I were to start thinking about that, I should have no time left for anything else. But it's an interesting question, and you can find some sort of answer to it in the book on cinema which I am writing at present together with a co-author. It is supposed to be coming out at the end of the year.

Is all the black-and-white footage in 'Mirror' documentary?

No, it's not. The dreams are black-and-white as well, they could not have been filmed in colour.

Are you going to make a film of 'The Idiot'?

I hope to.

Terekhova in 'Mirror' obviously doesn't love her children. Why not?

Why do you imagine she sells her ear-rings? Why doesn't she give the boy to her husband? And there are other episodes that illustrate her love for her children, you must have forgotten them.

Who is the woman in black? Why did you bring her in?

[*Turning to the audience*] What do you think, is it worth explaining? [*Unhesitating shouts of 'No, No!' from the hall.*]

Is the episode with the stammering boy significant at a personal or a social level?

Both.

[Tarkovsky's concluding words]

I should like to ask you all not to be so demanding, and not to think of *Mirror* as a difficult film. It is no more than a straightforward, simple story. It doesn't have to be made any more understandable.

On 'The Idiot'

With reference to the treatment already submitted for two films based on *The Idiot*, we wish to make the following points.

First: the reasons for our decision to make two films, as opposed to a series of perhaps two or three parts.

The basis for this decision lies above all in the architectonics of the novel. Interestingly enough, several film versions have used one of two basic lines of plot. For instance, the story of Nastasia Fillipovna, her leaving Totsky, her name-day party, her meeting with Myshkin. The first of the four parts of the novel were enough for I. A. Pyriev, for example, to make his film more than twenty years ago, and that version seemed to be a perfectly independent work of art. That, no doubt, was why the director felt no artistic need to work further on the film.

Other versions concentrate on Rogozhin, with the inspired final scene of the murder of Nastasia Fillipovna, and the game of cards beside the dead body, in old Rogozhin's house, which seems to have fallen silent for ever.

There are two epicentres in the novel, both creations of genius, separated by nearly five hundred pages. Between them lie two massive parts—the second and third, which are a kind of summary of the first explosion (Nastasia Fillipovna's name-day party)—and the start of a new exposition leading to Rogozhin's murder of his beloved.

This structure came about because the novel was not written all at once, but came out in serial parts; and so the first part was published two years before the book was actually finished. If one takes into account the fact that right up to the time of the separate (1874) edition the novel was still being completed and polished, it becomes clear that it was being written as it developed.

'The first part is in effect merely the introduction. The one thing it has to do is awaken a certain curiosity about what is to follow. . . .

In the second part everything has to be finally put into place . . .
The second part is decisive; it is the most difficult.'

'Most important of all is the character of the Idiot. Developing it.
He restores Nastasia Fillipovna's dignity, influences Rogozhin,
makes Aglaya human . . .'

In these and other remarks by the author we are constantly aware
that the demands of the 'development' of the hero and the novel—
which was written with long breaks over nearly five years—led
Dostoievsky to create a curious two-tiered work. One novel is built
on top of the other.

Long before the second part we have intimations of the earliest
structure, which for the sake of convenience we might call 'Nastasia
Fillipovna'. In this structure—defined by the triangle: Myshkin,
Nastasia Fillipovna, Rogozhin—we find plot, climax and finale,
namely the Prince's arrival, the name-day party, and Rogozhin's
attempt to kill the Prince at the Scales Hotel.

And so one novel is concluded, the triangle is resolved; perhaps
in a rather curious fashion, since it is by repulsion: all the main
characters move away from one another. Such a structure is legitimate; it is not unknown in the history of the novel, and it is duly
completed.

Dostoievsky's urge to 'develop' and 'widen' the available space
of the novel is reminiscent of a sportsman's attempt to break a world
record. This is typical of Dostoievsky's work generally, and particularly so for *The Idiot*, which several outstanding Russian writers
(including Lev Tolstoy and Mikhail Saltykov-Shchedrin) considered his best book.

It is important to look at two other factors, two tasks, which had a
bearing on the writer's extraordinarily stringent demands for this
novel. Dostoievsky saw as one of his most important tasks the creation of the 'positively beautiful man'.

'Beauty is an ideal, an ideal which neither our civilization nor
that of western Europe has yet come close to realizing.' Such was
Dostoievsky's grandiose aim; and such is the crux of the writer's
dissatisfaction with his first 'attempt', the first part.

Secondly, crucial to Dostoievsky's vision of the book was the
figure of Prince Myshkin in relation to post-reform Russia. Dostoievsky was not a writer who would shatter the equilibrium of life
through his characters' suffering, and fail to charge the upheaval
with a meaning of equal magnitude. He was bound to respond to the
stormy contemporary scene, the ferment of ideological arguments,

the new social phenomena, which could be summed up as the attraction and repulsion of three groups: collapsing landed gentry, emerging bourgeoisie, and the radicals—seminarian and democratic.

We shall return to this question later, but for the moment I want to look at the independent construction of the second novel. For the sake—again—of convenience, we may call it 'Rogozhin'.

Of course he does not occupy the main space of the second half of the novel. But it is in Rogozhin that all the lines of that part of the book intersect, he is at its climax (with the murder of Nastasia Fillipovna), and not only does he go on to continue his life, unbroken, having survived spiritually, but he is the only one to do so; with a genius's sureness of touch, the writer makes him the most robust social and moral type of contemporary Russia.

Nastasia Fillipovna is dead, Prince Myshkin has finally gone mad, Aglaya has embraced western Catholicism and cut herself off from Russia; only Rogozhin is going to go on. Even if he will be sentenced to penal servitude, and be 'deep in thought', he will have his own fate, which he has already accepted 'sombrely and in silence'.

The figure of Rogozhin leads on to so much else: to Dmitri Karamazov, to some of Leskov's heroes, to some of Gorky's, and surprisingly enough, even those of Chekhov and Bunin, who don't seem to have liked Dostoievsky, but who nonetheless could not entirely escape his influence. Nor, of course, could any of the other Russian writers who came after him.

The second part, the second *The Idiot*, is built on more complex architectonics. It fits, though only approximately, into the schema of a square: Prince Myshkin, Nastasia Fillipovna, Aglaya, Rogozhin.

Basically the action takes place in two settings, Pavlovsk and St. Petersburg. In the first there is almost a new exposition, a new situation for the characters. Here the author makes use of fresh air, a railway station, villas, walks, park benches, trees. He needs nature; just as he needed it in Switzerland for Myshkin's recovery, indeed for the latter to be able to return to Russia, to be able to live, to love and to 'pity'.

The trial which the characters are conducting, on their own and others' lives, is transferred back to St. Petersburg, to the city with which both author and characters have old scores. The corner of Gorokhovaya and Sadovaya, the dead house of Rogozhin with his crazed, happy old mother and the curious Pafnutievna—that is the setting for the final, apocalyptic resolving of the conflicts.

Again—the arrival of Myshkin, this time in Pavlovsk, again the ferment of passions, and a more elaborate pattern of relationships (Nastasia Fillipovna, Aglaya, Rogozhin, Prince Myshkin). There is a physical pressure driving events to a series of climaxes, which come rushing one after the other: Nastasia Fillipovna striking the officer with her whip, Ippolit's phoney suicide, the exchange between Aglaya and Myshkin, Pavlishchev's pretender son, the scene with Princess Belokonskaya, the exchange between Aglaya and Nastasia Fillipovna . . . and so on, until the final climax with Rogozhin's murder of Nastasia Fillipovna.

The second part of the novel, the second film, has to move fast, it must have a powerful impetus, for only then will the audience be aware of, and convinced by, the artistic and philosophical substance of the novel, as they have to be. They will see the main characters within the parameters of the definitive *mise-en-scène*, artistically ineluctable and whole.

All too often, after seeing an adaptation of a Dostoievsky novel on stage or on film, one is left with a thoroughly unpleasant impression by the endless insistence on the 'infernal' nature of Dostoievsky's characters. Only a few more steps in the same direction and people decide that Dostoievsky was not realistic, or try to believe that his driving force was despair, alienation from the world, the substitution of supernatural miracles for the laws of nature and society.

Such an understanding of Dostoievsky is part of the arsenal of those existentialists who set the 'absurd' against the immutable laws of nature and history, believing that belief itself is more powerful than all the laws which confront man in this world.

And here we have to declare our own position, firmly and unequivocally; and in doing so our first and greatest ally will be the writer himself.

Obedient to his spirit, his objectives, his great spiritual energy, we cannot extract from the novel—as is so often done—the sections that happen to suit us, and by skipping from one to the other arrive at the gory denouement, dismissing our critics with assurances that 'that was what Dostoievksy meant'.

Dostoievsky finds brilliant 'accidents' in his characters' moments of illumination, but he never has any accidents in the construction or motivation of the novel. It is one of the marks of his genius that every accident has been impeccably prepared.

That is the reason why it took so much work and time to discover what shape the adaptation of *The Idiot* had to have. A step by step treatment of the novel, in serial parts, is out of the question, it would contradict the spirit of the work. There is nothing step by step about it; it develops by explosions that come crowding one after the other; and each one is caused by a minutely detailed, comprehensive set of motivations.

The main problem of a film adaptation of Dostoievsky seems to us to be his own realism; his own affinity to cinema. The mature Dostoievsky is unthinkable without his repudiation of the 'natural school', but it may be that he denied it so vehemently precisely because it was so deeply embedded in him, incongruously side by side with that very denial. It was where he had started out, and it figures constantly in his great novels. What Dostoievsky most disliked about the 'natural school' was its protagonists' assumption that individuals were 'eaten into' by their milieu; but he himself was unable to move away from it, even though he found it deeply unsatisfactory. His own path tells us how we have to construct our future film. Dostoievsky made much of the contrast between himself and other writers because he sought to highlight the truth.

The power of the milieu over the individual is far more frightening in his work than in that of his fellow writers of the natural school. But whatever hell he may have painted within the human soul, Dostoievsky always longed passionately to free the individual from that hell.

For him, the mind relates to man's development, and the heart to what remains constant in him.

And the reason we require more film space for the screening of the novel (it is possible that each film may be made in two parts) is our wish—even anxiety—not to fail in the grave responsibility of bringing out the essence of those artistic contradictions, that artistic seeking, which, in Blok's words, 'have still not been reconciled by Philistine civilization, and never will be, for they will only be reconciled at the moment of that civilization's death.'

Without them there would be no Dostoievsky, that great Russian artist would not exist, and without him we should all be the lesser and the poorer both in mind and in heart.

For Dostoievsky, perhaps more than anyone else, spent his whole life in the expectation of a 'happier future awaiting mankind, and of the attainment of those ideals in which he believed, courageously and generously, all his life, precisely because he himself was capable of setting up an ideal. It is generally the lot of noble souls, of true lovers of humanity, to preserve that faith to the end.'

It is in *The Idiot* that these convictions are most fully reflected.

Such, then, are our reasons for envisaging *The Idiot* as two films. The first will start with Prince Myshkin's arrival in St. Petersburg. His entry into the Yepanchin household, the story of Nastasia Fillipovna, the scene at her name-day party, where there is an intersection of the main lines: Myshkin–Nastasia Fillipovna–Rogozhin. Then Moscow, their frenzied mutual repulsion, and at the end, when Nastasia Fillipovna deserts them both, the maturing of Rogozhin's decision to kill Myshkin, which he then tries to do at the Scales Hotel.

The material for the second film—and here we are talking not about concept and treatment, but actually about the material of the novel, which will be organized in the structure of the film—finds our heroes in Pavlovsk.

Once again they have moved away from each other, back to their original points of departure; they have been torn apart, even in terms of where they are living. They hardly know one another. Prince Myshkin is in Lebedev's house, Aglaya is in her parents' villa, Nastasia Fillipovna is with Darya Alekseevna, and, finally, Rogozhin is travelling daily from St. Petersburg. Either in reality or in their imagination, his feverish eyes follow the other characters around.

Again—the attempt to embody happiness in the highest degree possible in this life. Our heroes come together, almost as if for a duel, surrounded by the riff-raff of the Pavlovsk pleasure-grounds; the petty play of passions; self-interest; broken lives. They are the heroes of the novel first of all because their aspirations, their spiritual expectations of happiness—of happiness in this world—are higher and more whole than those of other people. And again, almost as if mocking, the writer takes the action back to the marriage of the Prince and Nastasia Fillipovna. And again she runs away from the altar. It is almost as if the author were rehearsing the same text, taken from life itself. And then, as if having assured himself that he did not make a mistake the first time, he composes the tragic, slow finale. It seems to us appropriate, and indeed absolutely essential— given the structure of the two films, separate and yet full of cross-references—that some episodes will have to be transferred from the first part to the second, and some the other way. It may be that material from the writer's other novels will have to be included in the screenplay, in order to clarify Dostoievsky's position. It is well known that he used to treat the same themes time after time; and we feel that this will be both necessary and artistically convincing.

However, these are questions that apply to actual work on the screenplays; for the moment we are asking to be allowed, finally, two years after presenting the treatment, to start work on the two screenplays based on Dostoievsky's *The Idiot*.

On 'Hamlet'

Why does Hamlet wreak revenge? Revenge is a form of expression for the blood tie of family, for sacrifice made for loved ones, a sacred duty.

Hamlet took his revenge, as we know, in order to set right a time that was 'out of joint'. It would be nearer the truth to say he did so in order to embody the idea of self-sacrifice.

We often display resolution or obstinacy in actions that do us nothing but harm. This, too, is a kind of search for self-sacrifice, self-denial, duty. Strange, absurd moments of deliberately putting yourself in someone's debt, of dependence, of being the victim—things that the materialist, Freud, would call masochism. The religious man would call them—duty. What Dostoievsky called—the desire to suffer.

This desire to suffer without any organized religious system can become simply psychotic.

In the end, it is love that has failed to find a form. But not Freudian love; spiritual love. Love is always the gift of oneself to another. And even though the word sacrificial (in the vulgar understanding of the term) has negative, outwardly destructive connotations, when it is applied to the individual who is sacrificing himself, the essence of that act is always love, that is—a positive, creative, Divine act.

Shakespeare has to be sought out and discovered. Sense of time, of the epoch—that is particularly important for me. You have to try to dig down to what Shakespeare was thinking. This tragedy is at once very complex and very simple. In some ways everything is amazingly simple! Mountains of books have been written about Shakespeare and *Hamlet*, but nobody has ever explained it totally, brought out the secret meaning. The only thing that is clear is that it is there. It is one of the greatest works of genius in the whole of art. In terms of inspiration, nobility, simplicity I know of no other play that can compare with *Hamlet*. You have the impression that it must have been written in the space of some fifteen inspired minutes. There are a great many puzzles, but they all resolve themselves as you go into the play, and everything becomes clear-cut and obvious. At the moment I have the feeling that I shouldn't be able to live without this production.

. . . I have not found anything! I don't know what to do! I have read the whole of Bulgakov, and it strikes me as naive, and not suitable for the stage. As for Leonid Andreyev, I don't see him at all.

Turgenev, Ostrovsky, Pisemsky—I can't see them, I don't understand them. With *Hamlet* I can see exactly what everything is and how it is . . . I really want Shakespeare. If it can't be *Hamlet*, then perhaps *Macbeth* or *Julius Caesar*? But in fact I want *Hamlet*, and I want Solonitsyn to play him, and Terekhova—Gertrude.

I should so like to work for a bit in theatre. The theatre has great, mysterious possibilities. I don't agree with Mikhail Ilych Romm, my VGIK teacher, that theatre is going to decline as cinema develops. Theatre is an independent and wonderful art form. It's not that I am no longer interested in film, just that for the moment I have proved to myself everything that I had to, particularly now that I have made *Mirror*. If there were something else I had to prove to myself, then I should not have any peace, the most important thing in any work is to prove something to yourself. At present I feel the need to work in the theatre. I don't know what the result will be, but I want to direct *Hamlet* on stage, and then, perhaps, we shall manage to make a film. And then it would be good to direct *The Final Sacrifice* on stage, and *Macbeth*.

Hamlet was well ahead of his time, and when he realizes that it is up to him to destroy that world, he starts to take revenge, and becomes the same as everyone else, and that is his downfall. That idea of Shakespeare is pursuing me. Can a man judge another, can one man shed another's blood? I do not consider that he can, that he has the right. Society can. Unfortunately—it can! And there is nothing to be done about that . . . But one drop of blood shed is equal to an ocean. I do not consider that a man has the right to kill another for the sake of the welfare of ten people. If I am told— 'Kill that man, and lots of people will be better off!'—I do not consider that I have the right to do so, and I would do better to kill myself, as one of our writers did at a particular moment of his life, after being obliged to sign death warrants. In the end he killed himself. Why . . . ? No one knows, but it seems to me that it was his inevitable end. The only pity is that he didn't come to that same decision at the moment when he had to sign the first death warrant. And that is Hamlet's tragedy. After he meets the Ghost, Hamlet dedicates his life to revenge, and that is why he perishes, he kills himself, it is suicide, he couldn't withstand the blood, good cannot be achieved through blood. In this connection it is very important to me that we do the 'Mousetrap' scene like this; I want the scene to be acted by the King, the Queen and the Ghost. How it is to be done technically we shall have to work out. But let us say that Claudius and Gertrude come to the play, climb on to a structure, and disappear off-stage, as if they were taking their places, out of view of the audience. Behind the scenes they put on some garment, or else take something off, anyhow, they change their appearance in some way, and after that they behave like players, miming the poisoning of Hamlet's father. It's important that it should all be seen as if through the eyes of Hamlet himself, just as he imagined it really happened. In my understanding of it, Hamlet does not perish at the end, when he dies physically, but immediately after the 'Mousetrap', as soon as he realizes that he is like the worthless Claudius.

Boris Leonidovich Pasternak is a wonderful poet, but his translation of *Hamlet* is staggeringly inaccurate; Morozov's translation is brilliant, superb! In fact we ought to be using it, it's only with him that I really have a sense of Shakespeare; I feel his roots, his beginnings. Let's try and make our own stage edition of Pasternak's translation, checking it against Morozov.

At first I was sorry we had no trap-doors, but now I think we don't need them. We don't want any tricks. There shouldn't be any tricks in theatre, they are the last thing theatre needs. In fact, altogether everything in theatre ought to be done very simply, amazingly simply . . .

I have never been an actor, but I feel that the fourth wall should never be broken down, nothing should ever be said specifically to people in the auditorium. That is bound to destroy something, I don't know what, but I am convinced that something is destroyed. Nothing should be explained. It's a terrible shortcoming with us, this tendency to explain things in art, to interpret things. Surely that is not the point of art?

I have just realized that we ought not to act the first scene. The

Ghost should not be shown in advance, and above all, we ought not to talk about him so much. In terms of the dramaturgy of the piece, the first scene should be the Queen. And the play will open in total darkness, with the outlines of the chamber being lit up very gradually, with the King and Queen's enormous bed. A figure is standing by the bed, looking at it sadly. We don't understand who it is, but it is the Ghost. Ideally we should create an illusion for the audience, through the lighting; as if there were something like a film in front of their eyes. Then the cock crows, and the Ghost walks out. But he walks out perfectly normally, factually, he doesn't vanish in a theatrical way. Altogether the Ghost ought to be the most real, concrete character in the play. (Just as in dreams we often see people close to us who have actually died.) All the pain is now concentrated in him, all the sufferings of the world. He could even have a handkerchief in his hand, and put it to his ear, as if he could still feel the poison there, as if it were still seeping.

Shakespeare's genius is in his masterly creation of atmosphere and of the times. I'd like to have one scene in the play, we shall have to find the right place, consisting of that discomfort, lack of structure, the chill of those times, and then suddenly in the middle of that cold there is someone sitting, cosily, feeling happy in his own house, as I feel when I arrive in my own house in the country, and I light the fire and sit down in front of it . . . and my family are all around me . . . It would be good to have that in the play.

To begin with, it's a family, a closely-knit family, they mustn't have the slightest inkling of all the miseries that lie ahead of them. They are very protective of each other, very dear to each other, they are all together. And that makes them happy! It is not a mere ritual conversation between a brother and sister before he goes away, and it's not a father lecturing his son, it's a scene where all three of them want to be together before the brother and son goes off, they want to be together again and again, to breathe together. We shall have to look for this scene in the relationship between them, in their own mental state, and not in the meaning of the text. We shall not be taking it from the beginning. Laertes and Ophelia will have been talking all night, she helped him to pack, they drank some wine, laughed, joked, and we come in on the end of their conversation . . .

I don't know what we're going to do without Terekhova, I feel helpless, I don't want to do any of it. All I want to do is go off to the country, I don't want to do anything else. . . . Get up early and be busy with something—sawing wood, painting, banging in nails . . . Anyhow, what does it mean to be a director in this country, when you can only do what you are told to do. Far better to go and saw wood!

She deliberately drinks the wine. She saw, she knows that Claudius put poison into the glass, she demands some wine, insists on having it. The role should begin with an amazing degree of happiness. She has to be happy to start with, she feels such well-being, it even has to be an innocent happiness. And then, very gradually, and intuitively, she becomes disillusioned in this man whom she loves to distraction, and starts to move away from him, because she is beginning to feel—and it is a question of feeling—that there is something frightening in Claudius, something she has never known, something daemonic. She senses that it is the King who is the cause of Hamlet's ravings, that the King is the key to it all. She begins to be afraid of Claudius, but she goes on loving him! That is very important, that is what we have to try to build up. A tremendous feeling of love for Claudius combines, disturbingly, with fear, cunning, and an almost childlike innocence. I know a woman like that. In the end Gertrude can bear it no longer and kills herself, I repeat—she drinks the poisoned wine deliberately, she realizes herself in death, in suicide.

The pile of corpses at the end of the play—is fate itself, it is vengeance. A pile of suicides! Because of course Laertes in his duel with Hamlet also kills himself, that is suicide as well:

> the foul practice
> Hath turned itself on me; lo, here I lie,
> Never to rise again.

He kills himself because he has completely lost his direction in life, he has lost his aim. I began by thinking that Laertes was not a personality, but now I realize that everyone in the play is a personality, it's a play of personalities.

We have to be clear about the causality of one other death—that of Polonius. What is it? Chance or destiny? Or perhaps another revenge? For what? . . . That requires more thought. Polonius is something unique, he is at court, he's a courtier, and yet he is simple, he is not at all the stereotype courtier, he is cleverer and more simple. He is well-mannered, educated, a real minister of state, and of course he is a true nobleman. He was the faithful liege of Hamlet's father, and meets his death under Claudius. His is a very dramatic role. Osric comes to take his place. I think he could even be in

Polonius' costume, but he is not Polonius! New commanders are always less good than their predecessors. All Osric has is the uniform. . . . I now see that when Hamlet stabs Polonius it has to be played like this: Polonius comes out of his hiding place and walks as he ever has, like a minister of state. And then he leans against something, sinks down, and dies with great dignity and calm. And again he dies like a minister of state, like a nobleman. I think that is the right way to do it, but we shall have to go on thinking about it . . .

I dare say *Hamlet* is the one play in world literature that has not been solved. And it is eternal; unlike the plays of some of our playwrights who are still alive, but are never put on because they were born dead.

I want to start rehearsals by working with individual actors. We have already worked out fairly clear concepts for each character, and the actors have to be initiated into the design, sketched into the basic schema. The actor must know where he starts from, where he finishes, through what he progresses from beginning to end. It is important to me to find a common language with each actor, to make each person aware of my own perceptions. The actors must be able to see all the cards straightaway, in theatre that is essential (in cinema I work quite differently with actors) and then they must be given total freedom, to the point where they must not even be constrained by the *mise-en-scène* that we have already decided upon as essential to the production. It is important that once I have given them their terms of reference, the actors should not be inhibited, slow down, waste time searching, lose their spontaneity. Those are things we have to beware of. An actor has to exist very easily on stage, and express even highly complex feelings very simply. It is not easy, it requires courage, but that is how I see the actor's art.

Stanislavsky was a genius! That applies both to his system and to the creation of the Moscow Arts Theatre. But I consider that Stanislavsky's system was for Stanislavsky only. He was the only one who could work by it and who could understand it. We take things from his system, but each of us interprets it in his own way, and that is not right, and it certainly isn't Stanislavsky.

In theatre today, in my view, the methodology and technique of acting are fraught with difficulties, above all in the aesthetics of means of expression. For instance, actors are often carried away by feeling, by bursts of temperament. Why? To show that they have these things? It's undignified to act emotions, quite simply indecent. Our profession is full of conventions, we can remind people about their feelings by means of thought, of ideas, we don't have to act them. In any case, once feeling is expressed openly, vividly, it immediately takes on something false, it becomes theatrical and ostentatious. No truly sincere person will ever express his feelings openly, true feeling always has some kind of veil. It is only false, insincere people who make a show of their feelings, apparently with the object of showing everyone else what wonderfully sensitive people they are. But it's not like that! In fact I absolutely do not accept powerful expressions of uninhibited, naked feeling and temperament, they always ring false. And something else! ... unfortunately we have completely forgotten how to make a text audible, we no longer know how. The only method we know is making everything louder. How pathetic! Again, there are some actors who mutter behind their teeth, on the grounds that the life going on inside them is so powerful, so real. Very clever!

We must avoid both extremes, I am afraid of them, and the more so when we have a play in verse. On no account must we hide the verse, we mustn't talk in prose. Here the actors will need help, the verse has to be there, and whatever happens they must derive pleasure from speaking in verse. Actors have a wonderful nature, we must love them as we love children, and then we can do anything with them.

NOTES

ON NAMES AND TITLES OCCURRING IN THE DIARIES

1970

p. 3   *Alexander (Sasha) Mishurin* (b. 1939): author of plays and screenplays, co-author of *Mirror*, played small part in *Solaris*, *Mirror*.
Anatoly (Tolya) Solonitsyn (1934–82): one of A.T.'s favourite actors, played in *Andrey Rublyov*, *Solaris*, *Mirror*, *Stalker*.
Vladimir Solovyov (1853–1900): Russian religious thinker and poet, exercised a major influence on the Symbolist movement.
Konstantin Leontiev (1831–91): philosopher, writer and critic.
Nikolay Berdyaev (1874–1948): Russian religious thinker exiled by Lenin, much read and highly regarded at the present time.

p. 4   *Evgeny Bazhanov*: sound mixer, Mosfilm Studios.
Vladimir Surin: predecessor of Nikolay Sizov as head of Mosfilm Studios.
Donatas Banionis (b. 1924): stage and movie actor, director of Panevezys Theatre, Lithuania, played in *Solaris*.
Nikolay Grinko (1920–89): Soviet actor; played in *Ivan's Childhood*, *Andrey Rublyov*, *Solaris*, *Mirror*, *Stalker*.
A. Massiulis (b. 1931): Lithuanian actor.
Yuri Yarvet (b. 1919): Estonian actor.
Maria Ivanovna Vishnyakova-Tarkovskaya (1907–79): mother of A.T.; actress.
George Stevens (1904–75): American director and cameraman.
Larissa (Lara, Larochka) Pavlovna Tarkovskaya: A.T.'s wife.

p. 5   *Irina (Ira) Rausch-Tarkovskaya*: director and actress, A.T.'s first wife, played in *Ivan's Childhood*, *Andrey Rublyov*.
Arseny (Senka, b. 1962): A.T.'s son by first marriage.
Nikolay (Kolya) Shishlin (b. 1933): worked in cultural section of Central Party Committee with responsibility for socialist countries; under Gorbachev, deputy chief of department of ideology; friend of A.T.

p. 6   *Yuly Karasik* (b. 1923): Soviet film director.
Andrey (Andriushka, Tyapa) Tarkovsky: son of Larissa and A.T.
Vera Rubina: make-up artist, worked on *Andrey Rublyov*, *Solaris*, *Mirror*.
Tamara Georgevna Ogorodnikova (T.G.): production manager, *Andrey Rublyov*; appeared in *Andrey Rublyov*, *Solaris*, *Mirror*.
Vadim Yussov (b. 1929): cameraman for all A.T.'s films up to *Solaris*.
Vladislav Dvorzhetsky (1939–78): Soviet actor, played Berton in *Solaris*.
Leonid (Lenya) Kozlov (b. 1933): Soviet film critic.

p. 7   *Friedrich Gorenstein*: writer of novels and screenplays, co-author with A.T. of *Solaris* script; now lives in W. Germany.
Vladimir Belyaev: at that time deputy chief commissioning editor, Mosfilm Studios.

p. 8   *Juxtapositions*: *A Book of Juxtapositions* was the title of the first version of

A.T.'s book on cinema, written in collaboration with the film critic Olga Surkova, which eventually appeared in English as *Sculpting in Time.*
Lev (Lyova, Leva) Vladimirovich Gornung (b. 1902): poet, translator, literary scholar, photographer; close friend of Arseniy Tarkovsky and Maria Ivanovna, A.T.'s parents.

p. 9   *Sergey Gerasimov* (1906–85): Soviet film director, actor and teacher, active from 1924 on.

p. 10   *Paul Heyse* (1830–1914): German poet.

p. 11   *Georgiy I. Kunitsyn*: worked under Pyotr Demichov, chief of ideology in Central Party Committee; instrumental in obtaining permission for the release of *Andrey Rublyov.*
Lao-Tzu: 6th–5th centuries BC, author of classical Chinese Taoist treatise.

p. 13   *Innokenty (Kesha) Smotkunovsky* (b. 1925): leading Soviet actor, was Narrator in *Mirror.*

p. 14   *Evgeny (Zhenya) Evtushenko* (b. 1933): well-known Siberian-born poet, who has recently turned to filmmaking.

p. 17   *Cesare Zavattini*: Italian writer, artist, film critic.
Valery Sirovsky (b. 1939): translator from Italian, worked in foreign department, Mosfilm Studios, accompanied A.T. to Venice.
Semyon Frehlich (b. 1920): Soviet film critic, author of screenplays.

p. 20   *Marina Tarkovskaya*: sister of A.T.; philologist.

p. 21   *Evgeny Zamyatin* (1884–1937): Russian writer, author of anti-Utopian novel, *Us.*
Sergey (Seryozha) Bondarchuk (b. 1920): Soviet actor and director.
Alla Gerber: journalist and critic.

p. 22   *Akutagawa Ryunosuke* (1892–1927): Japanese writer, author of *Rashomon.*
Grigory Chukhrai (b. 1921): Soviet film director.
Ariel: later called *Renunciation*, outline of a screenplay, never completed, set in a Russian monastery at the time of World War I. The hero, a monk, dreams of overcoming the laws of gravity through spiritual prowess and thus rising to heaven. (Levitation is a recurring theme in A.T.'s work.) He is subsequently killed in the war.

p. 23   *Evgeny Danilovich Surkov (E.D.)*: critic and publicist, worked in Goskino, chief editor of the journal *Iskusstvo Kino.*
S. Chernoutsan: Central Party Committee, film section.
M. A. Suslov (1902–82): Soviet statesman, chief of ideology, Central Party Committee.
Andrey (Andron) Mikhalkov-Konchalovsky (b. 1937): Soviet film director, writer of screenplays, co-author with A.T. of *The Steamroller and the Violin, Andrey Rublyov.* Played small part in *Ivan's Childhood.*
A. Saltykov (b. 1934): Soviet film director.
Gleb Panfilov (b. 1934): film director.
Nikolay Dostal: Soviet film director.

p. 24   *Vassily Solovyov* (b. 1925): author of screenplays, chief commissioning

editor of Mosfilm, 1968–71, chief editor of Central Screenplays Studios, 1974–80.
Nelly Fomina: costume designer, worked with A.T. on *Solaris, Mirror, Stalker.*
Mikhail (Misha) Romadin (b. 1940): artist, art director for *Solaris.*
Grigory Kozintsev (1905–73): Soviet film director, author of screenplays.
Alexander (Sasha) Gordon (b. 1931): Soviet film director, married to A.T.'s sister Marina.

p. 25   *Georgiy Malarchuk*: Moldavian writer, journalist.
Shavkat Abdusalimov (b. 1938): artist, designer, actor.
Alov Alexander (1923–83): Soviet film director, author of screenplays.
Vladimir (Volodya) Naumov (b. 1927): Soviet film director, worked with A. Alov.

p. 26   *Georgiy A. Scherbakov*: sold house in Myasnoye to A.T.
Tosia: Larissa Tarkovskaya's sister.

p. 27   *Felix Kuznetsov*: journalist and critic; was secretary, Moscow branch of Union of Writers.

p. 28   *Grigory (Grisha) Poshenyan* (b. 1922): Soviet poet, lived in Myasnoye.
A. E. Yablochkin: Director of Meyerhold Theatre.

p. 29   *Fyodor (Fedya) Rykalov*: official of Goskino, related to Larissa Tarkovskaya.
Nikolay Trofimovich Sizov (b. 1916): Soviet writer, Director, Mosfilm.

p. 30   *Margarita Terekhova* (b. 1942): theatre and film actress; played in *Mirror*, and in A.T.'s *Hamlet.*

1971

p. 33   *Pyotr Demichov* (b. 1918): Minister of Culture from 1974 until perestroika.
V. M. Kreiss: film critic.
Aleksey Romanov (b. 1908): former Minister of Cinematography of USSR, Chairman of Goskino, 1963–72.

p. 34   *I. Yefremov* (1907–72): Soviet science fiction writer, palaeontologist.
S. Gavrilov: set designer, Mosfilm, worked on *Solaris.*

p. 37   *Elem Klimov* (b. 1933): film director, currently Chairman of Union of Cinematographers.
Lev Kulidzhanov (b. 1924): film director, at that time first secretary, Union of Cinematographers.
E. Nagornaya: officially appointed production manager, *Solaris.*
Olga Barnet: played the mother in *Solaris.*
Natalia (Natasha) Bondarchuk (b. 1950): Soviet actress and film director.

p. 38   *Valerya Pogozheva*: at that time chief commissioning editor, Goskino.
F. T. Yermash: Chairman of Goskino, 1972–85.
Vladimir Baskakov (b. 1921): at that time deputy head of Goskino; Director of All-Union Institute of Film History until 1987.

p. 39   *Beata Tickiewicz*: wife of Andrej Wajda, the Polish film director.

p. 40   *Gordon Craig* (1872–1966): English theatre director, worked largely in Russia and Europe.

p. 41   *V. V. Stassov* (1824–1906): art and music critic.

p. 43   *V. A. Pozner*: Director of experimental studio of Mosfilm, subsequently moved to Paris.

p. 44   *Mikhail Ilych Romm* (1901–71): film director, writer of screenplays, artistic director of Mosfilm Studios, subsequently professor at All-Union State Institute of Cinematography (VGIK) and A.T.'s teacher.
Abram M. Room (1894–1976): Soviet theatre and film director.

1972

p. 49   *Stanislas Lem*: author of the book on which *Solaris* is based.

p. 52   *Georgiy (Gosha) Rerberg* (b. 1937): cameraman for *Mirror*.

p. 53   *Bagrat Oganessyan*: Armenian director, pupil of A.T., worked as student on *Andrey Rublyov*.

p. 55   *Vladimir Korolenko* (1853–1921): Russian writer of novellas and stories.

p. 57   *Vladimir (Volodya) Vissotsky* (1938–80): Soviet poet and singer.

p. 59   *Arayk Agoronyan*: worked on *Stalker* as student.
Alexander Kamshalov: current head of Goskino.

p. 60   *Yuri Ozerov* (b. 1921): Soviet film director.

p. 61   *Anna Semyonovna Yegorkina*: mother of Larissa Tarkovskaya.
Daniil Khrabrovitsky (b. 1929): Soviet film director and writer of screenplays, head of Gorky Studios.

1973

p. 66   *Strugatsky brothers*: *Arkady* (b. 1925) and *Boris* (b. 1933), co-authors of science fiction works, and of screenplay of *Stalker*.
Chinghis Aitmatov (b. 1928): Kirghiz writer.

p. 68   *S. G. Lapin*: Chairman of State Committee for Television and Radio from 1970.
Vladimir Ageyev: at that time head of Mosfilm group 'Comrade'.

p. 69   *Martyrology*: 'A History of Martyrdom'.
Vera Panova (1905–73): Soviet writer.
Sergey Urusevsky (b. 1908): Soviet cameraman.

p. 70   *Stanislav Rostotsky* (b. 1922): Soviet film director, from 1965 was secretary of executive committee of Union of Cinematographers.

p. 71   *Nikolay Pokrovsky*: historian, family friend.
Avar: member of an ethnic group inhabiting the Caucasus.
Svechev: art historian, specialist in Medieval Russia, expert in restoration.
Savely Yamschikov: Soviet art historian, consultant for *Andrey Rublyov*.
Nikolay Strakhov (1828–96): Russian thinker, publicist, critic.
Alexander Griboyedov (1795–1829): author of the play *Woe from Wit*.

p. 72   *Marlen Khutsiev* (1925–73): Soviet film director.

p. 73   *Grigory (Ghia) Danelia* (b. 1930): Soviet film director.

Vladimir Murashko (b. 1925): photographer, worked on *Solaris*, *Mirror*, *Stalker*.

p. 74 *Nikolay Dvigubsky* (b. 1936): Russian artist, now lives in France.

p. 75 *Maria (Masha) Chugunova*: assistant director, *Solaris*, *Mirror*, *Stalker*.

p. 77 *Ali Khamreyev*: (b. 1935): Uzbek film director.
Boris Pavlyonok: deputy head of Goskino, 1973–85.
Osman Karayev: film director, formerly deputy director of Mosfilm Studios.

p. 78 *Mark Zakharov*: Soviet theatre and film director.

p. 79 *Ivan Bunin* (1870–1953): Russian writer, emigrated to France in 1918, awarded Nobel Prize for literature in 1933.

p. 80 *Eduard Artemiev* (b. 1937): Soviet composer, worked on *Solaris*, *Mirror*, *Stalker* and A.T.'s stage production of *Hamlet*.

p. 82 *Boris Kremnev*: commissioning editor, Mosfilm.

1974

p. 89 *Anatoly Efros*: Soviet theatre director.

p. 90 *Svetlana Alliluyeva* (b. 1921): Stalin's daughter.
Vassily Shauro: head of cultural section of Central Party Committee from 1966 until perestroika.

p. 92 *Maurice Bessy* (b. 1910): French journalist, historian, writer of screenplays; Director, Cannes Film Festival.

p. 93 *Sergey (Seryozha) Paradzhanov* (1924–90): Soviet film director.
Victor Shklovsky (1893–1983): literary scholar and critic, author of screenplays.
Alexander Dovzhenko (1894–1956): Ukrainian director, whose early films A.T. greatly admired.

p. 96 *Tito Kalatozov*: son of film director Georgiy Kalatozov.

p. 97 *Nikolay Pomyalovsky* (1835–63): Russian writer.
Stanislav Kondrashev (b. 1929): Soviet journalist.
Evgeny Simonov: Soviet theatre director.

p. 98 *Yuri Nikulin* (b. 1921): film and circus artiste.

1975

p. 105 *Igor Zolotusky* (b. 1930): Soviet critic.

p. 106 *Shengelay brothers*: *Eldar* (b. 1933) and *Georgiy* (b. 1937), Georgian film directors.
Rolan Bykov (b. 1929): Soviet actor and film director, was in *Andrey Rublyov*.
Maya Plissetskaya (b. 1925): ballerina and actress.

p. 107 *Alexandrinka*: Alexander Theatre.

p. 108 *Igor Gorbachev*: Soviet actor, currently Director of Leningrad Dramatic Theatre.

p. 110   *Inna Churikova*: actress, wife of film director Gleb Panfilov.

p. 114   *Eleonora Barabasch* (b. 1929): member of artistic council of Mosfilm, deputy chief editor of Goskino (1973–6), then chief editor of Mosfilm Television Studios.

1976

p. 121   *Oleg Yankovsky* (b. 1944): Soviet theatre and film actor, played in *Mirror*, *Nostalgia*.

p. 124   *Tonino Guerra* (b. 1920): Italian poet and writer, author of screenplays, co-author with A.T. of *Nostalgia*; close friend of A.T.

p. 126   *Yuri Dobrokhotov*: then head of foreign publications of Mosfilm.

p. 127   *Villy Geller*: production manager of first version of *Stalker*.
Mikhail (Mishka) Marinin: Mosfilm production manager.
Olga (Olya) Kizilova: actress, daughter of Larissa Tarkovskaya, played in *Andrey Rublyov* and *Mirror*.

p. 129   *Lev (Leva) Kocharian*: film director, Mosfilm.

p. 131   *Vladimir (Volodya) Sedov*: theatre director, directed *Hamlet* with A.T. at Lenin Komsomol Theatre.

p. 133   *Alik Boim*: artist, worked on *Stalker*.

1977

p. 143   *Nikolay Sidelnikov*: composer, professor at Moscow Conservatoire; friend of A.T.'s family.
Pyotr Chaadayev (1794–1856): Russian philosopher.

p. 146   *Boris Konoplyov*: at that time chief engineer, Mosfilm.
Leonid I. Kalashnikov (b. 1926): cameraman, Mosfilm.

p. 147   *Nikolay Leskov* (1831–95): writer of novels and stories.

1978

p. 152   *Vladimir (Volodya) Burakovsky*: head of cardiological clinic.

p. 154   *Mikhail Kuzmin* (1875–1936): Symbolist poet and writer.

p. 156   *Vladimir Lossky* (1870–1965): Russian Orthodox thinker, lived in Paris.
Leonid (Lena, Lyona) Nekhoroshev (b. 1931): was editor for Mosfilm, now Prorector of VGIK.
Rudolf Steiner: German mystic philosopher; founded anthroposophy in 1913.

p. 158   *Rashid Safulin*: artist, worked on *Stalker*.
G. Zaruba: Central Party Committee.

p. 159   *Yuri Kochevrin* (b. 1932): economist, close friend of A.T.

1979

p. 165   *Eleonora (Lora) Yablochkina*: wife of Tonino Guerra, interpreter for A.T. for *Tempo di Viaggio*.

p. 168   *Ludmilla (Lucia) Feyginova*: editor of all A.T.'s films up to *Stalker*.

p. 169   *V. V. Sharun*: sound mixer, *Stalker*.

p. 172   *A. Surikov*: head of Sovexportfilm.

p. 174   *Peredelkino*: place near Moscow where Moscow artists and intellectuals have cottages; very prestigious.

p. 176   *Mikhail Prishvin* (1873–1954): Soviet writer, poet and publicist.
Dak (Dakhus): A.T.'s dog.

p. 180   *Emil Lotyanu* (b. 1936): Moldavian film director and poet.
M. Shkalikov: head of foreign relations department of Goskino, responsible for film festivals, roundly attacked at Vth Congress of Cinematographers.
Mikhail Zimyanin (b. 1914): Soviet statesman, from 1976 secretary of CC CP USSR. Member of Central Committee 1952–6, 1966.

p. 183   *Andrey (Andriusha) Smirnov* (b. 1941): Soviet film director, First Secretary, Union of Cinematographers.
Sergey Solovyov (b. 1941): Soviet film director.

p. 186   *Larissa Shepitko* (1938–79): film director, wife of Elem Klimov.

p. 189   *Ilyin*: worked in Soviet Embassy, Rome.
Franco Terilli: co-producer of *Tempo di Viaggio*.

p. 192   *A. Mossin*: Goskino official.

p. 193   *Enrica*: wife of Antonioni.

p. 194   *Galya Shabanova*: artist.

p. 196   *Luciano Tovoli*: Italian cameraman for *Tempo*.
Shtepsel: a popular, tall, lanky Soviet comedian.

p. 201   *Wrangel*: Commander-in-Chief of anti-Bolshevik forces in the 1920s.

p. 211   *Robert Sturua*: Georgian theatre director.
Julio Cortazar (b. 1914): Argentinian writer.

p. 214   *Nikita Mikhalkov* (b. 1938): Soviet film director, brother of Andrey Mikhalkov-Konchalovsky.
Vassily (Vassya) Shukshin (1929–74): popular Soviet writer, actor, scriptwriter, director, fellow student under Mikhail Romm, and friend of A.T.

p. 215   *Nikolay (Kolya) Burlyaev* (b. 1946): film actor and director, played in *Ivan's Childhood* and *Andrey Rublyov*.

p. 217   *Leonid Andreyev* (1871–1919): Russian writer, very popular in his day.
Father Pavel Florensky (1882–1943?): Russian theologist, priest, died in a concentration camp.

1980

p. 229   *Eldar Ryazanov* (b. 1927): Soviet film director.

p. 231   *Garik Pimkhazov*: photographer and friend of A.T.

p. 241   *Carlos Khotivari*: Georgian film director.
Giani Rodari: Italian children's writer.

Renzo Rosselini: executive producer, *Nostalgia*.
Canepari: deputy head of RAI 2.

p. 248   *Martine Offroy*: head of press section, Gaumont.

p. 249   *Yuri Tynyanov* (1894–1943): literary scholar, novelist.

p. 254   *Vika Tokareva*: author of novels and short stories.

p. 262   *Donatella Baglivo*: Italian documentary filmmaker, author of film on A.T., *A Poet of the Cinema*.

p. 265   *Andrey Bely* (1880–1934): Symbolist poet and prose writer.
Sergey Vassilevich Kalinkin: forester at Myasnoye.

1981

p. 269   *Alexander (Sasha) Sakurov*: Soviet film director.

p. 270   *Tatiana Storchak*: official of foreign relations department of Goskino.

p. 271   *John Roberts*: Director, Great Britian–USSR Association.
P. K. Kostikov: deputy head of foreign department, Goskino.

p. 273   *Zemfira Vassilevna*: doctor and friend, treated A.T. for heart attack.

p. 275   *Georgiy Ivanovich Gurdjiev* (1872–1949): Russian 'mystical' writer; lived and worked in Paris after emigrating.

p. 276   *Pär Almark*: at that time head of Swedish Film Institute.

p. 279   *Nikolay (Kolya) Dvigubsky* (b. 1936): artist and film designer, worked with A.T. on *Mirror* and other films, and also on A.T.'s production of *Boris Godunov* at Covent Garden, London, in 1983. Now lives in France.

p. 285   *Galya Brezhneva*: daughter of Brezhnev.

p. 286   *Pio de Berti*: head of RAI 2.

p. 288   *Alexander (Sasha) Medveyev*: young scientist friend of A.T., interested in directing.

p. 291   *Vyacheslav Ivanov* (1866–1949): Russian poet and theoretician for Symbolism.

1982

p. 299   *Claudio Abbado*: Director of Royal Opera House, Covent Garden, for whom A.T. directed *Boris Godunov*.

p. 301   *Yura Reverov*: film director, Lenfilm Studios.
Yosif Heifits (b. 1905): Soviet film director, author of screenplays.

p. 311   *Vera (Verochka) Semyonovna*: film director.
Giulietta Masina (b. 1921): Italian actress, wife of Frederico Fellini, friend of A.T.

p. 317   *Lilya Brik*: wife of Formalist critic, Osip Brik: their home was a Futurist salon; she was mistress of the poet Vladimir Mayakovsky.
N. Katanyanov: son of Lilya Brik.
Gideon Bakhman: musician.

Index

Index

Index

Lena (Larissa's protégé) 130
Lenin, Vladimir Ilyich 106, 185
Lenin Komsomol Theatre, Moscow 90, 110
Lenko, Rena 182–3
Lensoviet theatre 217
Leonardo da Vinci 153, 200, 320
Leone, Sergio 154
Leontiev, Konstantin 3
Leskov, Nikolay 147, 373
Lessons of Don Juan, The (Castaneda) 169
Letters to His Wife (about Cézanne) (Rilke 66)
Letters to Lucilius (Seneca) 288, 292
Letti, Franco 206
Lev Tolstoy (Shklovsky) 312, 313–14, 316
Li Bu-vey 23
Life Briefly Told, A (Hesse) 300
Life of Klim Samgin, The (Gorky) 96–7
Lika (Bunin) 305
Lina, Jure 276, 277, 311, 314, 320, 345
Lipotkin, Vladimir Aleksandrovich 116
Literaturnaya Gazeta 109, 127
Livanov, Vassya 34, 36
Lives of the Fathers 301–3
Lizzani, Carlo 189, 193, 200, 311
Lobechevsky, Nikolai 309
Locarno Festival 59
Lollobrigida, Gina 92
London, Tarkovsky committee in 337, 344
London Film Festival 74
London Film School 272
Lossky, Vladimir 156
Lotyanu, Emil Vladimirovich 180, 230, 308
Lozinsky (translator) 121
Luna, La (Bertolucci) 205
Lyubimov, Yuri Petrovich 337, 343–4

Macbeth (Polanski film) 365
Macbeth (proposed film) 121
Macbeth (Shakespeare) 379
Magic Mountain, The (Mann) 72, 77
Mahler, Gustav 145, 146
Malarchuk, Georgiy 25, 26
Man of Marble 247
Manin (Lenin Prize Winner) 8–9
Mann, Thomas 7, 21, 25, 28, 33, 58, 72, 77, 79, 80, 89, 98, 110, 174
Mao Tse Tung 130
Maraini, Dacia 98
Marina (actors' agent) 263

Marinin, Mikhail (Mishka) 127
Marshak, Samuel 295
Marx, Karl 237
Mashin, Volodya 308
Masina, Guilietta 311
Masliukov, Andrey 127
Massiulis, A. 4
Master and Margarita, The (projected film) 152, 153, 160, 211, 272
Mastroianni, Marcello 154
Matiushina (actress) 143
Matryona's House (proposed film) 14
Matryona's House (Solzhenitsyn) 29
Matveyev 272, 279
Maupassant, Guy de 89
Maximov, Vladimir 337, 338, 343–4
Medveyev, Alexander (Sasha) 288, 291
'Meetings Granted Me by Fate' (Birman) 40
Mersel, Professor van 321
Metamorphosis (Kafka) 133
Mikasian, Laura 277
Mikhailov, Yuri 19
Mikhalkov, Nikita 214
Mikhalkov, S. 298n
Mikhalkov-Konchalovsky, Andrey Sergeich (Andron) vii, 23, 216, 230
Mikheyev (engineer) 203
Mildenburg, Anna 145
Mirror (previously *The Bright, Bright Day*) 139, 156, 161, 300, 379; Antonioni and 115; awards 238; best film of 1978 (France) 161; and Cannes 92–3, 106–7, 368; completion of vii; Czechs publish script of 182; distribution 107; French buy 142, 259; and Institute of World Economics 159; Italians offer to enter for Donatello prize 178, 180; and Japan 335; letter to Shauro about 140–41; negatives taken to Rome 125; Paradzhanov on 100; premièred in Italy 160–61, 172; premièred in Paris 151; questions about 177–8, 212–15; reaches cinemas vii; screenplay 336; Sizov and 93, 97; success of 101, 109, 110; T despairs over 93; T's talk on 367–70; and Unita Festival 110; U.S. buys 161; Yermash rejects 96, 97, 98
Mishurin, Alexander (Sasha) 17, 68, 110, 114, 115, 161, 185, 252–3, 254; and Abalo

Index